POETICS OF THE PARANORMAL

KEVIN CHABOT

POETICS OF THE PARANORMAL

MCGILL-QUEEN'S UNIVERSITY PRESS
MONTREAL & KINGSTON | LONDON | CHICAGO

ISBN 978-0-2280-2273-2 (cloth)
ISBN 978-0-2280-2298-5 (paper)
ISBN 978-0-2280-2310-4 (ePDF)
ISBN 978-0-2280-2311-1 (ePUB)

Legal deposit fourth quarter 2024
Bibliothèque nationale du Québec

Printed in Canada on acid-free paper that is 100% ancient forest free
(100% post-consumer recycled), processed chlorine free

This book has been published with the help of a grant from the Federation for the Humanities and Social Sciences, through the Awards to Scholarly Publications Program, using funds provided by the Social Sciences and Humanities Research Council of Canada.

Funded by the Government of Canada | Financé par le gouvernement du Canada | Canada
Canada Council for the Arts | Conseil des arts du Canada

We acknowledge the support of the Canada Council for the Arts.

Nous remercions le Conseil des arts du Canada de son soutien.

McGill-Queen's University Press in Montreal is on land which long served as a site of meeting and exchange amongst Indigenous Peoples, including the Haudenosaunee and Anishinabeg nations. In Kingston it is situated on the territory of the Haudenosaunee and Anishinaabek. We acknowledge and thank the diverse Indigenous Peoples whose footsteps have marked these territories on which peoples of the world now gather.

Library and Archives Canada Cataloguing in Publication

Title: Poetics of the paranormal / Kevin Chabot.
Names: Chabot, Kevin, author.
Description: Includes bibliographical references and index.
Identifiers: Canadiana (print) 20240390733 | Canadiana (ebook) 2024039075X | ISBN 9780228022732 (cloth) | ISBN 9780228022985 (paper) | ISBN 9780228023104 (ePDF) | ISBN 9780228023111 (ePUB)
Subjects: LCSH: Ghosts in mass media. | LCSH: Ghosts in popular culture. | LCSH: Parapsychology in mass media. | LCSH: Mass media and culture. | LCSH: Spirit photography. | LCSH: Parapsychology.
Classification: LCC P96.G56 C43 2024 | DDC 302.23—dc23

Set in 11/14 Minion Pro with Trade Gothic LT Standard
Book design & typesetting by Garet Markvoort, zijn digital
Copyediting by Matthew Kudelka

CONTENTS

FIGURES

ACKNOWLEDGMENTS

This book was made possible by funding from the Social Sciences and Humanities Research Council of Canada. Chapter 4 of this book was previously published as "Tape: Videographic Ruin and the Lure of the Tangible" in *Quarterly Review of Film and Video* 39, no. 2 (2022): 442–63.

This book began with doctoral research undertaken in the Cinema Studies Institute at the University of Toronto. I am grateful for the support and mentorship of Charlie Keil, my PhD supervisor, without which this book would not have come to fruition. Charlie supported the project from the beginning and always encouraged me to take my ideas further, even when my research interests changed direction. His careful reading of drafts and his animated enthusiasm always kept me motivated and got me through the challenging climate of PhD work. I am thankful for his continued support. Angelica Fenner and Bart Testa were also instrumental in the shaping of this project as committee members for the dissertation version. Their insights and critiques provided valuable contributions to my thinking and made me a stronger writer. I am indebted to James Cahill and Jeffrey Sconce for their generous reading of the dissertation and for providing a pathway for post-dissertation revision through their sharp commentary and helpful feedback.

I am forever grateful to the community of colleagues and friends who have contributed directly or indirectly, intellectually or spiritually, to the completion of this book; without them I wouldn't have had the motivation or the intellectual stimulation to advance the work. Justin Morris, Celine Bell, and Amber Fundytus are near and dear to my heart and have been indispensable sources of support and joy. Thank you to Frederick Blichert, Jeff Clarke, Corinn Columpar, David Davidson, Eddie Farrell, Cyrus Ferguson, Nick Fernandes, Anjo-Mari Gouws, Amanda Greer, Karina Griffith, Morgan Harper, Brian Jacobson, Sean Kidnie, Daniel Laurin, Murray Leeder, Patrick Marshall, Dan McFadden, Erin Nunoda, Tony Pi, Brian Price, Carrie Reese, Katie Russell, Tom Russell, Nic Sammond, Sara Saljoughi, Meghan Sutherland, Ramtin Teymouri, Matt Thompson, Müge Tufenk, Jill Vasko, Joshua Wiebe, Blake Williams, Magda Yuksel, and Alberto Zambenedetti, all of whom provided much-needed professional and/or social support systems throughout my academic journey and beyond. An additional thank you to audience members at the annual SCMS and FMSAC conferences for their spirited questions and engagement with my ideas.

My editor Jonathan Crago has been a pleasure to work with (and incredibly patient!) as I conducted further research and adapted the work for its present version. I was lucky to secure a SSHRC postdoctoral fellowship at Dalhousie University that allowed for further time and resources to pursue my academic research. Jason Haslam and Shannon Brownlee have been wonderful colleagues, offering me opportunities to share my work and new research with the Dalhousie community. I am also indebted to my students who indulged my interests in all things supernatural with vibrant class discussion in CIN44H1S – Spectral Media (U of T) and FILM4390 – Spectral Media (Dalhousie).

Lastly, I'd like to thank my family for emotional and sometimes financial support of my academic endeavours. My parents Celine and Mike, brothers Dan and Jason, sister-in-law Allecia, and niece Charlie. A sense of community is something I strive to cultivate, and I am grateful for my family, friends, and colleagues.

POETICS OF THE PARANORMAL

1 A GHOST STORY

David Lowery's *A Ghost Story* (2017) follows a young unnamed couple played by Rooney Mara and Casey Affleck (the characters are identified as "M" and "C" respectively on the IMDb) who live in a rural bungalow. Despite M's desire to move out of the home and search for another place to live, C feels a heretofore unexplained connection to the home and is resistant to leaving. "What is it you like about this house so much?" M asks C. "History," he replies. A musician and composer by trade, C's melodies reverberate throughout the home's hardwood floors and plastered walls of muted blues, greens, and browns. One night while in bed, the couple hears a sound coming from the living room. It is the calamitous keys of the piano being struck discordantly. The familiar timbre is ordinarily comforting but is here disconcerting, given both the inexplicability of its occurrence and its atonality. The pair returns to their bedroom as C adopts a contemplative glance directed at the piano. This is familiar; he has heard this before.

When C is unexpectedly killed in a car accident, his ghost remains behind to observe M's grieving process and the fate of his beloved home. The film's elliptical narrative structure transports the spectator through distinct periods of time, depicting the home's deterioration and demolition before jumping ahead decades to portray a bustling metropolis in what was once an isolated rural town. The film then folds back upon itself: C's ghost is shown observing his former self and M as they tour the home with a real estate agent before making the purchase. We then follow C's ghost as he observes his former life with M in the house. This temporal refracture in the film's narrative suggests that C's attachment to the home and its history stems from an unconscious connection with his own ghost – the house was always already haunted by the ghost of C's future. The film makes this clear when the clang of the piano keys heard at the beginning of the film is revealed to be C's ghost sitting with a thud upon the piano, eliciting a Barthesian *frisson* "over a catastrophe that has already occurred."[1] The film's cyclical narrative thus reveals the present tense of the film's discourse to be contaminated by C's past and future, emblematized by the haunting presence of C's ghost. The temporal heterogeneity and narrative circularity in *A Ghost Story* are echoed visually in the representation of C's ghost as a billowing white sheet with eyeholes and in the prismatic light formations that represent the invisible presence of his ghost. The folds of the sheet and the refracture of light represented in the film come to signify the ethereal ontology of the ghost, one that defies homogeneous time and temporal linearity.

A Ghost Story's narrative structure and representation of ghosts as flowing sheets foreground the fundamental liminality of the ghost as a figure, one that belies binaries of visibility and invisibility, materiality and immateriality, past and the present, and presence and absence. The presence of C's ghost functions to mark the absence of his living body; he is enshrouded within a sheet that maintains the shape and outline of his material body, but he is kept hidden behind its veil. Moreover, despite the materiality of the sheet, ghosts in the film remain invisible to those still living. Yet the film emphasizes the waves and folds of the sheet itself, a material presence that drags on the ground as C saunters about various spaces like a spectral *flâneur*. The sheet evinces mass and weight as it flows downward from C's head into a pool of fabric at his feet; ripples of its folds and creases register C's movement through space. Moreover, the sheet begins as a crisp, freshly laundered garment and accumulates dirt and grime as the film goes on, attesting to the deleterious effect of friction in space and endurance through time. Akin to a photograph, the ghostly shroud constitutes an indexical marker of the passage of time through its degradation, registering wear and tear as the film unfolds.

A Ghost Story, then, accentuates the materiality of the sheet despite both the invisibility and ethereality proper to the ghost. Its deterioration confers a timeliness upon an entity that is, ostensibly, outside of time and beyond the entropic decay bestowed upon all organic materials by the ceaseless momentum of temporal progression. The sheet's creases and folds, waves and flows convey the ontological condition of

FIGURE 1.1 | C'S MATERIAL GHOST, *A GHOST STORY.*

the ghost as a figure that disrupts a linear conception of sequence and progress in favour of overlap, flux, and circularity. These waves and flows further manifest themselves structurally in the film's narrative as C's ghost bears witness to both the future and the past from the perspective of an indeterminate, indiscernible present.

What *is* a ghost? The standard definition describes the spirit, soul, or essence of a dead individual that has either remained on, or returned to, the living, human plane of existence; that is, it has not "moved on" to a metaphysical realm such as Heaven or what Spiritualists called Summerland. Ghosts, however, have exhibited a wide variety of characteristics in both form and function across time, depending upon the cultural, religious, and historical milieu in which they manifest. Prior to the Protestant Reformation in Europe, for example, ghosts were conceptualized as souls trapped in Purgatory, an intermediary state of punishment and/or reflection before the final adjudication of a soul's salvation or damnation. This decidedly Catholic explanation would require significant revision when Luther's Reformation eliminated purgatory from Protestant theology in favour of a soul's direct route to its final destination upon death. In both cases, ghosts appeared before specific individuals, bearing information, a warning, or a message to impart to the living. The ghost harbours unfinished business and seeks to set the record straight, restore the natural order of things, facilitate problem solving, and repair broken relations, a motivation that continues to animate ghostly visitations in popular culture today. The ghost returns, as Colin Davis has articulated, "*in order to be sent away again*," to be permitted to rest interminably upon the successful resolution of a problem or the completion of a task.[2]

By the nineteenth century, the ghost in Western culture had lost its sense of purpose. While some spirits continued to visit the living in order to enact change, others simply lingered, hovering between absence and presence, failing to fully vanish. Such listless ghosts are indicative of "residual" hauntings, a category created by paranormal investigators and psychical researches to describe ghosts that do not interact with the living and, indeed, are not self-aware. Such ghosts are akin to echoes; they are reverberations of the past that continue to repeat in perpetuity, which explains why some ghosts are repeatedly seen performing the same functions (e.g., walking down stairs) at the same time (e.g., every night at midnight). Dennis and Michele Waskul identify two subcategories of residual haunting: anniversary and historical hauntings. The former describes ghosts who reappear on a specific date or time of year, as in a ghost appearing every year on the anniversary of their corporeal death, while the latter describes the appearance of ghosts at historically important sites, such as the Gettysburg battlefield.[3] The Waskuls describe such residual hauntings as a "compulsion to repeat" wherein ghosts, unlike the attention-seeking and self-aware entities of "intelligent" hauntings, re-enact the past without conscious agency.[4] As we will encounter throughout this book, residual ghosts are often analogized with recording media as their (re)appearances are akin to a looped reel of film or tape recorder. Such hauntings are stuck on replay; fragments of the past are continuously (re)enacted like an ethereal rerun.

The Waskuls further identify distinct, though not mutually exclusive, *kinds* of ghosts within their topology, demarcating specific types of returns and motivations that differentiate spectral visitations. Their categories include apparitions (visual manifestations), phantasms (which appear in dreams or altered states of consciousness), wraiths (spirits that appear just before or after their corporeal death), poltergeists (quintessential "noisy ghosts" that manipulate objects), spectres (menacing presences perceived to be threatening), and phantoms. The afterlife, then, is a decidedly cosmopolitan realm with multiple iterations of ghosts that vary in form and function. Whether intelligent or residual, purposeful or indifferent, helpful or threatening, comforting or terrifying, what unites the shifting conceptions of ghosts across time in Western popular culture – in fiction, visual art, and folklore – is their status as *remnants*, the lasting traces of persons (or sometimes animals) after their corporeal death. The ontology of the ghost is one that defies linear standardized time and therefore bears a unique relationship to history, temporality, and media, a relationship that will be explored throughout this book.

Attempts to define with certainty an entity that is by its very nature elusive, ambiguous, and indeed perhaps non-existent, are, of course, futile. As the incredulous investigator Benjamin Radford of the *Skeptical Inquirer* writes, "There are a half dozen or so different definitions of ghosts, and there's equal evidence for all of them. Trying to classify inherently unknown entities whose very existence and nature remains unproven is a fool's errand: How many types of ghosts are there? As many as you want there to be."[5] Ghosts evade epistemological capture precisely because, as Jacques Derrida argued, they exist outside knowledge and refuse incorporation into a logocentric system of thought.[6] This explains why even contemporary ghost hunters, despite the myriad television shows, documentaries, and YouTube channels dedicated to paranormal investigation and their increasingly technologized investigative methods, "still don't know what ghosts are."[7] Indeed, contemporary ghost hunters seek to document through image and sound that which belies the precepts of evidentiary recording: entities beyond time whose existence remains necessarily unverifiable. This book does not set out to solve the question of the existence of ghosts or define their metaphysical operations; rather, *Poetics of the Paranormal* aims to discern how media representations have constructed our Western cultural conceptions of ghosts, and, conversely, how ghosts have constructed our media. There exists a spectral reciprocity between ghosts and media technologies in terms of the preservation and mediation of time, history, subjectivity, and memory, refracted via the medium-specific qualities of photography, film, television, video, and digital networks. Ghosts are transmedial figures in that they reveal the unique haunted qualities of our media while highlighting their own mediumistic qualities. If we accept in the most general terms the conviction that ghosts are the spiritual remnants of individuals after death, as is widely represented across media, we are left with an even more perplexing and fascinating question: what do ghosts look like?

ON APPARITIONAL POETICS

Poetics of the Paranormal addresses the visual and aural construction of ghosts and haunting in contemporary media. Although ghosts are the central figure under investigation in this book, it should be noted that the terms "supernatural" and "paranormal" may refer to a variety of phenomena that challenge contemporary understandings of the rules and laws of nature. Derived from the Latin *supernaturalis* – beyond or above nature – the supernatural may include angels, demons, psychic visions, telekinesis, witchcraft, zombies, fairies, vampires, and other entities and phenomena that violate our conception of the natural world. Murray Leeder notes that "supernatural" was most often used in relation to religion before it accrued a more secular understanding in the nineteenth century, distinct from strictly theological matters.[8] The term "paranormal" similarly describes that which contradicts established natural laws, with the Greek prefix *para*, denoting "alongside of," "past," or "beyond," affixed to the Latin *normalis*, meaning "conforming to," or "governed by rule."[9] Paranormal is the more recent term developed in the twentieth century, and it expresses a more scientific, and even agnostic, disposition regarding such phenomena. Paranormal, for example, might describe cryptids like Bigfoot, the Loch Ness monster, and the Jersey Devil as well as extraterrestrial life, in that these are all entities that may defy current scientific fact but do not necessarily pose an existential challenge to the natural world. In this way, paranormal refers to phenomena that may be beyond explanation but are not beyond the domain of scientific investigation. As adherents of the Spiritualist movement discussed in chapter 2 attest, such terminology has been disputed for the ways in which it frames phenomena as being beyond or opposed to nature; believers, by contrast, often situate such phenomena as rooted in the mysterious and as yet scientifically unexplainable natural flows, vibrations, and functions of the world. In other words, the paranormal and supernatural may be beyond the human mind's comprehension but not beyond nature. Although the term paranormal describes an array of phenomena and entities, *Poetics of the Paranormal* uses the terms "paranormal" and "supernatural" synonymously, while focusing on the specific figure of the ghost. The ghost, I contend, remains *the* paradigmatic, exemplary figure of the paranormal and supernatural, as it both collapses and exceeds the distinctions between these very terms that seek to identify, categorize, and master its elusive constitution.

Rather than investigating the veracity of ghosts as actual existing entities – a question that is ultimately unanswerable and relegated to the domain of faith – I examine in this book how ghosts have come to shape our conceptions of media ontologies and, conversely, how media have constructed the paranormal as an aesthetic system. Following David Bordwell's formulation, poetics, derived from the Greek *poiesis*, describes a creative production, "a process that includes a craft component (such as rules of thumb), the more general principles according to which the work is composed, and its functions, effects, and uses."[10] "Any inquiry," Bordwell continues, "into the fundamental principles by which artifacts in any representational medium are constructed, and the effects that flow from those principles, can fall within the domain of poetics."[11] In the discipline of film studies, such research would encompass an analysis of *mise-en-scène*, cinematography, editing, music, and sound design in order to discern how colour, movement, lighting, blocking, rhythm, and sound work to produce effects and affects. One might consider how camera framing, shallow focus, low-key lighting, deep staging, and cacophonous sound work together to achieve a jump scare effect in horror cinema.[12] A poetics, then, emphasizes the formal and aesthetic construction of a work of art, but it also takes into account historical and cultural contexts that explain and add nuance to our understanding of artistic conventions. For example, the technological and industrial conditions that facilitated the transition to synchronized sound in the late 1920s advance our understanding of the creative employment of sound and its emerging conventions during that period. By investigating a poetics of the paranormal, then, I aim to uncover the means by which our ghosts *take shape*, taking into account the visual and sonic characteristics of ghosts as they have appeared in media texts. So, what do ghosts look like? They look like photographs. And moving images. And television broadcasts. And electronic video playback. And digital signals. Ghostly poetics is as variable as the media employed to visualize ghosts.

The whimsically clichéd representation of ghosts in *A Ghost Story* as white sheets with eyeholes conjures not only the comical (and lazy!) Halloween costume ubiquitous in popular culture, but also key questions concerning the iconography and visual history of ghosts. As John Harvey has noted, the iconography of ghosts and spirits varies historically and across cultures.[13] In the Middle Ages, for example, "ghosts were believed to be corporeal and assume several forms."[14] Graphic illustrations depicted ghosts as indistinguishable from living subjects until the moment of materialization or vanishing.[15] Importantly, the material base upon which depictions of ghosts were illustrated inevitably contributed to the visual conventions of ghostliness. On cheaply made woodcuts, the insubstantiality of ghosts and their distinction from living humans was far more difficult to convey visually than with steel-plate engraving.[16] As Harvey details, fine-line engraving was better able to depict gradations of light, texture, and outline as well as represent vaporous and translucent materials such as clouds, mists, and, of course, spirits.[17] While descriptions of ghosts as transparent remained almost entirely absent from the twelfth to nineteenth century, the advent of steel-plate engraving made their representation as transparent, wispy entities possible thereby demonstrating the importance of material media in the visual construction of the ghost.[18] As chapter 2 will explore in greater detail, the development of photography in the mid-nineteenth century – a medium itself associated with fluids, vapours, transparencies, and materialization – further contributed to the conventional iconography of the ghost as transparent in Europe and North America.[19]

Susan Owens has traced the convention of ghosts in white sheets to the clothing used in burial, which traditionally consisted of undyed linen or wool. Owen notes that in England, a 1666 law mandated that English wool must be used in burial shrouds, further cementing the association between white sheets and the dead.[20] *A Ghost Story* echoes this history when C's body, dead on a table in the hospital morgue, lies covered in a white sheet. When C sits up on the table, he remains shrouded in the sheet, embodying the iconic image of a ghost. Ghosts clad in white not only reflected the practice of burial clothing used in England but also the imagery that accompanied funerary rituals in the sixteenth and seventeenth centuries. "Engraved memorial brasses and carved stone effigies usually show the dead dressed in contemporary costume," Owens writes, "but it was not uncommon for them to be represented wearing grave clothes, in anticipation of their resurrection at the Last Judgement."[21] This iconography was incorporated into gothic poetry and broadside ballads as a recognizable convention to differentiate spirits from living human beings. Such iconography ensured that readers would immediately identify the figure as a ghost, eliminating any confusion or doubt about what was being represented. As Owens details, broadside ballads "depict ghosts full-length, shown from the side, and wearing voluminous shrouds tied up in a bunch at the top of the head but loose at the feet to facilitate movement, and with schematically represented faces visible in profile. Almost invariably they carry a burning torch with one hand and gesture or point with the other."[22] Importantly, this representation of ghosts was produced, in part, by the production processes of broadside publishing, whereby an image was cut into a block of wood, rendering details difficult to engrave. Echoing Harvey's observations on the drawbacks of wood-cut illustration, Owen remarks, "The heavy, vertical folds of the ghost's pronounced drapery, its schematic form and stick-like arms were all ideally suited to this printing method."[23] This visual convention would remain dominant well into the late eighteenth century.[24]

Ghosts lost their fleshy corporeality amidst the shifting technological landscape of the eighteenth and nineteenth centuries, during which visual entertainments appeared dematerialized and uncanny. Paul Philidor is credited with inventing the phantasmagoria show in 1790, a visual spectacle developed out of the legacy of magic lantern performances in which images of ghosts, skeletons, demons, and all manner of supernatural entities were projected to simulate movement, to the delight and horror of audiences. The apparatus of projection was hidden from view, creating the illusion of free-floating phantoms moving about the auditorium. Projectionists would physically move the projector to make the ghostly images appear to fly, growing and shrinking in size, and a translucent screen, or even billowing smoke, would be used to display the otherworldly images. Undoubtedly a thrilling experience, this veritable technologized séance anticipated the shimmering moving images of the cinema, which would similarly glisten on silver screens before audiences in a darkened theatre. The supernatural imagery in phantasmagoria shows was necessarily translucent, for the apparatus utilized illustrated (usually hand-painted) slides projected onto diaphanous screens, generating translucent images. Phantasmagoria, then, constituted a larger-scale and much more theatrical version of the magic lantern performances that were so popular in the seventeenth century.[25]

In addition to movement, a central attraction of phantasmagoria was metamorphosis and substitution whereby "through the use of two slides, one image would magically transform into another image."[26] These spectacular performances were not presented as genuinely supernatural events, unlike the séances of the Spiritualist movement in the nineteenth and twentieth centuries, but rather acknowledged the illusory effects of imaging apparatuses. Images of ghosts and other supernatural phenomena were understood to be products of technology, the result of manipulating optical science. As such, phantasmagoria shows ostensibly aligned themselves with the Enlightenment project of demystification, of revealing rational, scientific explanations for supposedly paranormal events. However, in concealing the apparatus of projection from audiences and hiding how such images were generated, phantasmagoria, perhaps inadvertently, contributed to the evolving association of visual technologies with conjuring machines. Leeder suggests that claims that phantasmagoria had a didactic function were merely "lip service at best."[27] Similarly, Stacey Abbott argues that in attempting to demystify and debunk the supernatural, phantasmagoria ended up mystifying the technology.[28] As theatrical spectacle, phantasmagoria perpetuated a decidedly disembodied visual representation of ghosts, one that emphasized the ghost's ability to suddenly (re)appear, vanish, transform itself, and move through solid objects. In this way, the popular entertainment reinforced already existing perceptions of how ghosts manifest themselves but altered their constitution from corporeal entities that appeared and vanished to dematerialized vapours that were never fully present to begin with.

Another device that mystified its image-generating mechanism was known as Pepper's Ghost. This optical trick was utilized on theatrical stages in order to produce transparent images of ghosts that would interact with actors live onstage. Significantly, Pepper's Ghost also perpetuated the novel representation of ghosts as transparent, a departure from the corporeal ghosts of previous centuries. Like other visual arts, theatrical stage productions had previously represented spirits as corporeal. This was largely out of necessity, since living actors would portray ghosts onstage alongside their living counterparts. The ethereal status of stage ghosts was signified through a variety of special effects such as smoke, flames, coloured lights, and thunderous sounds that announced the appearance of an otherworldly being.[29] The radical alterity of ghosts onstage was also marked by their peculiar manner of arrival; they would emerge out of a trapdoor in the stage from "those theatrical nether regions that the Elizabethans called the 'cellarage' or even 'Hell.'"[30] Pepper's Ghost, however, which employed light and a large pane of glass to project an actor's performance, allowed a vaporous and ethereal spirit to share the stage with living actors. Developed by John Henry Pepper in the early 1860s, the optical trick involved placing a pane of glass on the stage between the actors and the audience at a forty-five-degree angle. Beneath the stage, the actor playing a ghost was lit with bright light, which bounced the image of the actor onto the pane of glass, thereby creating the illusion of a transparent spectre onstage.[31] Pepper's Ghost made its debut on 24 December 1862 in the London stage adaptation of Charles Dickens's *The Haunted Man*, creating considerable buzz about the new special effect.[32] The copresence of embodied actor and transparent projected image onstage actualized the uncanny experience of an apparitional encounter, one in which the spirit image's paradoxical absent presence was juxtaposed with the physical concreteness of the living actor. Arguably, the Pepper's Ghost trick inverted the spatio-temporal constitution of spirits; in contrast to the traditional understanding of the ghost as an entity outside of time but occupying a shared space, Pepper's Ghost depicted a haunted encounter shared in time but separated in space. The actor playing the ghost was actually underneath the stage, separated from

FIGURE 1.2 | MARLEY'S GHOST APPEARING BEFORE SCROOGE IN CHARLES DICKENS'S *A CHRISTMAS CAROL*, ILLUSTRATION BY JOHN LEECH, 1843.

their co-star, in order to maintain a real-time haunted interaction. In this way, while Pepper's Ghost succeeded in producing a convincing illusion of ghostly manifestation live before audiences, it did so in a manner that challenged dominant conventions about ghosts. Importantly, another work by Dickens was highly influential in the dissemination of such conventions and would continue to shape the form and function of ghosts for generations to come. That work, of course, was the incomparable *A Christmas Carol*.

First published in 1843, *A Christmas Carol* describes the ghost of Marley explicitly as transparent, a marked departure from ghost stories in literary history. While Marley's ghost first appears as a face in Scrooge's door, his second appearance displays his entire body, with Scrooge being able to see through his body. This description was accompanied by John Leech's famous illustration in the book's first edition, depicting the scene inside Scrooge's chamber. Leech conveyed the transparency of the ghost by having the wood panelling on the wall behind Marley appear on his chest, creating the impression of the wall showing through the ghost. Phantasmagoria, Pepper's Ghost, and, as we will see in chapter 2, photography, all contributed to the visual dematerialization of the ghost in Western popular culture, a new insubstantiality that Dickens perpetuated in *A Christmas Carol* and that Leech expressed in his illustration. The ghost's transparency was made possible by developments in visual technologies and popular entertainment, and such techniques better expressed the liminal status of the ghost as an entity occupying a position between life and death, presence and absence. After the publication of *A Christmas Carol*, Owens writes, "purportedly true accounts of cloudy or see-through ghosts began to be recorded."[33] Only after these developments in the visual representation of ghosts did people begin to report ghost sightings that conformed to the recent convention of transparency. These visual technologies of the eighteenth and nineteenth centuries, which strongly influenced the emergence of cinema, thus created the modern ghost while simultaneously "mak[ing] sense" out of ghostly behaviours and characteristics. Their ethereal transparency would stand metonymically for their ability to suddenly materialize, vanish, and move through walls.[34] For Owens, "It is paradoxical that it should have been advances in technology, in the shape of back-projection and the science of photography, which provided new ways of 'seeing' such age-old phenomena as ghosts."[35] Rather than paradoxical, I view this dynamic in terms of reciprocity. Technology conjured ghosts in increasingly graphic representations while ghosts began to function technologically.

This book focuses on representations of ghosts and haunting across photography, film, television, video, and networked new media – that is, the internet – in order to identify the aesthetic conventions that define what ghosts are and what they look like. Using case studies in each chapter, the book moves beyond simply identifying the codes and conventions that construct the paranormal in media to argue that ghosts are constructed as *photographic*, *cinematic*, *televisual*, *videographic*, and *networked* when visualized in these respective media. Ghosts and hauntings are therefore *transmedial* in orientation, exhibiting qualities that are proper to their medium of manifestation and, crucially, revealing the haunting qualities of media. These technologized methods of ghostly representation betray a desire to visualize the imperceptible, an epistephilic drive to bring the supernatural within the bounds of knowledge, while also demonstrating a persistent investment in media as compensatory vision – as able to access and document that which escapes our perceptive capabilities.

Poetics of the Paranormal contributes to a body of scholarship that engages with questions of ghosts, haunting, and spectrality that first gained traction in the 1990s. Roger Luckhurst identified what he called a "spectral turn" in the humanities and social sciences, a turn initiated by the publication of Jacques Derrida's *Specters of Marx* in 1994.[36] In that book, Derrida advances a philosophy of the spectre that is imbricated within a larger project of deconstruction. In what he calls hauntology, Derrida argues that all concepts are fundamentally imbued with an irresolvable contamination and undecidability. "It is necessary to introduce haunting into the very construction of a concept," Derrida writes. "Of every concept, beginning with the concepts of being and time. That is what we would be calling here a hauntology."[37] Hauntology, especially in the French *hauntologie*, occasions a homonymous relation with ontology, a shadowy projection or inverted doubling that attests to the essential equivocality of "ontology, history, inheritance, materiality, and ideology."[38] Spectrality and haunting thereby contribute to an upending of Western organizations of thought structured by binary oppositions, as ghosts defy such classificatory schemas through their boundary-collapsing liminality. The "paradoxical incorporation" epitomized by the ghost, a figure that is neither wholly body nor wholly spirit, also "desynchronizes time" in rendering the past, present, and future as coeval temporal flows.[39] The ghost represents a radical challenge to reigning political-economic forces that seek to fix neoliberal subjectivity within a strictly forward-moving schema of temporal progress. It is not surprising that the collapse of the Soviet Union conjured such hauntological discourses since the apparitional promise of a post-capitalist future seemed to vanish, dematerializing into thin air. Haunting, though, is a stubborn praxis; "it is about refusing to give up the ghost," as Mark Fisher has written, "or, – and this can sometimes amount to the same thing – the refusal of the ghost to give up on us."[40] Ghosts and haunting became a natural subject through which to stage myriad social, cultural, economic, and industrial analyses in the humanities and social sciences, with particular attention paid to the production of invisibilities and absences within systems of subjugation. For postcolonial theory, for example, spectrality has been an especially useful tool to challenge the hegemony of empire by illuminating the peoples, practices, and cultures that are relegated to the margins of global capital, themselves rendered absent presences.

Dipesh Chakrabarty, like Derrida in *Specters of Marx*, takes aim at what Michael Roth calls the "vulgarized Hegelian historicism" espoused by Francis Fukuyama's declaration of the end of history upon the collapse of the Soviet Union.[41] Chakrabarty advances this critique as an entry point through which to interrogate the sociopolitical and economic dominance of Europe. In Fukuyama's statement, capitalism is synonymous with modernity and both are presumed to have originated in Europe, spreading globally over time.[42] This problematically situates Europe as the centre and generator of progress, thereby erroneously constituting the West as superior to other world regions. As such, Europe constructs itself as the pinnacle of civilization, modernity, and Enlightenment to which all other regions must strive. As Bliss Cua Lim elaborates, this colonial understanding of "time-as-space," wherein the metropole occupies the central and therefore most "advanced" state, consigns colonized nations and peoples to a state of perpetual belatedness, always falling behind the steady march of progress.[43] Such logic has been used as a justification for colonialism and as a means to bring "civilization" and "modernity" to "primitive" peoples; it also functions to maintain this hierarchy of domination and subservience even in postcolonial contexts. As Chakrabarty explains, modernist liberalism preaches the virtues of self-governance and self-determination even while African, Indian, and indigenous peoples are consistently banished to the "imaginary waiting room of history," told they are not yet ready for self-rule, that they have not yet arrived in time, that they have not yet caught up.[44] "This waiting," Chakrabarty asserts, "was the realization of the 'not yet' of historicism."[45] The legacy and continued manifestations of colonialism thereby construct colonized peoples as spectral subjects, as embodiments of primitivism and pastness within the present, as having been occluded and marginalized by the homogeneous empty time of European modernity.

Lim considers what she calls "modern time consciousness" to be a form of "exercising social, political, and economic control over periods of work and leisure; it obscures the ceaselessly changing plurality of our existence in time; and it underwrites a linear, developmental notion of progress that gives rise to ethical problems with regard to cultural and racial difference."[46] For both Lim and Chakrabarty, belief in the occult and the supernatural acquires a distinct political dimension in its refusal of secular modernity and the capitalist rationalization of time. Employing India as an exemplar of postcolonial struggle, Chakrabarty writes that scholars "have assumed that for India to function as a nation based on the institutions of science, democracy, citizenship, and social justice, 'reason' had to prevail over what was 'irrational' and 'superstitious' among its citizens."[47] Therefore, the presence of superstitious and/or supernatural belief systems in contemporary life constitutes "human embodiments of anachronism," the presence of "premodern" modes of thought within contemporary modernity.[48] As such, supernatural belief systems and the ghosts and spirits that lie therein problematize modern time-consciousness, which conceptualizes time as linear, homogeneous, standardized, rationalized, and decidedly disenchanted.

As philosophical praxis, then, spectrality paradoxically asks us to remain cognizant of that which lies outside knowledge, of that which both precedes and exceeds the conditions of the present in its knowability. Hauntology demands, therefore, that we remain attuned to that which is unable to be thought, that we remain aware of those presences that dwell beyond the threshold of comprehension. To live with ghosts, to *be* with them, is to initiate an ethico-political relation with individuals of the past and the not yet present, to demand and indeed to compel justice.[49] "If I am getting ready to speak at length about ghosts, inheritance, and generations of ghosts," Derrida writes, "which is to say about certain *others* who are not present, nor presently living, either to us, in us, or outside us, it is in the name of *justice*."[50] So, while an invisible and unacknowledged presence, the ghost is also, and interminably, a figure of the future, a being not yet present, for its ontology rests upon its assured repetition and return. "A specter is always a *revenant*," Derrida asserts. "One cannot control its comings and goings because it *begins by coming back*."[51] A lingering trace of the past within the present that simultaneously anticipates the future in its ineluctable return, the ghost, through the activity of haunting, "demands justice, or at least a response."[52] When the ghost of Hamlet's father – perhaps the paradigmatic ghost in Western literature – returns in Act I, scene v, he demands that the young Prince of Denmark avenge his murder by killing the duplicitous Claudius. In that it begins with the return of a spectre, *Hamlet* epitomizes for Derrida not only the demand for reparative justice but also the recursive temporality occasioned by the presence of ghosts. A haunting as a return in order to generate a future response; indeed, the time is out of joint.

Both postcolonial theory and the publication of *Specters of Marx*, then, have contributed to a flurry of academic interest in spectrality as a means to interrogate the hegemonic construct of modern time-consciousness. Lim incorporates the cinema into this discourse in her examination of ghost films and the fantastic. The ghost film's engagement with alternative modes of temporal flow extends beyond non-linear narrative trajectories and the superimposition of multiple times within a scene; the cinematic apparatus is itself, she argues, a conjurer of ghosts. In the darkened space of the cinema auditorium, images of absent subjects are projected onto a screen, a chimerical shimmer of light and shadow. While the projection of equidistant photograms at sixteen or twenty-four frames-per-second marks film as a kind of clock, as a mechanism of time measurement, the fantastic genre and its mode of world-making elicit the potential for temporal multiplicity, the "uncanny hint of untranslatable times" constitutive of immiscible temporality as such.[53] Yet the temporal critique advanced by ghost films, particularly in the postcolonial context, is not limited exclusively to the fantastic genre or the medium of film. Lim writes, "The critique of homogeneous time is reducible to neither the cinema nor the fantastic; compelling temporal critique has been elaborated in anthropology, historiography, philosophy, experimental video, and elsewhere."[54] While Lim privileges the cinema and its photographic base in order to frame her argument, she acknowledges that haunting and spectrality are intermedial and interdisciplinary concerns. Lim's incorporation of cinematic ghostliness and temporal critique therefore serves as a key conceptual frame for this book's examination of spectrality and the transmediality of the ghost.

TRANSMEDIAL GHOSTS

Bliss Lim's characterization of spectrality as an interdisciplinary and intermedial concern intersects with the work of Tom Gunning and Jeffrey Sconce, who have similarly explored the relationship between technologized modes of visuality and the supernatural. While we have seen how postcolonial theory and *Specters of Marx* spurred scholarly interest in temporal critique and alternative temporalities, including haunting and spectrality, Gunning and Sconce examined how media have been understood as ghostly in themselves and have been used as ghost-hunting tools in attempts to authenticate supernatural encounters. Whereas scholars have tended to distance themselves from the pursuit of ghosts, Gunning and Sconce are explicitly interested in exploring the relationship between ghosts and technology, both as a conceptual metaphor through which to comprehend the wonderment associated with sonic transmission and visual illusion and also as literal ghost-hunting apparatuses.

In *Haunted Media: Electronic Presence from Telegraphy to Television*, Sconce argues that the history of electronic telecommunications is imbued with ghosts and associations with the supernatural. "Sound and image without material substance," Sconce writes, "the electronically mediated worlds of telecommunications often evoke the supernatural by creating virtual beings that appear to have no physical form."[55] Sconce charts the development of the telegraph, wireless telegraph, radio, and television in order to demonstrate that "we still so often ascribe mystical powers to what are ultimately very material technologies."[56] Central to the associations of these electronic technologies with the supernatural are the properties of instantaneous transmission and simultaneity. Like the ghost, telecommunications entail a collapse of space and time, occasioning an uncanny experience of liveness and presence. "The ethereal 'presence' of communications without bodies," Sconce argues, "suggested the possibility of other similarly preternatural interlocutors, invisible entities who, like distant telegraph and wireless operators, could be reached through a most utilitarian application of the technology."[57] For Sconce, then, the development of telecommunications functioned to support belief in the supernatural and the possibility of communication with the dead, since disembodied communication was regularly practised through telegraphy, radio, and television.

Nineteenth-century developments in technology, science, and telecommunications provided a key context in which the Spiritualist movement flourished. As Tom Gunning writes, "Science and technology envisioned a reality that teetered on the brink of nothingness." "Rather than rational reassurance," Gunning continues, "the invisible realm revealed through scientific discovery generated a sense of deep uncertainty, an entrance into a new, unfamiliar world that seemed ghostly and insubstantial."[58] While the emergence of telecommunications seemed to eradicate temporal delay and spatial distance in transmitting messages instantaneously, visual technologies such as photography, telescopes, microscopes, and X-ray photography brought invisible worlds into view. If electronic telecommunication demonstrated the ghostly possibility of disembodied presence, then photographic technologies unveiled alien worlds, both infinitesimal and cosmic. Visual technologies proved superior to human sight in their ability to capture natural phenomena beyond the purview of human biological vision. The new media of the nineteenth and early twentieth centuries, then, opened up new regimes of time consciousness and new scales of worldly phenomena, including the pseudo-scientific world of spiritual energies and ghostly communication.

Gunning attributes the development of analogue photography and film in part to the positivist drive for knowledge, which sought novel modes of technologized knowledge production. "We could call this potential for uncovering new visual knowledge," Gunning writes, "the gnostic (from *gnosis*, knowledge) mission of cinema."[59] Significantly, experiments conducted by Eadweard Muybridge, Étienne-Jules Marey, Albert Londe, Georges Demenÿ, and others aimed to attune photographic processes to increasingly ephemeral and instantaneous events in nature, marking the revelation and visual capture of ethereal and invisible phenomena a central motivation of photographic development.[60] The confluence of microscopy and cinematography, for example, is used to great effect in key scenes in F.W. Murnau's *Nosferatu* (1922), a film Gunning argues is intimately invested in the uncanny powers of the cinema.[61] Early in the film, Professor Bulwer (John Gottowt) delivers a lecture to students concerning the predatory characteristics that define the natural world. Microscopic photography excerpted from contemporaneous scientific films depicts a Venus flytrap catching and ingesting a fly, a vampirous operation used in the film as a clear analogy for Count Orlok (Max Schreck). Later in the scene, another microscopic shot depicts a polyp in close-up as it ingests its microbial victim. Gunning notes that the film's intertitle has Bulwer refer to the polyp as a phantom, a "transparent, almost ethereal" creature.[62] With a close-up of Bulwer mouthing the word "phantom," Gunning states that the film also points to the phantom presence of the voice in silent cinema – visualized through facial movement yet inaudible.[63] *Nosferatu*'s use of microscopic imagery from scientific films not only functions to emphasize Count Orlok's vampirism as an exemplar of the predation found in nature but also demonstrates the possibilities of photography and the cinema. "*Nosferatu*," Gunning argues, "explored the play between the visible and the invisible, reflections and shadow, on- and off-screen space that cinema made possible, forging a technological image of the uncanny."[64] *Nosferatu* therefore deviates from the theatrical precepts of German Expressionism and its reliance on distorted *mise-en-scène* in order to convey an uncanny visuality

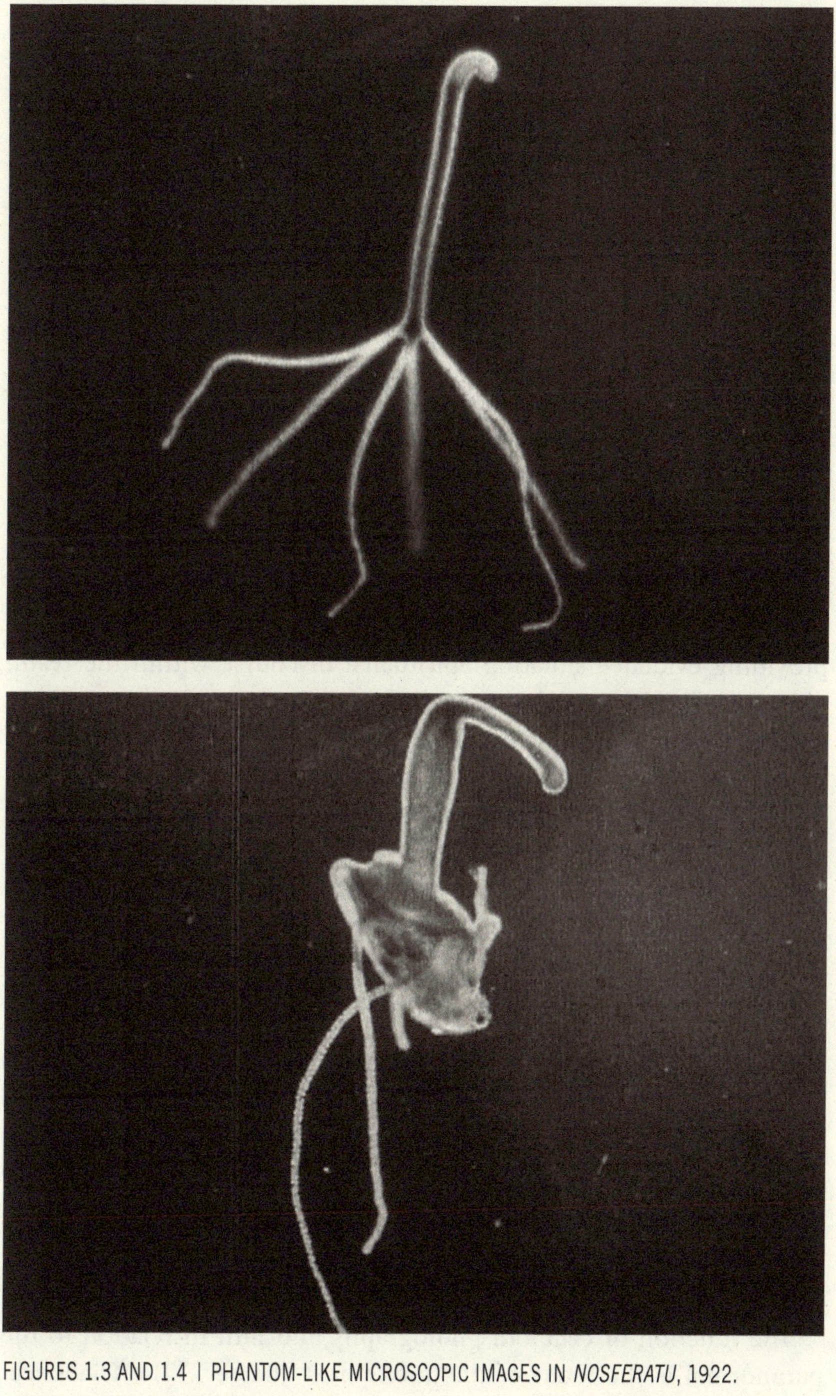

FIGURES 1.3 AND 1.4 | PHANTOM-LIKE MICROSCOPIC IMAGES IN *NOSFERATU*, 1922.

that is uniquely cinematographic. Such practices for Gunning demonstrate the "ambiguous relations woven among visuality, technology, knowledge, representation, and entertainment in modern culture."[65]

In their capacity to document and reveal the machinations of the natural world and facilitate a renewed vision, visual technologies of the nineteenth century occupy the precarious boundary between authenticating evidence and illusory optical trick. While photography is itself the product of scientific developments in chemistry and optics that lend it an air of indexical objectivity, it also generates a "parallel world of phantasmatic doubles," rendering the medium particularly conducive to occult and supernatural associations.[66] As chapter 2 details, the Spiritualist movement initiated by the Fox sisters in the 1840s seized upon these novel technologies of telecommunication and visuality as a means to assert the supernatural as scientifically verifiable. Invoking contemporaneous developments in electricity, telegraphy, chemistry, and biology, Spiritualism aimed to distance itself from religion and superstition by emphasizing the role of media in providing evidence situating Spiritualist discourse within the realm of empirical science rather than faith. As Gunning reiterates, "Since spiritualists saw their revelation as fundamentally modern, casting out the outmoded Calvinist beliefs in original sin and hellfire damnation, they welcomed evidence that their new revelation of the afterlife could be established 'scientifically.'"[67] As with the medium of photography, Spiritualism required an embodied medium, often a woman, who was similarly understood to be *sensitive* and *receptive* to spiritual communication. Media and intermediality therefore served important functions within Spiritualism in particular and paranormal investigation more broadly. Despite the ghost's refusal of linear temporality, this book is structured chronologically, examining a distinct medium in each chapter. In isolating the chapters according to the media of celluloid photography and film, television, video, and the internet, I hope to show the ways in which haunting operates intermedially and demonstrate how the ghost is constructed as a transmedial figure, with each medium contributing to the cultural imaginary of spirits and haunting.

The function of celluloid photography and film in relation to the paranormal is the focus of the book's next chapter, "The Diabolical

Image: Photography, Cinema, and Haunted Celluloid." The chapter unpacks the explicit association between the photographic image and the supernatural evident throughout canonical writings of classical film theory. Writers as varied as Jean Epstein, Béla Balázs, Siegfried Kracauer, and Dziga Vertov all aimed to define the specificity of the photographic and cinematographic image as revelatory, both augmenting and substituting for the biological deficiencies of human sight a mechanical mode of vision. Malcolm Turvey has characterized this tendency within classical film theory as the "revelationist tradition," a tradition that celebrates photography and film as superior forms of sight that exceed human perception and thereby represent a reality inaccessible to the human sensorium.[68]

The revelationist tradition of classical film theory resonates strongly with Spiritualist discourses of the nineteenth century in which the photographic image was celebrated as a method for documenting the presence of ghosts. If classical film theorists argued that photography and film accessed temporalities and realms of experience beyond human sight, then Spiritualists literalized this notion in imbuing the spiritualist camera with the power to capture the supernatural. Here, I explain the Spiritualists' investment in technologized modes of vision and its importance to the practice of mediumship. As this section argues, both classical film theory and Spiritualism advance a conception of photography and film as technologies that compensate for the limitations of human vision and reveal the reality of ghosts, entities that often remain invisible to human sight. To demonstrate this celebratory position vis-à-vis film and revelation, I analyze Nick Murphy's *The Awakening* (2011), a film that takes place in the 1920s and follows a researcher played by Rebecca Hall as she aims to debunk claims of haunting. Hall's character Florence Cathcart begins the film as a staunch skeptic, but her investigation of a supposedly haunted boarding school shakes her fundamental disbelief in spirits. Through various early twentieth-century investigative technologies, and especially celluloid photography, the haunting at the heart of the film's narrative is proven, attesting to the power and evidentiary status of the photographic image.

While *The Awakening* is aligned with the tradition of classical film theory and Spiritualism in its representation of celluloid film as revelatory and compensatory vision, 2012's *Sinister* (Scott Derrickson) depicts celluloid film as a malevolent and illusory medium. The next section situates *Sinister* within the broader discourse of contemporary film theory that regards with suspicion the reality effects of cinematic representation. For apparatus theorists of the 1970s, particularly those associated with the journal *Screen* such as Jean-Louis Baudry, Christian Metz, and Laura Mulvey, the immersion of the spectator in the illusory reality of the cinematic image constituted nothing short of ideological interpellation and psychic manipulation. Here, the reproduction of Cartesian perspectivalism and identification with the image and protagonists in mainstream narrative film pose a direct threat to the spectator; realist aesthetics produce a passive spectator who, in turn, uncritically accepts hegemonic social order. Because the cinema disguises its status as fictional construct and material apparatus for the duration of the film, such theorists consider mainstream narrative films to be exercises in deception that trick the spectator into accepting and internalizing a false image of the world.

Sinister reproduces this anxiety concerning the illusory status and affective power of the cinematic image in representing celluloid film as literally haunted by a demonic presence. When Ellison Oswalt (Ethan Hawke) discovers and views a series of old Super 8mm film reels, the demonic entity residing in the very emulsion of the filmstrip negatively affects his sense of reality. Ultimately, as the section will demonstrate, Oswalt's viewing of the haunting celluloid image effectively conjures the presence of the demon, leading to the demise of Oswalt and his family as they are subsumed by the film image itself. The chapter concludes, then, by arguing that the return of celluloid film in contemporary horror films can be categorized within these two broad tendencies: the celebration of analogue photography as revelatory, evidentiary, and compensatory vision, or its demonization as illusory, manipulative, and threatening. Given the release of *The Awakening* and *Sinister* in the 2010s, I suggest that the rise of digital image production has spurred renewed interest in analogue photography and film, sparking reconsiderations of its relationship to reality and illusion.

Chapter 3 shifts from photography and film to examine the medium of television. Titled "Televisual Ghosts and Paranormal Investigation," this chapter provides an analysis of ghost-hunting reality TV epitomized by the popular SyFy series *Ghost Hunters* (2004–16). The chapter first engages with theories concerning televisual medium specificity with an emphasis on temporality. The uniqueness of television and its distinction from cinema has often been attributed to the capacity of TV to produce live transmission, to broadcast an event simultaneously with its occurrence. Because of this temporal simultaneity as well as the presence of the television set in domestic spaces, André Bazin argued that television, more so than cinema, offered a uniquely intimate spectatorial experience.[69] Television's temporal order is often articulated as a "*this-is-going-on*" in contrast to the "*that-has-been*" of photography.[70] The chapter continues to survey scholarly engagements with televisual time, including the work of Bazin, Stefan Andriopoulos, Mary Ann Doane, and Jane Feuer, before turning specifically to paranormal reality television.

Karen Williams argues that paranormal reality television contributes to a broader lineage of ghostly media from the magic lantern and phantasmagoria shows onward, thereby perpetuating into the twenty-first century the dichotomy between "earnest authenticating" and "spectacle and effect" that characterizes displays of fantastic technologies.[71] Sarah Juliet Lauro and Catherine Paul argue, however, that paranormal reality TV exudes a postmodern ambivalence concerning our faith in technologized modes of evidence. When shows like *Ghost Hunters* present night-vision footage, thermal images, and sound recordings, the home viewer is presented with a choice: "she might accept that the technology has captured something ranging from inexplicable to proof of spirits, *or* she might find the technological medium of the show itself an obstacle to acceptance."[72] Such hesitation presented by the fact of mediation itself initiates what the authors call the "postmodern fantastic": the undecidability of technologized forms of visual evidence.[73] I argue, however, that *Ghost Hunters* and paranormal reality television advance a geological rationale of haunting in which the material landscape, the Earth's very bedrock, becomes a medium for the storage and transmission of spiritual energies. The ghost hunter is constructed as a kind of temporal archaeologist, excavating the heterogeneous temporalities accumulated by landscapes and the residual traces of spirits entombed therein. Through the notion of residual haunting, *Ghost Hunters* presents a conception of haunting as sedimented, fossilized within the present-pastness of the landscape as palimpsest.

Chapter 4, "Tape: Videographic Ruin and the Lure of the Tangible," builds upon the previous chapters by examining the resurgence of videotape in contemporary horror film. The chapter examines the found-footage subgenre of horror film specifically as it displays a significant investment in videotape as ruin. Through the act of discovery in found-footage horror film, I argue, videotape is imbued with the tactile and affective properties of historicity and memory. Videotape is transformed, then, through the process and act of discovery, from a simple storage format into the more complex formulation of technological ruin. The chapter begins by defining found-footage horror, providing on overview of its historical development and its narrative and formal characteristics. The chapter then provides an analysis of the relationship between videotape and horror film in that the latter was central to the development of a viable home video market in the late 1970s and early 1980s. I then discuss the demise of videotape and the ascension of DVD as the pre-eminent home video format before turning to the re-emergence of videotape on the consumer market.

The next section explores the problematics of video and medium specificity. Through a historical and theoretical analysis of the format, I suggest that video constitutes a contaminated medium, one that incorporates both cinema and television while not wholly belonging to either. Due to its liminality and its status as a contaminated medium, video materially embodies properties of the ghost in its category-bending interstitiality. The resurgence of videotape in the digital era, then, presents a unique opportunity to re-examine questions concerning medium specificity and intermediality. The chapter's analysis of the *V/H/S* series (2012–14) highlights the collapse of medium specificity as well as the allure of tangible media amid the ubiquity of digitization.

Chapter 5, "Hyperlinked Hauntings: Digital Horror and Networked Spectrality," investigates the internet as a digital archive of supernatural evidence. Today, amateur paranormal investigators may sift through innumerable webpages, blogs, and YouTube channels in search of the most persuasive and compelling evidence of haunting. The chapter argues, however, that our cultural understanding of the internet as an infinite archive, as a site of plenitude, freedom, and accessibility, is only made possible through orchestrated processes of control, curation, and erasure. That is, the fragility, degradation, and erasure of online digital files paradoxically render storage and accessibility possible. As Alexander Galloway has argued, the governing principle of control guided the development of the internet from its beginnings, despite its cultural associations with freedom and limitless access.[74] What I call networked horror films, those that depict the internet as a central threat in their narratives, explore the dichotomy between access and loss constitutive of the internet as a medium. I argue that networked horror represents the internet as an agent of contagion and erasure, thereby foregrounding anxieties concerning the influence of the internet in contemporary culture as well as its function as digital archive. While many networked horror films, including *Pulse* (Kiyoshi Kurosawa, 2001), *Feardotcom* (William Malone, 2002), *Halloween: Resurrection* (Phil Rosenthal, 2002), *The Den* (Zachary Donohue, 2013), *Unfriended* (Levan Gabriadze, 2014), and *Unfriended: Dark Web* (Stephen Susco, 2018), attest to this central anxiety, I employ the YouTube web series *Marble Hornets* (2009–14) and the Slender Man mythology as my chief case study.

The first section, "Contagion," illuminates the internet's function as a conduit for viral contagion. In *Marble Hornets*, the Slender Man is a mysterious supernatural humanoid creature who is abnormally tall, has elongated limbs, wears a suit, and, most disturbingly, lacks a face. The all-white, faceless figure stalks its victims, slowly driving them insane. Victims of the Slender Man experience memory loss and physical illness after being exposed to the creature. Importantly, once one has spotted the figure in person or in archival footage, one risks becoming the target of its haunting countenance. The Slender Man's threat is articulated in part as a viral contagion, moving from victim to victim via electronic exposure. This narrative characteristic is reminiscent of the actual spread of the Slender Man as a fictional mythological creature on the internet. First created on the message boards of SomethingAwful.com, the character gained popularity as a "creepypasta" and developed a significant fanbase. Moreover, *Marble Hornets* effectively began as a post on the Something Awful message board before uploading its first instalment on YouTube. The narrative of *Marble Hornets* takes place over a variety of social media platforms including YouTube, Twitter, and Instagram, marking the series as a transmedial work. In the development of the Slender Man as a character and the narrative threat it poses in *Marble Hornets*, viral spread and contagion are central, serving as a comment on the status of the internet and digital distribution.

The next section, "Erasure," focuses on the negative effects of the Slender Man on the protagonists of *Marble Hornets*, with particular attention paid to memory loss, time gaps, and the aesthetic convention of the glitch. Here, the glitch constitutes a visual manifestation of error and rupture, phenomena the characters experience psychically through amnesia and delusion. The mental gaps and absences produced through encounters with the Slender Man are mirrored in the discontinuity of *Marble Hornets*, structured as it is by a sequence of entries uploaded in non-chronological order. As is made clearer in the chapter, the series' narrative jumps back and forth in time, assembling fragments of digital video footage that constitutes the content of the series. With its discontinuous episode structure, emphasis on memory loss, and extensive use of digital glitches, *Marble Hornets* reflexively engages with the gaps and absences that structure the internet as digital archive.

Poetics of the Paranormal offers a new perspective for engaging with media and their relationship to the supernatural, one that demonstrates how media shape ghosts and how ghosts have shaped our media. The guiding question this book seeks to answer, then, is not simply "What do ghosts look like?"; it is also "What do ghosts make visible?" That is, what do ghosts allow us to understand about media, technology, and theory? Paranormal investigation in contemporary horror, I contend, does more than ask us to productively reconsider the function of evidence during our current climate of media change; it also encourages an interrogation of technologized spectrality. The horror narratives explored in this book across media bring to the fore a convergence of proof, belief, and indiscernibility that so defines our contemporary experiences of the postmodern fantastic.[75]

2

THE DIABOLICAL IMAGE: PHOTOGRAPHY, CINEMA, AND HAUNTED CELLULOID

"COULD CINEMA IN ITS ESSENCE BE EVIL?"[1]
TOM GUNNING

In 1915, cinema's capacity for evil was put on trial. The Ohio state legislature passed a law in 1913 creating a state film censorship board that required films to be submitted for approval before they could be exhibited in the state. With a mandate to approve films of a "moral, educational or amusing and harmless character," the board imposed penalties on exhibitors for screening films that had not been submitted and approved for public exhibition.[2] Mutual Film Corporation, a notable distributor, however, had refused to abide by the Ohio state law. Arguing that the law placed unwarranted restrictions on interstate commerce, that the law granted an exorbitant amount of legislative power to an unaccountable administrative body, and, most significantly, that the law violated Mutual's constitutional rights of freedom of speech and the press under the First Amendment, Mutual's lawyers fought the regulations in the US Supreme Court.[3] In *Mutual Film Corporation v Industrial Commission of Ohio*, the Supreme Court ruled unanimously in favour of the Ohio law upholding the state's right to censor films, thus denying motion pictures First Amendment rights under the constitution.

The decision, authored by Justice Joseph McKenna, stated, "It cannot be put out of view that the exhibition of moving pictures is a business, pure and simple, originated and conducted for profit."[4] Cinema's status as an industrial, commercial product, McKenna argued, prevented the medium from enjoying the kinds of protections extended to the press; although the press certainly constituted an industry in its own right, it also provided a service in the interest of the public good. According to the Court, motion pictures, by contrast, were "capable of evil, having power for it, the greater because of the attractiveness and manner of exhibition."[5] In further differentiating the cinema from print journalism, Justice McKenna asserted that films were "mere representations of events, of ideas and sentiments published and known, vivid, useful and entertaining no doubt, but as we have said, capable of evil."[6] The Court's decision would remain in place until 1952, when it was finally overturned, thereby granting motion pictures the rights and protections of the First Amendment.

McKenna's written decision articulates a suspicion not of any individual film or its content, but of the medium of cinema itself, citing the "attractiveness and manner of exhibition" as particularly worrisome. According to the Court, the *dispositif* of theatrical exhibition that placed spectators in a dark auditorium with strangers facing a luminous screen as images were projected at sixteen to twenty-four frames per second posed a unique threat to the physical and psychological constitution of the spectator. More than theatre, more than photography, and more than print journalism, it was claimed, the cinema wielded undue influence over the spectator in its ability to arouse involuntary physical reactions, such as jolts or screams. More sinister than such corporeal excitation, however, was the cinema's capacity to affect the mental state of the spectator through the manipulation of sense perception, "an attraction," Gunning writes, "compared to bewitchment, hypnosis, casting a spell, or putting the viewer/audience into a trance."[7] Although the Court acknowledged the utility and entertainment value of the moving image, the cinema's potential to enthrall and immerse the spectator within its spectacle, the Court found, carried "evil" potentialities and risked negatively affecting viewers' aesthetic, moral, and political judgment.[8] Anxiety over the influence of the cinema upon unwitting audience members, it should be noted, also carried classist and sexist implications; in this context, women, children, and the working class were perceived to be particularly vulnerable to the affective power of the moving image, for they supposedly lacked the cultural refinement and the intellectual competence to adequately absorb the visceral stimulation of the cinema.[9] Like Uncle Josh in Edwin S. Porter's *Uncle Josh at the Moving Picture Show* (1902), such spectators, it was claimed, might take the projected image to be that of reality itself, unable to discern a two-dimensional reproduction from its profilmic reality. In this way, the Supreme Court levied a critique against the cinematic apparatus that laid bare anxieties concerning the affective power of the medium and its propensity to project an illusory representation of the real.

The *Mutual* decision crystallized a tension that has haunted photographic media – still photography and motion pictures – since their development in the nineteenth century. As products of developments in optical science and in visual spectacle and entertainment, photographs manifest a positivist, empirical desire for objective and automatic mechanical documentation of reality as well as, simultaneously, the spectacle of optical illusion and visual trickery. The photographic image offers a mediated transcription of external reality: the camera registers automatically whatever is present before its lens, yet at the same time it generates an uncanny double of the represented material. A portrait photograph of one's grandmother, for example, both is and is not *her*. The photograph may capture her likeness with precision and detail unrivalled by preceding visual media, but it remains a likeness, a two-dimensional object that one can hold, exchange, and preserve. This tension between the photograph as an authentic slice of the real, on the one hand, and the photograph as a fabrication that only, and perhaps insidiously, *appears* real, on the other, has also defined central debates within classical and contemporary film theory, discourses that have long sought to define the ontology of the cinema, its status as an art, and its ideological effects on spectators.

As this chapter will show, many classical film theorists from the 1920s through the 1940s maintained that the cinema, because of its photographic foundation, accessed and revealed profound truths about the world, subjectivity, and reality itself. Film, it was argued, was able to capture and express characteristics beyond our common human perception. Cinema held the power to elevate reality, to move us beyond the doldrums of everyday existence, to enable us to capture the essential beauty at the heart of even the most ordinary situations. Cinema encouraged us to perceive our surroundings differently; it provided an accurate and authentic representation of reality, certainly, but that representation was one that transcended the blinding forces of habit, routine, and immediate utility. It allowed us to see, to perceive, anew. This was the lofty promise the relatively new medium made to spectators. Classical film theorists endowed the medium with unique representational power as well as access to a reality that otherwise would have been largely obscured by the machinations of modern life. For film theorists of the late 1960s and 1970s, however, cinema did not reveal but rather *distorted* reality precisely through its claims to the real. According to them, the narrative cinema of Hollywood constructed a false image of the world under the guise of representational realism, which was, in actuality, an illusion constructed through form, style, and editing techniques. That illusion masked the film's status as a construct and, more importantly, as an industrial commodity, thus advancing an erroneous impression that the world being presented to the audience was unmediated and directly accessible. Ultimately for such theorists, this photographic prestidigitation resulted in the pacification of spectators, thereby inoculating the political economy of capitalist states against meaningful challenge from the masses. The cinema was, these theorists reiterated, an industrial commodity; as such, it sought to reproduce the conditions that made its existence possible. In producing an illusory and fictitious representation of an unmediated reality, popular narrative cinema masked the actual precarious, tumultuous, and disastrous conditions of capitalist existence.

A diabolical duality thus coheres in film's photochemical verisimilitude, one that understands the cinema as accessing greater degrees of truth on the one hand and as constructing an erroneous, illusory impression of truth on the other. These debates subsided in the 1980s and 1990s in favour of a new historicism in film studies, among other interventions in the field, but they re-emerged with a new inflection at the turn of the millennium amidst the shift toward digital cinema production and exhibition. Now that cinematic images could be generated wholly or in part by software applications without the use of film or even cameras, the relationship between cinema and reality was once again up for passionate debate. What interests me here is that the status of photochemical film as either revelatory or illusory has become a central site of negotiation within several films in the first decades of the new millennium, particularly supernatural horror films that take as their subject the evidentiary quality of the photographic image. I argue that these films explicitly restage the binary opposition of photochemical photography as objective and revelatory on the one hand and as manipulative and illusory on the other. To this end, I examine Nick Murphy's *The Awakening* (2011) as an exemplar of the former tendency and Scott Derrickson's *Sinister* (2012) as an exemplar of the latter.

The Awakening takes place in 1920s London and follows Florence Cathcart (Rebecca Hall), an author dedicated to the debunking and demystification of claims of haunting. Enlisted to investigate a supposedly haunted boarding school in rural England, Cathcart sets out to scientifically determine the cause of various strange happenings at the school, employing a variety of instruments including thermometers, barometers, chemicals, and photography. *Sinister* similarly concerns itself with the evidentiary status of celluloid film. Ellison Oswalt (Ethan Hawke), a true-crime writer, discovers in the attic of his new home a cache of Super 8mm home movies as well as a projector. Far from documenting idyllic family gatherings, the films contain grisly scenes of murder committed by an unknown assailant. Determined to take on this investigation independently from the police, Oswalt learns that the Super 8mm images are literally haunted by a demonic spirit, a presence that threatens to doom Oswalt and his family for having viewed its image. Both films engage with the relationship between celluloid film and the supernatural, exploring the ways in which the photographic image captures and expresses a reality beyond conventional human perception. As such, *The Awakening* and *Sinister* are indebted to the legacy of Spiritualism, a nineteenth- and twentieth-century belief system that espoused the veridical status of the spirit world as well as our ability to communicate with spirits through physical, psychical, and technological mediumship.

These are just two examples of the re-emergence of analogue photography and film in contemporary horror cinema. *The Blair Witch Project* (Daniel Myrick and Eduardo Sánchez, 1999) incorporates both 16mm black-and-white cinematography and video footage of a haunted forest, rendering the landscape an uncanny labyrinth through which the characters must navigate as they attempt to document the existence of a legendary witch. The twist ending of Alejandro Amenábar's *The Others* (2001) is predicated upon the discovery of a post-mortem photograph that exposes those whom we previously believed to be living as the ghosts of the deceased. More recently, *Insidious* (James Wan, 2010) depicts various analogue methods for spirit detection in an effort to rescue the son of the protagonists, who has become trapped in an ethereal void known as "the further." In *Red Lights* (Rodrigo Cortés, 2012), a team of researchers attempt to debunk the claims of a renowned psychic (Robert De Niro) using an assortment of tests and high-tech equipment, only to discover that analogue photography and polaroid film lend credence to his claims to have supernatural powers. *The Conjuring* (2013), also directed by James Wan, follows demonologists Ed and Lorraine Warren, who employ analogue photography to detect the presence of spirits in this dramatization of a supposedly true story of domestic haunting in 1970s Rhode Island. As well as static photography, the Warrens employ a 16mm film camera in their investigation, thus contributing to a portfolio of evidence to present to the Catholic Church in order to justify an exorcism. As these texts demonstrate, such a return to analogue photographic methods in the beginning of the twenty-first century amidst the increasingly ubiquitous availability of digital recording technologies yields significant insights into the cultural value we place upon certain methods of image production, insights that in horror film more broadly, and supernatural horror films in particular, are predicated upon the evidentiary status of the image.

But what accounts for this renewed fascination with material, analogue media? To be sure, various media have functioned as haunted objects, including television (*Poltergeist* [Tobe Hopper, 1984]), VHS tapes (*Ringu* [Hideo Nakata, 1998]; *The Ring* [Gore Verbinski, 2002]), the internet (*Feardotcom* [William Malone, 2002]), and cell phones (*One Missed Call* [Takashi Miike, 2003; Eric Valette, 2008]). With *Sinister*, we can add Super 8mm film to this list of haunted media within horror film. While horror cinema has certainly expressed an interest in seeking out novel objects to infest with evil autonomy,[10] it strikes me as significant that at the very moment traditional film has been supplanted by digital image production and exhibition, analogue photography and film have resurfaced as haunted objects. In the case of *Sinister*, the anachronistic presence of Super 8mm film is cause for suspicion, as the technology has no logical place in a contemporary home. Like an antique artifact, celluloid film here is depicted as a historical curiosity that must be investigated, its mysteries solved.

While the haunted quality of the Super 8mm image in *Sinister* is tied to the film gauge's senescence and aesthetic of decay, other supernatural horror films represent analogue media as superior conveyors of evidence and truthful renderings of physical reality. If digital technology is often argued to have abandoned the indexical quality of the image (a discussion that will be addressed in more detail in chapter 5), such films represent the return of analogue as a reassurance of the real, often affirming the existence of the supernatural realm. Contemporary supernatural films oscillate between these two tendencies: existential reassurance and diabolical illusionism. As such, the next section of this chapter will examine the former tendency in *The Awakening* and the following section will examine *Sinister* in relation to the diabolical image. Although Walter Benjamin famously declared that mechanical reproduction had brought about the decay of the aura of the art object as it "substitutes a plurality of copies for a unique existence,"[11] analogue photography and celluloid film have returned as media of originality and uniqueness despite epitomizing the very process of mechanical reproduction endemic to industrial modernity. In a moment when digital images are often said to be wholly immaterial and cut off from any existential bond to reality, analogue media emerge as a visual tether, linking us to a material reality thought lost.

PHOTOGRAPHY AND THE INVISIBLE: HAUNTED PORTRAITURE AND CLASSICAL FILM THEORY

In *Theory of Film*, Siegfried Kracauer argues that two main tendencies of the cinema presented themselves at the moment of its origin in the works of the Lumière brothers and Georges Méliès respectively. In works such as *L'Arrivée d'un train en gare de La Ciotat* (1895), *La Sortie de l'usine Lumière à Lyon* (1895), and *Repas de bébé* (1895), the Lumières fixed the lens of their *cinématographe* upon ordinary happenings, on the banal and the mundane. According to Kracauer, the Lumière films "pictured everyday life after the manner of photographs,"[12] exploiting the basic property of the medium as a photographic device by capturing physical reality through movement. "Film," Kracauer asserts, "is uniquely equipped to record and reveal physical reality and, hence, gravitates toward it."[13] It is significant that Kracauer considers this recording function to be a *basic* property of film; although film has technical properties unique to the medium (he singles out editing as particularly indispensable), the basic property of recording reality takes precedence over technical skill; he describes the former as "responsible for the cinematic quality of a film."[14] A film exhibiting the greatest feats of technical virtuosity would thus be seen as *less* cinematic precisely because of its betrayal of the basic property.[15] If the actualities of the Lumière brothers epitomize the realist tendency of film, then the fantastic cinema of Georges Méliès is, for Kracauer, emblematic of the formalist tendency. Works such as *Le Voyage dans la lune* (1902) and *Le Voyage à travers l'impossible* (1904) literally envision impossible journeys to exotic distant worlds, while *Le Manoir du diable* (1896), *L'Auberge ensorcelée* (1897), and *Le Revenant* (1903) reveal the invisible realm of ghosts and spirits. Employing elaborate stage sets and trick photography – the splice and superimposition in particular – Méliès understood film to be an extension of stage magic, uniquely capable of conjuring illusion.

These binary oppositions of documentation versus illusion and reality versus fantasy are of course permeable, and Kracauer acknowledges that most films combine attributes of both, citing dream sequences as salient examples.[16] However, Kracauer argues that "artistic films," that is, those which defy realism and revel in fantasy, move the medium away from its primary purpose of revealing reality, ironically rendering the most artistic films the least cinematic.[17] Even while pointing to the inherent realism of the medium, though, Kracauer suggests that even the most fantastic films cannot completely do away with nature,[18] for the camera is always confined to recording the raw material in profilmic space. "All of these creative efforts," he writes, "are in keeping with the cinematic approach as long as they benefit, in some way or other, the medium's substantive concern with our visible world."[19] Craftsmanship and artistry are thus permitted by Kracauer so long as they contribute to, rather than detract from, cinema's vocation as a realist medium.

Along with classical film theorists Jean Epstein, Dziga Vertov, and Béla Balázs, Kracauer belongs to what Malcolm Turvey has called the "revelationist tradition" in film theory, a tradition that champions the cinema's ability to exceed human perception and access reality.[20] Principally concerned with defining cinematic ontology and the unique artistic attributes of the medium, classical film theorists in the revelationist tradition define the medium as uniquely able to access and re-present something of authentic reality, a reality that remains invisible to human sight. The revelationist tradition posits that human vision is unable to provide authentic views of the world and that photography and film overcome its limitations with techniques such as the close-up, slow motion, and time-lapse photography.[21] Jean Epstein cites science and nature films as demonstrating the cinema's capacity to augment our human perception of time and proffer "amazing glimpses into the life of plants and crystals."[22] "Time hurries on or retreats, or stops and waits for you," Epstein writes. "A new reality is revealed, a reality for a special occasion, which is untrue to everyday reality just as everyday reality is untrue to the heightened awareness of poetry."[23] By slowing down or speeding up the flow of time, cinema can offer us access to hitherto imperceptible phenomena such as the growth and movement of plants. Epstein laments the privileging of story over image and critiques the dominant cinema's production of literary and stage adaptations; for him, the medium becomes an art form when it exploits the medium-specific qualities of *photogénie* – that which is enhanced by filmic production. More specifically, Epstein describes as photogenic any instance wherein the moral character of subjects and objects is enhanced through cinematic reproduction, a morality that lies in the capturing of the soul.[24]

The term *photogénie* is borrowed from Epstein's contemporary Germaine Dulac, who similarly defined cinema's ontology as one of revelation. "If machines decompose movement and set out to explore the realm of the infinitely small in nature," Dulac writes, "it is in order to visually reveal to us beauties and dramas that our eye, a feeble lens, does not perceive."[25] Dulac repeats this claim in an earlier essay from 1925 in which she likens the cinema to a superior eye, a more powerful optical instrument through which to visualize the world.[26] Like

Epstein, Dulac suggests that the essence of humanity – its spirit or soul – is rendered visible in film, erasing cultural and national differences in favour of a universal humanism.[27] Walter Benjamin argues a similar point, suggesting that the close-up and slow motion reveal "entirely new structural formations of the subject," that is, our optical unconscious.[28] These authors agree the cinema offers a compensatory view of reality, exhibiting the detail and the intricacy of movement that remains imperceptible in ordinary experience.

Like these writers, Béla Balázs champions the cinema's penetrating eye, but he fixes his analytic gaze upon the human face, arguing that an emotional, intellectual, and, indeed, spiritual truth is rendered visible in the on-screen faces of human subjects. Balázs asserts that the invention of the printing press "rendered illegible the faces of men" due to its primacy of language over the visual;[29] he then credits silent cinema for once again turning our attention to visual culture. Specifically, Balázs celebrates the close-up for its ability to communicate the spirit of the filmed individual without the use of words. Of the close-up, Balázs writes, "What appears on the face and the facial expression is a spiritual experience which is rendered immediately visible without the intermediary of words."[30] Unencumbered by words, the silent film close-up offers a new kind of transparency, bringing the human soul or spirit into focus. Of particular importance for Balázs is the polyphonic nature of the face and its expression of multiple, sometimes contradictory, emotions at once. Likened to chords in musical composition, the face becomes a melodic site upon which the interplay of harmonious, although distinct, thoughts and emotions are laid bare.[31] It is the scale, intimacy, and duration of the cinematic close-up projected onto a large theatre screen that allows one to perceive the machinations of the face, the micro-physiognomy of a twitch of the eye or curl of the mouth, that reveal the soul of the subject.

Balázs is not alone in finding musical analogies with cinema. In "The Birth of the Sixth Art," Ricciotto Canudo celebrates film as the unification of the "rhythms of space" and the "rhythms of time," combining the materialist plastic arts of painting and sculpture with the temporality of musical performance.[32] "The new manifestation of Art," Canudo contends, "should really be more precisely *a Painting and a Sculpture developing in Time*, as in music and poetry, which realise themselves by transforming air into rhythm for the duration of their execution."[33] Canudo, publishing in 1911, is not prepared to declare the relatively new medium of moving images a bona fide art form on par with painting, but he suggests that the cinematograph "points the way" to achieving not only the consolidation of materialist and temporal rhythms but also a "new aesthetic function" that epitomizes the modern age.[34] For Canudo, rhythm, movement, and duration align film with music, distinguishing the medium from the stillness of the plastic arts and promising to provide an aesthetic experience akin to "a glimpse of the spirits."[35] Similarly, Élie Faure suggested that the cinema, or the art of cineplastics as he called it, "incorporates time in space," allowing for the playful and artistic manipulation of time that was previously the province of music alone.[36] In 1919, Marcel Gromaire declared that cinema, "like music, is an autonomous art" that transforms its material into a unique expression distinct from any adapted material it may be based upon, likening a cinematic adaptation of a literary work to an "opera for the eyes."[37] Like these writers, Léon Moussinac identified the rhythm of moving images as the cinema's most compelling aesthetic attribute, writing that musical and cinematic rhythm share a unique relationship to memory in that the listener and viewer assimilate disparate elements into a cohesive whole to form a perceptual impression of the complete work.[38] These comparisons between cinema and music all highlight the importance of temporality, movement, and flow to defining the uniqueness of film as an art form as well as the relationship between the fragment and the whole – that is, the single element of the film frame vis-à-vis the complete work. All these writers contend that in experimenting with different temporal rhythms through the manipulation of the materiality of celluloid in shooting speed and projection speed, the cinema offers alternative views and experiences of time that portray its true condition of flow and flux, even while escaping the conscious perception of modern subjects. Cinema's alternative temporal regimes offer an experience of time divorced from the regimented standardization of mechanical time ordered by discrete units of hours, minutes, seconds.

The reality revealed by virtue of photography's profilmic verisimilitude, however, accrues a melancholic pedigree for Kracauer, as the photograph's relationship to time, memory, and history renders it inextricable from mortality. Photographs not only age, decay, and disintegrate but also lose their referentiality to a living present, becoming fragmented abstractions. A photographic record of the real is not eternal; it withers. Referring to a photo of a twenty-four-year-old woman taken in 1864, Kracauer asks: "Is this what *grandmother* looked like?"[39] The photographed woman bears little resemblance to the memories her grandchildren hold of her, and this relegates verification to the testimony of others rather than to the material photographic print itself. The photo is further alienated from the present due to the outdated clothing worn by the woman, signifiers that place her firmly in a distant past. Excised from its original time and place, the photograph "wanders ghost-like through the present, like the lady of a haunted castle."[40] Although the woman's outmoded garments and hairstyle may draw laughter from contemporary viewers, Kracauer notes that this laughter is a symptom of disavowal that is simultaneously accompanied by a shudder of recognition: recognition that this time too shall pass and that the present will flow irrevocably into the past, where we will all become (dead) historical remnants for the future. "Laughter is not the only response provoked by antiquated photography," Kracauer writes. "It presents what is utterly past, and yet this detritus was once present."[41] What is preserved in the photograph is the instant of time during which the human subject before the lens, as the photograph ages, is reduced to a "mannequin" modelling temporally estranged garments, signifying the inevitability of obsolescence. As Miriam Hansen articulates, "The grandchildren's giggles are a defense against dread, a shocklike, visceral recognition of their own contingency and mortality, of a history that does not include them."[42] "Ghosts," Kracauer concludes, "are simultaneously comical and terrifying."[43]

In capturing an instant of time as a spatial configuration – as a material print – the photograph, Kracauer maintains, is susceptible to the degenerating effects of time's flow, a deleterious constitution of the image that is, albeit incompletely, overcome by film and its construction of motion through a composite of still images. The photograph lays bare the certitude of death and the assurance of one's mortality, even while simultaneously revealing fragmentation and contingency as defining features of modernity; thereby, it challenges a bourgeois historicism and aesthetic regime predicated upon continuity, wholeness, and unity. Because film is composed of such fragments in the form of still images, it poses the possibility of recombination and reformation in radical new ways that allow for novel avenues of perception and a "liberated consciousness."[44] The turn to the mass circulation of photographic media represents what Kracauer provocatively calls the "*go-for-broke game* of history," an unprecedented opportunity to reshape thought and society as a challenge to industrial capitalism, as in the radical montage aesthetics of Sergei Eisenstein's *Battleship Potemkin* (1925), or, conversely, the reification of capitalist social relationships. The fate of modernity and the direction of history effectively rest on whether (and how) photographic media will mobilize the working-class masses to actualize their self-interest, or whether they will instead serve to reproduce and perpetuate the conditions that subjugate the masses to the ruling class.[45]

In the liberatory potentiality of the photographic image and its relationship to fragmentation and death, Kracauer finds a surprising ally in the metaphysics of Spiritualism, which similarly sought to liberate consciousness through the visual representation of death via residual manifestations of ghosts in photographs. Like the classical film theorists discussed here, Spiritualists argued that the photographic process rendered the camera a superior eye able to visualize that which eluded our deficient corporeal sense of sight. Thus, the nineteenth and early twentieth centuries witnessed the mass production of haunted portraits claiming to depict the actual souls of the dead. In Nick Murphy's *The Awakening* (2011), Spiritualism itself becomes the subject of investigation as its protagonist aims to disprove and debunk the existence of the supernatural and the movement's appropriation of pseudoscientific methods.

The Awakening begins with a title card featuring a quote from the fictitious author Florence Cathcart, the protagonist of the film, from her book *Seeing Through Ghosts*. It reads: "Observation: Between 1914 and 1919 war and influenza have claimed more than a million lives in Britain alone. Conclusion: This is a time for ghosts." Cathcart, an avowed atheist and skeptic, has devoted her career to investigating and debunking claims of haunting and paranormal activity, claims that have increased in the immediate aftermath of the First World War. And indeed, Cathcart is haunted by ghosts of her own, for her fiancé died in combat. Rather than attempt to contact his spirit, however, Cathcart uses this fact as a point of authentication when attending séances. In the first scene, Cathcart, using a pseudonym, presents a photograph of her deceased fiancé to a woman overseeing a séance so as to demonstrate the sincerity of her desire to contact the spirit world. Cathcart is permitted to enter to the séance room and joins a table of patrons similarly seeking spiritual contact. In a dimly lit parlour room, she takes her seat around a large table along with several other participants. The group joins hands as the theatrics of the séance begin; a raven is sacrificed, a woman's nose begins to bleed, candles mysteriously go out, and the apparition of a young girl is seen in the reflection of a bell jar. Cathcart puts an end to this spectacle of the supernatural by exposing the spirit as a little boy in a wig. With the assistance of her detective partner, Cathcart opens the drapes, illuminating the room while explaining to the bereaved how the mysterious happenings were accomplished: fake blood capsules, string attached to candles pulling out the wick, and, of course, classic misdirection. "You're charlatans," Cathcart admonishes, "and poor ones at that." In demystifying the paranormal event as nothing more than illusion and trickery, Cathcart aims to demonstrate that belief in the supernatural more broadly is a farce perpetuated by greedy opportunists taking advantage of vulnerable people in mourning. Cathcart's crusade is thus against the central tenets of Spiritualism: that spirits exist and are able to communicate with the living.

In the United States, Spiritualism originated in Hydesville, New York, in 1848 when the Fox family began to experience unexplained disturbances in their home. In March of that year, the family's young daughters Kate and Margeretta decided to engage with the disembodied sonic phenomena in an attempt to discern their origins and purpose. Using a system of one knock for "yes" and two knocks for "no," the sisters had ostensibly succeeded in communicating with the spectral presence occupying their home, as the entity correctly answered, via knocking, specific questions, including the ages of the Fox children and how many of the Fox family were alive and dead.[46] News of the Fox sisters' supposed success in communicating with the dead quickly spread and initiated a new movement that claimed to authenticate the existence of a spiritual realm; indeed, and more importantly, this realm could be accessed through communications media. Spiritualism held that a direct link between the earthly material realm and the metaphysical spiritual realm – primarily through the participation of mediums (i.e., clairvoyant individuals who claimed to have a unique sensitivity to the presence of spirits) – could be established wherein entities from the ether could communicate with those still living. Spiritualism, as a religious and political movement, became extremely popular, with séances even reportedly held in the White House,[47] and initiated "the modern fascination with séances, spirit circles, automatic writing, telepathy, clairvoyance, Ouija boards, and other paranormal phenomena."[48] Photographic processes in particular had a strong impact on Spiritualism, for they not only authenticated belief in the supernatural but also helped spread the movement to others: the display and exhibition of such photographs would convert the skeptical.

Photography was highly persuasive in both spiritualist and scientific discourses because it was viewed as automatically reproducing an objective image of reality. From the silvered glass plates of the daguerreotype made commercially available in 1839 to William Henry Fox Talbot's innovation of the calotype process using sensitized paper negatives, photographic images supposedly offered direct transcriptions of external reality, its mediation limited only by the frame of the image and the choice of lens and camera angle.[49] Photography was conceptualized as the "pencil of nature,"[50] and its use by the sciences testified to its value as the supposedly objective recording instrument *par excellence*. Images produced via the automated photographic process – itself a scientific development in optics, chemistry, and mechanization – enjoyed a privileged relationship to reality, authenticity, and objectivity. Indeed, as Clément Chéroux has noted, since its inception, "photography had always benefitted from a scientific aura whenever it was discussed."[51] Similarly, Philippe Montebello and Jean-Luc Monterosso write, "A unique characteristic of photography has always been its ability to record the visible, material world with truth and accuracy."[52] From its earliest introduction, then, photography was understood to be a mechanical, automated process that faithfully reproduced reality within its images, a conception that not only was essential in defining the new visual medium as distinct from existing modes of visual representation in painting but also heralded as a novel form of knowledge production. As such, photography conceived as a scientific instrument rather than an an artistic medium contributed to broader positivist ideologies of the nineteenth century that understood the physical, natural world as something able to be decoded, classified, and rationalized through empirical observation.

In supplanting the previous standard of drawings and watercolours for identifying, recording, and categorizing specimens such as microscopic bacteria, the photograph with its mechanical objectivity promised an unprecedented degree of authority as evidence. Jennifer Tucker has shown that at a time when the existence of germs and their impact was being debated, it was photographic evidence of microbes that finally persuaded the scientific community of their importance.[53] Confronted with visual evidence, the medical community could no longer question or deny the fact of bacterial contagion and its relationship to disease. As such, the photographic apparatus functioned as a "harmonizing mediator" that could settle factual disputes with empirical precision. Writing of photomicrography in particular, photographer and chemist Dr Hermann Wilhelm Vogel stated in *The Chemistry of Light and Photography* (1875), "Nowhere has photography shown itself a more brilliant auxiliary or substitute for the art of drawing than in the reproduction of microscopic objects."[54] Pragmatically, photography eliminated the laborious task of creating detailed artist's renderings of specimens, a time-consuming process that inevitably fell short of creating a complete, comprehensive record. Photographs had this added benefit: they could be copied, published, and distributed so as to allow increased access to research among scientists and, later on, with the introduction of illustrated journals and magazines, among the public at large.[55] As such, photography served a democratic function in increasing access to scientific knowledge.

This sense of a democratic science was shared by the first president of the American Society for Psychical Research, William James, brother of the famed novelist Henry James. Trained in psychology, William James led the ASPR beginning in 1884. It was the American branch of the Society of Psychical Research, founded in England in 1882. James prized the slowness of empirical observation and data collection in both psychology and psychical research, a fastidious methodology that James saw as essential to the accumulation of sound, verifiable evidence. He understood this to be a slow and patient endeavour; thus, the goal of the ASPR was to simply collect and record data over several decades rather than assign definitive conclusions to supernatural questions.[56] Recording data and reports from a variety of individuals over a vast geographical and historical period conformed to James's broader aspirations toward a pluralist democracy in which the variety of perspectives offered by a heterogeneous citizenry produced a "richer articulation of reality."[57] This ideal of democratic pluralism was limited, however, to a white, middle-class, and mostly male constituency that typically defined conceptions of citizenship in the late nineteenth century. As Alicia Puglionesi remarks, referring to the emphasis on testimony and witnessing in psychical research and the empirical sciences more broadly, "The knowledge that people prize most highly emerges from their own direct experience or from the accounts of others whom they perceive as like them."[58] In privileging direct participation from non-scientists in the reporting and recording of observational data, psychical research took inspiration from similar methods adopted in meteorology and astronomy, fields that shared with psychical research the task of "identify[ing] and fix[ing] fleeting phenomena encountered only in their indirect emanations."[59] Such phenomena proved elusive and difficult to capture photographically, for they required that personal accounts and eyewitness testimony be gathered and systematized.

Puglionesi has described how ill-equipped the ASPR was to administer and catalogue the trove of documentation sent to its offices, for it lacked the staff and resources necessary to efficiently categorize and store the materials. In a section titled "Tedium," Puglionesi describes the challenge of going through the ASPR's files: "what a tedious task lies before me – everything is out of order, none of the names mean anything, terrible penmanship is the rule – my day will be an aimless drift through the flotsam of the unremembered dead."[60] Encouraging participation and submissions of documents detailing phenomena established psychical research as a science open to the amateur wherein one need not possess disciplinary expertise in order to contribute to the field. Amateurs and non-experts would remain a central component of paranormal investigation into the contemporary era, in which everyone from plumbers to stand-up comedians to Jack Osbourn and

Kesha lead investigations of haunted places weekly on their respective reality TV programs. The inclusion of non-expert amateurs in its endeavours would, however, further stoke public interest in the activities of the ASPR and contribute to a broader spectacularization of science that was well under way in the nineteenth century.

Photographic copies of specimens and natural phenomena circulated among the intelligentsia and the social elite and were also exhibited as attractions in fairgrounds and at carnivals. Notably, these venues would also prove significant in the display of the first motion pictures during the late nineteenth and early twentieth centuries. Scientific photographs here became forms of visual entertainment, contributing to what Tucker has described as the "spectacle of science."[61] Once illustrated journals and newspapers became increasingly widespread after the 1890s and into the early twentieth century, scientific photographs were published with more regularity and commanded more attention from the public at large. Such publication benefited the scientific community, for it cultivated public interest in scientific research, which in turn justified government and private investment in various projects, besides contributing to the positivist ethos of the time, which valued above all else empirical observation as a guarantor of knowledge. This democratization of seeing at the height of the age of discovery had quasi-utopian implications, for it promised to solve the mysteries of nature and reveal its secrets.

Cathcart epitomizes this ideology in *The Awakening*. As a stalwart skeptic, she has made a career of revealing the natural causes and/or the intentional deceptions behind supposedly supernatural phenomena. After the events of the séance that begin the film, Florence Cathcart (Rebecca Hall) returns to her London home, where she is approached by Robert Mallory (Dominic West), a teacher at an all-boys boarding school. He explains that when the school was a private residence many years ago, a child was said to have been mysteriously murdered. Ever since, tales of the child's ghostly presence have plagued the school and terrified its pupils. "So you're here about a death that may or may not have happened however many years ago?," Cathcart asks, incredulously. But Mallory informs her that another death took place three weeks ago, the death of a student who had claimed to have seen the ghost of the murdered child. Because the students of the school are

2.1 | PANORAMIC CLASS PHOTO WITH GHOSTLY "EXTRA" IN *THE AWAKENING*, 2011.

convinced of the existence of this ghost, Mallory implores Cathcart to visit the school and determine what, if anything, explains the unusual sightings.

The key piece of evidence that Mallory presents to Cathcart is a series of panoramic school photographs that depict all the students standing in rows in front of the school. He points out the ghostly, transparent figure of a boy standing at the edge of the row. Cathcart dismisses these images as the result of an old school prank that exploits an essential deficiency of the photographic apparatus: long exposure time. She explains that as the camera tracks across the rows of students, a boy from one end runs across to the other side, reaching the end of the row as the camera completes its lateral tracking motion. Such a prank not only produces a doubled image of the student occupying two spaces simultaneously but also potentially produces a semi-transparent image of the boy. Mallory, familiar with this prank, explains that all the boys were accounted for in each photograph, eliminating the possibility of a student performing this photographic trick. Moreover, Mallory gestures toward the background of the most recent class photo wherein the transparent figure of a boy is visible in an upper-story window of the school. While unconvinced by this evidence, Cathcart nevertheless agrees to visit the school, debunk the claims of haunting, and put the fears of the students to rest.

While travelling to the school, Mallory asks Cathcart why she is committed to people believing in nothing. Cathcart responds, "No, without science, people don't believe in nothing. They believe in anything, including sprits ... I believe in evidence." After they arrive at the school, a montage sequence introduces various instruments Cathcart will be using in order to accrue evidence: "Pocket Premo twelve exposure pack with meniscus lens; sound recorder, part Bell-Tainter;[62] Fumigator for measuring contact traces; Marconi magnetic field detector." And finally, a series of trip wires that, on being activated, will open the shutter of an attached camera for one thirtieth of a second while an electrical charge ignites a powdered mixture of magnesium and potassium chlorate, thus providing enough light for the photographic plate to register a coherent image. Marvelling at the virtuosity of this scientific demonstration, Mallory opines, "They must hate you." "Who? The Spiritualists?," Cathcart responds. "No, the ghosts." Clearly, judging from such a battery of instruments and tests, no ghost, and indeed no human, is meant to escape the penetrating eyes and ears of scientific surveillance.

It is striking that all the methods of gathering evidence employed by Cathcart are understood to be irrefutable precisely because of their indexicality; in terms of the semiotics of Charles Sanders Peirce, these indexical signifiers all testify to the previous existence of the referent by way of lasting trace or imprint. As Mary Ann Doane elaborates, "it is the indexical sign that acts as a temporal trace and has an existential relation to its object."[63] In addition to examples such as a weather vane, which is physically affected by the direction of the wind, the photographic image is considered an indexical sign because of the photochemical reaction of light hitting the film or glass plate. Tom Gunning summarizes the indexical quality of the photograph as "the transformation of light sensitive emulsion caused by light reflecting off the object photographed filtered through the lens and diaphragm."[64] The photograph thus understood becomes an index of light that existed in the instant the photograph was taken. "The footprint, the weathercock, the photographic image," Doane continues, "all testify to the fact that the referent was present and left its legible trace directly in representation."[65] While Cathcart suggests that Spiritualists may hate her because she employs instruments that, because of their indexicality, provide irrefutable proof of fraud or forgery, this sense of the photograph-as-trace that testifies to the prior existence of an object in time and space is consistently echoed in Spiritualist discourse regarding the centrality of photographs as evidence. In fact, Spiritualists, like the scientific community, held that photography did indeed reveal the hidden truths of nature with its unique mechanical and photochemical vision. Spirits, it was argued, were material, natural phenomena that had simply escaped our human empirical faculties. Photography as a scientific instrument revealed and documented the invisible worlds of bacteria; in much the same way, Spiritualists maintained that photography was revelatory of an alternate plane of existence as substantial and material as our own.

In his 1894 work *The Veil Lifted*, John Taylor provides the following list of five criteria that define spirit photographs:

1 Portraits of psychical entities not seen by normal vision.
2 Portraits of objects not seen or thought of by the sitter or by the medium or operator; such as flowers, words, crosses, crowns, lights, and various emblematic objects.
3 Pictures which have the appearance of being copied from statues, paintings, or drawings.
4 Pictures of what are called materialised forms visible to normal sight.
5 Pictures of the "wraith" or "double" of persons still in the body.[66]

As this list demonstrates, Spiritualists adopted and advocated for different techniques in photographing spirits, techniques that would prove to be a point of contention within Spiritualist circles.[67] To be sure, Spiritualists often did not believe that *all* photographs claiming to depict the presence of spirits were authentic, and charges of technical incompetence and fraud were levelled by Spiritualists and skeptics alike. Lest one assume that nineteenth-century subjects uncritically accepted photographic images of the supernatural as inherently genuine, such conflicts even within Spiritualism itself suggest otherwise.

Nevertheless, in terms of definition, a spirit photograph consisted of a living individual posing for a photographic portrait; upon developing the negative, a semi-transparent figure would appear adjacent to the sitter. This characterizes the majority of William Mumler's photographic works, in which identifiable dead individuals appear with their living family members in the finished photograph. Central to the authenticity of the spirit photograph, then, was the appearance of a recognizable and *identifiable* dead individual within the same image as that of the sitter. Simone Natale notes that the evidential status of spirit photographs hinged upon expert testimony and the recognition of the spirit; only then would it be accepted as authentic. This demonstrates the importance of corroboration in Spiritualist practices and psychical research.[68] Frederick Hudson's spirit photographs, although sharing many conventions of Mumler's portraiture, differ regarding how the spirit is represented. Here, the ghostly figure is an embodied and corporeal being (i.e., not a transparent entity), clothed in long, flowing white robes, signifying its phantasmatic status.[69]

Thirteen years after the Fox sisters had made contact, William Mumler made a startling discovery upon developing one of his photographs. A jeweller by trade and a self-confessed amateur when it came to photography, Mumler is considered the first person to claim to have captured a spectral countenance in a photograph.[70] Mumler initially dismissed his ghost photograph as the result of his own inexperience with the photographic process; however, as he made further photographs, the ghostly presence appeared increasingly more vivid on different glass plates, thus testifying, for Mumler, to the veracity of the spirit images. Recounting Mumler's first experience with spirit photography, John Taylor wrote, "[Mumler] surmised that [the spirit photograph] arose from an image having been previously on the plate, and its having been imperfectly cleaned off."[71] Taylor continued, "Subjected to a more thorough cleaning, the form appeared again more strongly marked than before, and he could offer no explanation than the one given," that being, that the image was the result of a ghostly presence in the same room as the camera.[72] Mumler was initially hesitant regarding the Spiritualist movement appropriating his photographs as proof of the paranormal, but quickly saw an economic opportunity in the enterprise of spirit photography. As Crista Cloutier writes, "At a time when standard photographs were selling for about a quarter apiece, [Mumler's] fee was ten dollars per sitting, with

FIGURE 2.2 | PHOTOGRAPHIC PORTRAIT BY WILLIAM MUMLER OF A MAN IDENTIFIED AS HARRY GORDON WITH A TRANSPARENT “EXTRA” BEHIND HIM, APPEARING TO HAND THE SITTER A CRUCIFIX.

FIGURE 2.3 | PHOTOGRAPHIC PORTRAIT BY WILLIAM MUMLER OF AN UNIDENTIFIED MAN WITH TRANSPARENT "EXTRA" BEHIND HIM.

no guarantee of obtaining the desired image."[73] Although Spiritualists utilized the photographs as authentications of their beliefs, Mumler's spirit photographs were not without their skeptics; several individuals, including prominent photographer James Wallace Black, challenged Mumler, requesting that they be permitted to supervise him while he made such photographs.[74] The controversy surrounding the credibility of the photographs culminated in Mumler's arrest in 1869 and his subsequent trial.

The trial took place in the Tombs Police Court, New York City, with Justice Dowling presiding. Mumler was charged with two felonies and a misdemeanour: "fraud by false pretenses, cheating under the common law definition, and larceny by trick and device."[75] The trial attracted much public attention, not only to Spiritualism as a practice and spirit photography in particular, but also to the role of photography as evidence. Witnesses for both the prosecution and the defence all agreed that the photographs were indeed proof, and they concurred that the photographs did constitute evidence of *something* important to the case, but they interpreted the images in diametrically opposed ways.[76] In her study of the historical role of photography in court cases, Jennifer Mnookin examined the Mumler trial and the ways in which photographs were positioned as evidence. She argues that the case was about more than proving the guilt or innocence of Mumler himself; also on trial was Spiritualism's relationship to the burden of proof: "Was it the defense's obligation to prove that the photographs were actually produced by spiritual means, or did the prosecution have the burden of proving that they were produced mechanically?"[77] In her analysis of the testimony produced at the trial, Mnookin identifies three distinct stances taken toward the photographs as evidence. (1) Supernatural realism: the photographs were proof of the supernatural precisely because they were *photographs*. In other words, the photographs themselves were enough to compel some individuals to believe in the supernatural. (2) Mechanical illusionism: the photographs themselves proved the images to be obvious forgeries. This position emphasized the many ways in which photographs could be manipulated to produce the results Mumler had presented. (3) Anti-evidentialist: this position, held by Mumler's lawyers, posited that the photographs could not be considered evidence at all because they did not reveal their means of production. To discern how the photographs were made, one must examine the process rather than the end product.[78]

Ultimately, Judge Dowling agreed with Mumler's attorneys, deciding that the photographs did not prove the existence of spirits but that neither did they prove that fraud had taken place. Mumler was acquitted of all charges. "The tremendous variation in the understanding of these images as constituting proof of ghosts, proof of fraud, or no proof at all," Mnookin writes, "reminds us that we cannot assume that a photograph has a singular and unproblematic meaning."[79] As with the controversial interpretation of the meaning of Mumler's photographs, Mumler's acquittal was itself variously understood as proving the photographs to be fakes or proving Mumler to be a genuine spirit photographer. The mechanical objectivity of the photographic apparatus was argued to be a guarantor against the possibility of fraud.

In *Photographing the Invisible*, a book written in defence of spirit photography from a scientific point of view, James Coates celebrates Mumler's exoneration as well as that of spirit photography as a practice: "The evidence in favour of spirit photography which was produced at this trial was overwhelming."[80] Essential to Mumler's acquittal and the legitimizing of spirit photography, according to Coates, was the testimony of respectable, intelligent individuals who, because of their social status and reputations, were perceived to be objective, rational, and authoritative voices.[81] Similarly for Taylor, that the photographs and Mumler had been investigated by respectable, professional men held in high regard testified to the legitimacy of the photographs themselves.[82] These writers championed Mumler's court battle as a secular, impartial, and thus objective confirmation of the spirit photographs and of Spiritualism as a legitimate movement; but others viewed the trial as proving spirit photography to be fraudulent, thereby placing Spiritualism as a whole into question. Renowned showman P.T. Barnum, for example, was brought in to testify during the trial; there, he denounced Spiritualism altogether.[83] Moreover, the photography section of the American Institute, "the voice of the scientific establishment," released a statement two weeks after the trial declaring that spirit photography was trickery.[84] As Cloutier suggests, more than Mumler and his photographs, the court case "put spiritualism itself on trial."[85]

Barnum's participation in the trial gestures toward the extent to which spirit photography, and Spiritualism more broadly, had become a popular form of entertainment in the Victorian era, as it would be well into the twentieth century. As noted in this book's introduction, superimposition techniques were already familiar to those who frequented phantasmagoria performances, during which multiple slides would be used to simulate movement, transparency, transformation, and superimposition. David Brewster, inventor of the kaleidoscope, wrote in his 1856 book on the stereoscope that the optical instrument could be used to generate "amusements" for the purposes of entertainment. A photographer might "give a spiritual appearance to one or more of his figures" and "exhibit them as 'thin air' amid the solid realities of the stereoscopic picture."[86] Furthermore, Natale has shown how the emergence of Spiritualism was integrated with the Victorian visual entertainment and popular culture in the course of which spiritualist tools and psychic mediums became commercial commodities and famous celebrities, respectively. Natale notes, for example, that talking boards (Ouija boards, as they are more popularly known) were used in séances and subsequently commodified as parlour games.[87] Renowned psychic mediums like Eusapia Palladino, Daniel Dunglas Home, and the Fox sisters would go on tours, charging admission to audiences to view their spectacular psychic feats live on stage. Many mediums also had agents and would advertise their performances, thereby aligning mediums with popular entertainment figures of the era.[88]

Responding to charges of trickery, Coates maintained that to deny the visual powers of the photographic camera was to expose one's misunderstandings and fundamental ignorance regarding the operation of the medium: "To say that the invisible cannot be photographed, even on the material plane, would be to confess ignorance of facts which are commonplace – as, for instance, to mention the application of X-ray photography to the exploration of the muscles, of fractures of bone, and the internal organs. Astronomical photography affords innumerable illustrations of photographing the invisible."[89]

Here, Coates asserted that photography's capacity to render invisible objects and processes legible was already accepted by the scientific establishment, thereby refuting claims that photography could not reveal the invisible. Coates continued, citing what he called N-rays, or magnetism, and photo-phonography, or the photographing of sounds, as further proof that invisible phenomena were already being captured photographically.[90] Thomas Slater, described in Coates's text as an "optical and philosophical instrument maker," expressed a similar criticism of skeptics in a letter to the editor of *The Spiritualist* dated 8 May 1872. As excerpted in Georgiana Houghton's *Chronicles of Spirit Photography*, Slater wrote, "We naturally ask ourselves what is the meaning of it? … And for the present, we must be content to say, 'We don't know!'… Perhaps it may be to correct our erroneous impression that spirit is less tangible, less real than matter."[91] For both Coates and Slater, then, the apparitions appearing in spirit photographs were not the revenants of a superstitious, religious past, but a physical, material presence that was only made visible through the photographic apparatus. In this way, spirit photography positioned itself as a subset or subgenre of scientific photography. As with scientific photography, whether spirit photographs were recognized as authentic evidentiary documents hinged upon whether photography was understood as a scientific technical process that not only transcribed but also *physically impressed* a trace of the real onto the image. Cathcart begins *The Awakening* convinced that her indexical scientific instruments will reveal the trickery behind the ghostly occurrences at the school; to her astonishment, they continue to point to the veracity of the paranormal.

The initial stage of Cathcart's investigation seems to have solved the mystery: she observed a student wandering the school grounds at night with the intent to scare others. However, strange sounds and sightings continue to occur even once all the students have vacated the school. Cathcart herself continues to hear a child's voice and claims that she has seen glimpses of a child moving about the school undetected. Her suspicions are confirmed when she witnesses the apparition of a man holding a shotgun in a hallway. Shocked, Cathcart backs away from the figure, triggering a series of trip wires that begin taking photographs of the space. The figure points his gun at Cathcart just as the explosive ignition of the photographic apparatus is initiated, creating a visual allusion to Marey's photographic gun. Cathcart falls to the ground in fear, and the figure disappears. Having witnessed this extraordinary event, she asks Mallory to accompany her to a makeshift darkroom, where they develop the photographs. One by one, they expose the photosensitive papers to a light source and submerge them in a chemical bath. Before our eyes, the images begin to materialize, depicting intermittent instants of Cathcart's movements. There, in the background corner of one of the photographs, is the image of a child, a transparent ghost, confirming within the film's narrative that the haunting is genuine.

This darkroom scene is the focal point of the film: more forcefully than any other, it confirms for both Cathcart and the audience the legitimacy of the haunting and, more significantly, asserts the inextricability of photography, illumination, and knowledge. In the darkroom, Mallory ruminates on the affective and metaphorical power of darkness. "The dark used to bother me," he confesses. "Later of course it came to mean safety [during the First World War]; no sniper fire or shells. But as a lad I'd huddle into my bed, wanting to see what was there but too frightened to open my eyes. It's never darker than when we close our eyes and yet we keep them shut. Why is that?" As the images begin to emerge in the chemical bath, Mallory pointedly asks Cathcart, "Why do you keep your eyes closed, Florence?" This question becomes all the more significant, given the twist ending of the film, which reveals that the child ghost haunting the school is, in fact, Cathcart's stepbrother, who, along with Cathcart's mother, was murdered by their father with a shotgun. Having repressed these memories for most of her life, Cathcart only recalls and accepts her traumatic past when confronted with visual evidence that, in the film, is represented as indexical and thus irrefutable. *The Awakening* thus positions analogic, indexical media such as photography, barometric measurements, footprints, fingerprints, and the like as registering a physical truth – the existence of a ghost – which then unlocks the deeper historical truth of Cathcart's childhood.

The Awakening's portrayal of 1920s Spiritualism in the United Kingdom reproduces questions concerning the role of photography, its status as an evidentiary tool, its relationship to reality, and its function as a paranormal investigative instrument for twenty-first-century audiences. The film perpetuates a revelationist conception of the photographic image that was previously articulated by Spiritualists and classical film theorists alike. Photography, according to the film's discourse, not only captures an impression of the real, a physical trace of an instant of time, but also transcends human perception by rendering visible that which escapes ordinary vision. In its historical phantasy of 1920s London arising fresh from the Victorian era's gothic obsessions, the film portrays an era of modernization and scientific advancement, one in which photography, already nearly a century old at the time of the film's setting, achieves a renewed veneration. The film thus mirrors and recasts the technological landscape of the turn of the millennium during which new media forms are overtaking older ones. *The Awakening* rearticulates in 2011 what Spiritualists and classical film theorists argued in different contexts, albeit in strikingly similar supernatural terms, in the late nineteenth and early twentieth centuries: analogue photography reveals a reality beyond what our human faculties of vision can perceive. Such a statement in a film released in 2011 constitutes a mournful elegy for an analogue format in the process of disappearing.

Like *The Others*, *The Conjuring*, and *Insidious*, *The Awakening* exemplifies one tendency within supernatural horror films that position analogue media, and photography in particular, as having privileged access to reality, its status as mechanical instrument not only conferring a sense of unbiased objectivity to the analogue image but also superseding the human capacity of vision, for it reveals hidden truths embedded in biologically imperceptible wavelengths and in distant pasts. Indeed, as Tom Gunning has shown, the growing attempts to improve and perfect the photographic medium and the development of early cinema both owe a great debt to an epistephilic impulse that drove the motion studies of Muybridge and Marey, both of whom are implicitly referenced in *The Awakening*.[92] Here, analogue photography re-emerges as the objective medium *par excellence*, accruing authentic pieces of evidence and creating new visual knowledge that reveals the truth. The Spiritualists insisted that ghosts are physical components of nature that can be uncovered using the physics and chemistry of light and shadow. The mechanical eye, as Dziga Vertov would have it, presents to us a clearer vision of the world as it is; however, as these films suggest, it is up to us to open our eyes.

In addition to spirit photography, another spiritualist photographic subgenre emerged in the twentieth century that claimed to capture not only the spirit of a dead individual but also its astounding emanation from the bodies of psychic mediums. Such photographs graphically depicted amorphous and delicate cloth-like substances protruding from the mouths, nostrils, breasts, and genitalia of mediums in a process known as materialization. Unlike the spirit photographs of William Mumler, materialization photographs depicted the process of visualization itself: a nebulous white form would take shape from out of the medium's body before vanishing. Spiritualists referred to this mysterious substance as *ectoplasm*, a spiritual film in the literal sense that accrued mucus-like consistency and texture. During a séance, the materializing medium would retreat to her spirit cabinet and emerge when the ectoplasm began to flow from her orifices. At times, the ectoplasm remained an amorphous, abstract flow of material, its spiritual status derived from a spectacular self-referentiality; at other times, the ectoplasm would form recognizable images of faces and even life-sized reanimations of spirits. The ephemeral materiality of the ectoplasm, its corporeal connection to the medium, and its capture *in process*, that is, in time, were central criteria of this decidedly tactile form of spirit photography.

The photographic image, while heralded as a revelatory technology within Spiritualism generally, was here incapable of fully representing the phenomenon of materialization, for the stillness of the photograph omitted the ectoplasm's emergence in time. Psychical researcher Theodore Besterman, for example, lamented that "even six or eight cameras, of however varied kinds, cannot do more than register what is before them at the moment of the flashlight exposure. They cannot record the *development* of the phenomena, or, what is often vital, the sequence of various, often seemingly insignificant, events."[93] Of course, by the turn of the twentieth century, the means to represent duration photographically had been invented in the form of film. This made the absence of moving images especially conspicuous as spirit photography progressed into the twentieth century. Besterman, then, was pining for a recording technology that already existed; "he wants the movies," as Karen Beckman states. Andreas Fischer notes that the séance space was lit somewhat like a film set and that stereoscopic cameras were sometimes used to approximate the three-dimensionality of the materialization performance.[94] Yet frustrations regarding photography's inability to represent motion and movement remained common.[95] In his book-length study of psychic materializations titled *Phenomena of Materialization*, first published in German in 1913, Dr Albert von Schrenk-Notzing reproduces still images from the séances of mediums Eva C. and Stanislava P.[96] While most of the book's still images reproduce the live events in which photography functioned to fix the ephemeral, evanescent ectoplasm in an instant of time before it disappeared, Schrenk-Notzing did utilize a *cinématographe* on two occasions in 1913, both of which involved recording séances conducted by Stanislava P. The two filming sessions produced 360 and 400 film frames, respectively, and depicted the emergence and retraction of ectoplasm from and back into the medium's mouth. Despite the capture of this footage purportedly depicting the event in motion, Schrenk-Notzing makes the baffling decision to reproduce in his book not a sequence of film frames, but disparate frames from the filmed material that are non-contiguous; thus he elided any sense of motion that would have accompanied a series of images published in succession. "Schrenk-Notzing," Beckman concludes, "turns the longed-for films back into photographs."[97]

Spiritualists' opposition to moving images, even though psychical researchers were crying out for such images to be made, offers us significant insights into the status of both the cinematic image and the constitution of the ghost. Ghosts are never fully present to begin with; as such, film, composed of temporal fragments of sixteen to twenty-four frames per second, could never truly recompose such elusive spectral presences. Motion in film is an illusion generated by projection: it does not represent time as duration, as flow, but rather a series of still images in quick succession. In documenting séances and spiritual happenings, Spiritualists opted for the instant of still photography and rejected the illusory manufacturing of motion made possible by film. As such, film "is the unnamed ghost haunting twentieth-century spirit photography," given the clear allusions to motion that nevertheless remains absent.[98]

In its reproduction of an illusion of motion, the cinema accrues a decidedly sinister character in contemporary film theory, one that highlights the manipulative power of the image and its ability to fool the senses of spectators. While the photographic image was celebrated by classical film theorists and Spiritualists alike as revealing a natural truth that lay beyond the limited field of human perception, the moving image for contemporary film theorists beginning in the 1970s represented a threating representation of a false reality predicated upon an illusion of cohesion, wholeness, and unity that disguised its status as a construct composed of fragments. While this first tendency in contemporary paranormal films evinces a faith in the objective truth of the analogue image, Gunning is quick to remind us that this is nevertheless *faith*, that is, a conception of the truth-power of the medium that borders on the occult.[99] The remainder of this chapter examines a film that takes the occult faith in the image seriously: Scott Derrickson's *Sinister*. Rather than celebrating the mechanical objectivity of the photographic and cinematic image, *Sinister* proffers a nightmarish vision of cinema's mesmeric power, conjuring the anxieties and paranoia surrounding the medium at the turn of the nineteenth century.

The film follows true-crime writer Ellison Oswalt (Ethan Hawke) and his family, who move into a new home, where Ellison plans to embark on a book project based on an unsolved murder that occurred in the area. The family has made a habit of moving into neighbourhoods that have been sites of vicious crimes – Ellison's wife Tracy (Juliet Rylance) nervously asks, "We didn't move in a few houses down from a crime scene again, did we?" – but this time, Ellison has chosen the *precise house* in which the crime took place, intentionally keeping that fact from the family. While carrying miscellaneous boxes up to the attic for storage, Ellison makes a curious discovery. In the middle of the attic there is a box containing five reels of Super 8mm film and a film projector, apparently left behind by the previous ill-fated owners. Intrigued, Ellison sets up a makeshift screening room in his home office and projects the first reel of film. The reel begins with an idyllic family enjoying their backyard on a bright summer afternoon;

the footage appears to be a home movie like any other. Suddenly, an unexpected jump cut occurs, dramatically altering the scene. Against a dreary grey sky, a family of four stand with hoods over their heads underneath a large, ominous tree branch, with nooses tied around their necks. In eerie, oneiric slow motion, the family is hanged by an unseen force.

Labelled "Family Hanging Out," the reel constitutes a disturbing reversal of the typical home movie, in that it documents the destruction of a family rather than its joyous, celebratory moments. According to Patricia Zimmerman, the primary function of the home movie is to document "the most important and consuming narrative of all – the grand, happy epic of nuclear family life."[100] The Super 8mm footage in *Sinister* obliterates this function, using the same small-gauge film format meant to secure domestic happiness. As Haidee Wasson has shown, the first home movie format, 16mm, was specifically marketed by Kodak in the 1920s as a household appliance that would bring families together and contribute to the idealization of the modern, efficient, bourgeois family. Wasson writes that while millions may have had access to this new technology, "the millions [were] not those of cinema's mass audience but a series of intimate and familial groups with children happily gathered around Mother."[101] In the 1920s, then, 16mm was understood as a technology of the private sphere, and, as Wasson continues, this domestic ideal "was held together by the ubiquitous image of the efficient home and the consuming housewife tasked with operating the electrical appliances and machines that were increasingly central to middle-class domesticity."[102] Thus, 16mm film allowed families to create and project their own personal films,; although lacking the image quality of 35mm, this format was sufficient for the recording and preserving of events in a family's history.

The smaller-gauge 8mm was introduced in 1932, and by the 1950s it had supplanted 16mm as the preferred gauge for filming and projecting home movies. As Stacey Johnson notes, this shift is explained in part by "[the] ever expanding association of 16mm productions with television, documentary, education and semi-professional production."[103] As 16mm became institutionalized and more professional, 8mm took its place as the primary home movie film gauge. Like 16mm before it, 8mm became associated with domesticity and pre-existing notions of sentimentality, recreation, and the documenting of family history. As Johnson reiterates, "8mm became synonymous with activities of families and less so with diversely creative and artistic pursuits."[104] It was not until 1965 that Eastman Kodak announced another development in amateur film with the introduction of their new Super 8mm technology. This gauge shrank the perforations on the side of the filmstrip, allowing more space for the image track, resulting in improved image quality.[105] *Sinister* implicitly references this history: the earliest film reel Ellison discovers is labelled 1966, corresponding to the introduction of the new gauge. Moreover, each reel Ellison views takes the form of a home movie, thereby attesting to the use of amateur film gauges as a private, intimate, and familial pastime. Although Ellison eventually becomes accustomed to projecting celluloid, its status as an old and out-of-date technology is always at the forefront, including the degraded film grain and the requisite scratches and damage on the filmstrips he projects.

Such amateur films were intended to be used in the private sphere of the home, which would seem to eliminate a central concern surrounding cinema – its public exhibition in front of a heterogeneous audience. However, the potential for evil in *Sinister* lies not so much in the exhibition context as in the material base of cinema itself. At the end of the film, the malevolent Super 8mm reels are revealed to be haunted by a demonic presence called Bughuul, an entity that lives within images and has the power to manipulate those images as well as the perceptions of the spectator. In an iChat conversation, Dr Jonas (Vincent D'Onofrio), a local college professor specializing in the occult, describes Bughuul's mythology to Ellison: "Early Christians believed that Bughuul actually lived in the images themselves and that they were gateways into his realm … The ancient church believed that he would take possession of those who saw the images and cause them to do terrible things. Or, in some cases, he could even abduct the viewer into the images themselves. Children exposed to the images were especially vulnerable to Bughuul's possession and/or abduction."

Here, Dr Jonas is articulating the demonic power of the image as capable of possessing those who view it and transporting them into the realm of the imaginary. Importantly, Jonas emphasizes that children were understood to be particularly vulnerable to the lure of the image, an anxiety evident in the 1915 Supreme Court ruling denying motion pictures First Amendment rights.[106] While Jonas frames this information as a myth, as the ancient beliefs of a primitive and superstitious past, the narrative affirms its veracity.

Indeed, the strange occurrences that accumulate throughout *Sinister* become increasingly aligned with the Super 8mm film and projector. The first inclination of the diabolic ontology of the image become evident when Ellison projects the third reel of film, labelled "Pool Party." As with the other reels, "Pool Party" begins as a pleasant home movie capturing a happy family enjoying their backyard pool on a sunny afternoon. Then a jump cut occurs and we are transported to a night scene. The jittery hand-held camera reveals the family members bound to poolside chairs as they are pulled into the pool and drowned. The previous reels failed to depict the culprit of these murders; this one depicts Bughuul for the first time, who is standing underwater at the bottom of the pool watching the victims drown. Ellison quickly pauses the image, halting the succession of the filmstrip through the projector. He stands up and approaches the screen in order to examine Bughuul's ghostly visage when the film suddenly begins to burn in the projector. The image disintegrates as the emulsion of the film stock melts away and Ellison runs to the projector to put out the flames.

Here, the material base of cinema as singular photographic images (or photograms) is displayed to the audience. Moreover, the film stock is represented as a delicate and highly combustible material. The potential for film to burst into flame while being produced, exhibited, and stored posed a serious safety risk during the first decades of cinema, when film stock was nitrate based rather than made of more stable acetate. As such, the image burning while stopped in the gate of the projector would not be considered an unusual happening; however, confronted with the image of the demonic countenance of Bughuul, Ellison has set the haunting into motion. As we learn by the film's end, Bughuul's demonic manifestation and possession is initiated by the viewing of its image. In this way, the stilled image of Bughuul's skeletal face functions as a *memento mori*, a reminder and guarantor of the inevitability of death, an inevitability metaphorized in the ceaseless forward momentum of projection.

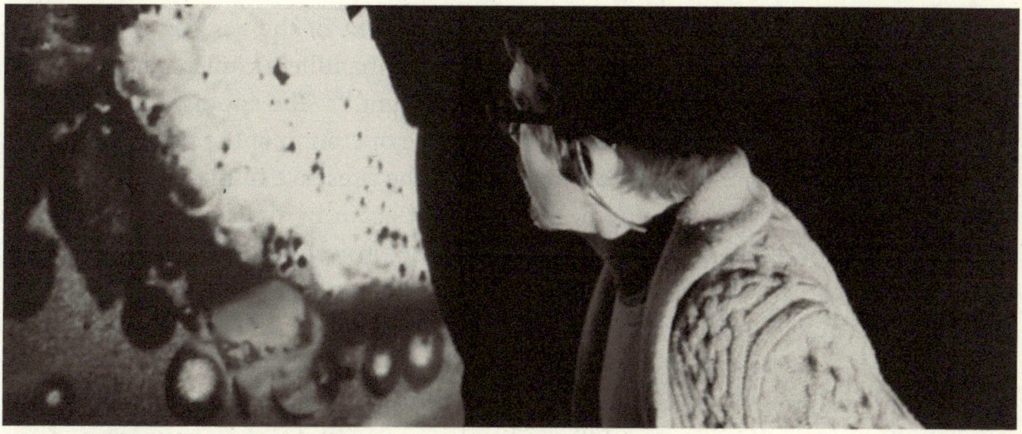

FIGURE 2.4 | BURNING CELLULOID OBSCURES THE DEMONIC VISAGE OF BUGHUUL IN *SINISTER*, 2012.

Like the material filmstrip, the Super 8mm projector is represented as an uncanny haunted object. After Ellison views the first reel of Super 8mm film, for example, there is a dramatic low-angle shot of the projector, which zooms into the lens, creating an ominous and threatening image of the projector. Later in the film, Ellison is watching the final reel, titled "Lawn Work," in which a lawnmower runs over the captive family members. Significantly, the sound of the projector shutter is amplified on the soundtrack to mimic, or at least suggest, the sound of the lawnmower's motor. As with the first reel of film, this viewing is accompanied by the low-angle zoom into the projector. Such cinematographic techniques occur regularly throughout the film, usually following the exhibition of the reels. Additionally, on several occasions, the sound of the projector's shutter and the succession of the filmstrip disturbs Ellison while he is sleeping. On the first occasion, he walks to his office and discovers the reel "Family Hanging Out" playing on the screen, without explanation. Ellison checks on his children and his wife, all of whom remain sleeping in their beds, begging the question of how the projector was activated. The second occurrence, however, is a much more traumatic affair for Ellison.

This sequence begins with a long shot of Ellison sleeping in his bed. Suddenly, a spotlight, the source of which remains off-screen, illuminates Ellison's sleeping face. Reminiscent of the aesthetics apparent in the film reels of the murders, the handheld camera moves toward Ellison, accompanied by the spotlight.[107] The spotlight shuts off and Ellison wakes up, again hearing the operation of the projector. There is no one in his bedroom, leaving the presence of the spotlight an eerie mystery. Having been woken yet again by the sound of the projector, Ellison checks his office, but the projector is not there. He follows the sound and discovers that the stairs leading to the attic have been pulled down and that a light is emanating from the attic. Ellison climbs up the stairs to investigate and sees the ghosts of the five missing children watching the Super 8mm films. Suddenly, Bughuul manifests himself in front of Ellison, his demonic countenance occupying a full close-up,[108] accompanied by a loud extradiegetic musical cue on the soundtrack. This traumatic experience forces Ellison to take action: he collects the projector and Super 8mm reels, walks into the backyard, and proceeds to burn the equipment. Close-ups of flames engulfing the filmstrips and projector linger onscreen as he resolves to take his family back to their old home that very night.

Having destroyed the haunted film and returned to their previous home, Ellison and the family prepare to settle back into a life of ordinary domesticity. While placing boxes in the attic, however, Ellison again finds the box of the Super 8mm reels and the projector, which have apparently survived the attempt to destroy them and somehow materialized in their old home. In an envelope labelled "extended cut endings" are five small rolls of Super 8mm film. Ellison examines where the filmstrips have been cut and, using his previously learned techniques, splices the films back together. He sets up the projector and views the reels with the new extended endings.

Where the earlier films simply went to black, these new extended endings reveal the missing child of each family committing the murders. In a twist ending, after having viewed these extended endings, Ellison's daughter Ashley (Clare Foley) proceeds to drug the Oswalt family, allowing her to restrain their bodies, and kills them with an axe, all the while filming the act with a Super 8mm camera. As with the previous families in the Super 8mm reels, Ellison and his family have become the subjects of a snuff film, their reel similarly labelled with the seemingly innocuous title "House Painting," referring to images painted on the wall of their home in the family's blood. Following these murders, Bughuul manifests himself behind Ashley. The demon picks up Ashley and, while the Super 8mm projector continues to project images onto a screen in the home, escorts her through the diegetic cinema screen into the realm of the image, where she joins the spectres of the other children. The myth of Bughuul has been proven true; the Oswalt family has fallen victim to the diabolical power of the image and been possessed and murdered by the cinema.

In *Sinister*, the threat of the cinematic image espoused by Justice McKenna is literalized; a demonic presence residing within Super 8mm filmstrips is materialized through the act of projection and exhibition, negatively affecting the mental state of the spectator. Ultimately, the image ends up possessing a child, a demographic singled out by McKenna as especially vulnerable to what Jean Baudrillard would later call the diabolical seduction of the image.[109] In *Sinister*, the photographic and cinematic image is not a facsimile of reality, a penetrating and revelatory technology superseding the insufficient capabilities of the human eye; rather, it is an invasive and parasitical agent that takes possession of the subject. Unlike the classical film theorists of the revelationist tradition, contemporary film theorists are beholden to the tradition of apparatus theory advanced by Jean-Louis Baudry, a tradition that is mirrored in *Sinister*'s portrayal of the image as threat. While Baudrillard does not belong to this group, his argument that the image becomes its most diabolical when it is mistaken for truth or reality essentially restates the central tenets of contemporary film theory, a discourse that is highly suspicious of mimetic representation.

As the political tumult of the 1960s culminated in the May 1968 student and worker strikes in Paris, film theory shifted from venerating this medium-specific capacity for revelation to assuming a decidedly more suspicious approach. Influenced by the linguistic turn in critical theory more broadly, film theorists began to understand cinema as a signifying system, one that did not share privileged or neutral access to the real, but actively produced meaning. Adopting Saussurian semiotics, Lacanian psychoanalysis, and Althusserian Marxism as distinct methodologies, 1970s film theory, as proliferated in the highly influential journal *Screen*, saw the aesthetic category of realism as an ideological effect that functioned to reproduce the social conditions of industrial capitalism, thus sustaining dominant power relations. Deploying Cartesian perspectivalism and disavowing the material, technological, and economic conditions of cinematic production, these theorists argued that the cinematic spectator is encouraged to occupy a position of passivity and thereby uncritically and unconsciously absorb dominant ideological messages. Unlike in the revelationist tradition of film theory, cinema is here defined as a medium of mystification allying the spectator with those of Plato's cave, shackled in place and viewing shadows, which are mistaken for reality.

A seminal figure in contemporary film theory and a proponent of apparatus theory specifically, Baudry employed the allegory of Plato's cave in order to draw connections between the shackled prisoners and the cinema spectator. In "The Apparatus: Metapsychological Approaches to the Impression of Reality in Cinema," Baudry asks: "Isn't it curious that Plato … would imagine or resort to an apparatus that doesn't merely evoke, but quite precisely describes in its mode of operation the cinematographic apparatus and the spectator's place in relation to it[?]"[110] Baudry cites Plato's description of a dark, cavernous underground space in which the prisoners are chained. Behind the prisoners and from a higher plane, a fire burns, projecting shadows onto the cave wall. This configuration of the cave in Plato's allegory, Baudry suggests, is analogous to the conditions of cinematic theatrical exhibition, in which a spectator is situated in front of a screen while a projector, situated behind the spectator in a higher position, projects shimmering images of absent objects. This viewing situation initiates a process of regression wherein the spectator loses their sense of time and space, is secured within the reality effects of cinematic representation, and unconsciously absorbs the dominant ideological position that has been implicit in Western visual art since the *quattrocento* development of linear perspective: the transcendental subject.

This all-too-brief outline of Baudry's application of Plato's allegory of the cave to the cinema requires some unpacking. First, Baudry's emphasis on the immobility of the spectator may strike one as dubious as it pertains to one's experience of theatrical exhibition. To be sure, one may leave the cinema auditorium at any point for refreshments or a washroom break, and one is likely to notice when fellow cinemagoers enter and exit the space. It is thus more accurate to suggest that the cinema spectator, while perhaps experiencing periods of immersion in the film, also experiences regular and predictable interruptions of this immersion. Additionally, as I discuss in the following chapters, the rise of home video and non-theatrical sites of exhibition challenges the centrality of immobility and darkness to the experience of cinema. Our case study *Sinister* depicts one such example of non-theatrical moviegoing as Ellison views the film reels within the comfort of his home. However, Baudry makes clear that physical chains are not necessary in order to keep the prisoners in place within the "subterranean screening room."[111] Baudry argues that the condition of forced immobility is internalized such that the prisoner would elect to remain in the cave even if freed from the shackles. Baudry turns to psychoanalysis to explain this conundrum.

The forced immobility caused by the chains is analogous to Lacan's imaginary in Baudry's reading of it – the infant, experiencing a state of wholeness, pleasure, and continuity with the body of the mother, lacks conscious control of their own motor reflexes. Because the infant's entry into the symbolic order and their constitution as a subject is marked by the loss of this sense of wholeness and pleasure, the regression into the imaginary initiated by the cinema is thus a pleasurable experience of return. Through the primary identification with the film as discourse and secondary identification with on-screen characters, the cinema spectator experiences the pleasure of identification as ego-ideal – the ideal-I – a state of coherence, power, and totality wrought by the image yet absent in the everyday experience of the subject. Christian Metz argues the same point when he defines the cinema as an imaginary signifier, its re-enactment of the mirror stage endemic to, and constitutive of, cinematic spectatorship.

But it is in the illusory nature of the false identification with the screen/mirror that the cinema accrues ghostly and indeed insidious effects. In order for immersion and identification to be sustained throughout a film, one must disavow the operation and existence of the cinematic apparatus. As such, Baudry describes the cinema as living on the "denial of difference" whereby the spectator disavows their knowledge of the singularity of each photogram in order to maintain the illusion of motion.[112] The vanishing of the apparatus from the consciousness of the spectator ensures the illusion of totality, a complete and transparent representation of perceptual reality. What is denied, then, is the cinema as a *work*, as a material product of the manipulation and transformation of raw material (filming, editing, post-production) that is then consumed by the spectator.

In "The Tutor-Code of Classical Cinema," Daniel Dayan expands on the ideological stakes of the concealment of the apparatus. Dayan likens the film shot to a traditional painting in that both consist of framed images composed according to the principle of linear perspective. Such a composition constructs a single point of view that the subject inhabits when viewing the image, effectively determining how the painting will be read by the subject. Summarizing Jean-Pierre Oudart's theorization of classical painting, Dayan describes the entrapment of the subject within the painting's classical representational codes, which portray as natural, objective, and universal a particular point of view of the world. "The Romantic landscapes of the nineteenth century," Dayan writes, "submit nature to a remodeling which imposes on them a monocular perspective, transforming the landscape into that which is seen by a given subject."[113] The adherence on the part of the spectator to a particular perspective determined by the painting renders the *subject* the actual product of this system of signification; for what is produced in this viewing relationship is the transcendental humanist subject, one that adopts a (false) vision of a total, cohesive world observed from afar. "The representational painting is *already unified*," Dayan argues, "the painting proposes not only itself, but its own reading."[114] Retroactively called Cartesian perspectivalism, linear perspective in painting contributed to the modernist project of mastery over nature in its depiction of mathematical certainty, rationality, and order. Martin Jay points out that such a rationalization of space through linear perspective grew out of a medieval fascination with the metaphysics of light, rendering geometric order and logic a divine truth. "Light as divine *lux* rather than perceived *lumen*," Jay writes, "linear perspective came to symbolize a harmony between the mathematical regularities in optics and God's will."[115] A depiction of the world from the outside, an Apollonian, God's-eye view, the scopic regime of Cartesian perspectivalism disembodies vision, aligning the spectator with a transcendental, "objective" perspective. That such codes produce an impression of reality – an *effet-de-réel* in Oudart's terms[116] – is what constitutes the work as ideological, in that the actual codes of signification are rendered invisible and taken to be a natural, true representation of the world.

Following the *telos* of modernist thought, photography and film more fully satisfy this bourgeois desire for the reproduction of reality, for their mode of mechanical, automatic reproduction does away with the hand of the artist in favour of an indexical imprint of light. Dayan reminds us, however, that classical narrative cinema equally depends upon Cartesian perspectivalism in order to secure a cohesive diegesis. Unlike the painting or the photograph, though, cinema poses a unique problem: the spectator is confronted with many images, which often shift in angle and point of view. As such, how is the cinemagoer implicated in this system when it depends upon the disavowal of the presence of the apparatus in order to function? Dayan posits that classical cinema employs the technique of "suture" to stitch the viewer into the narrative world of the film. In any given shot, once the spectator becomes aware of the existence of the frame, she realizes that the shot is imposing a particular view on her and that it neglects to represent an authentic totality. It becomes clear that the frame is an arbitrary demarcation of the visual field. The spectator then becomes suspicious that some other authority is determining what and how she sees. Of the film shot, she begins to ask "Who is viewing this?," "Who is ordering these images?," and "For what purpose are they doing so?"[117] This invisible authority is conceived as a ghostly presence, the entity that has true control and possession of the image rather than the subject. This ghostly presence is what Oudart will call "the absent one."[118] Theoretically, classical narrative cinema solves this problem by providing a reverse shot subsequent to the current shot, thereby filling in the gap created by the knowledge of the frame and completing the illusion of a fully constituted narrative universe. This system of suture – this shot/reverse shot process – functions to keep the spectator within the realm of the imaginary, unaware of the cinematic apparatus.

Simply put, according to the apparatus theorists, whom I have just summarized, what the spectator sees is not there, for the cinema fundamentally consists of the reanimation of absent objects brought to life through the projection of light on-screen. Present as an image in alternating light and darkness yet materially absent, such a conception of the cinematic signifier aligns closely with the figure of the ghost. Itself a projection of the soul or spirit of a deceased individual, the ghost is an image of an absent body, literally photo-graphic, written in light.[119] Additionally, the suspicion of an invisible presence orchestrating the viewing experience is a more explicit ghostly phenomenon as it is articulated in suture theory. This suspicion is proven true in *Sinister* as the demon controls the parameters of viewing.

The cinema's reanimation of life places the medium within what Noël Burch has described as the "Frankensteinian ideology" of the nineteenth century: "the recreation of life, the symbolic triumph over death."[120] From the development of the daguerreotype to the cinema, Burch argues, nineteenth-century positivist historiography contextualized each technological development as a step toward the complete reproduction of the illusion of reality.[121] However, contemporary film theorists such as Baudry advocated for the demystification of the cinema in order to expose the ideological operation haunting the image. In *Sinister*, the evil demon of images, the deceitful manipulator of the real, is exposed.

As if to metaphorize the ideology of bourgeois realism haunting the progression of technology, we find in *Sinister* a depiction of an evolutionary conception of visual media. We are shown ancient carvings and drawings associated with the demon, Ashley paints the demon's portrait on her wall, demonic symbols are painted in the family's blood at the film's gruesome conclusion, and, in addition to the Super 8mm films, we see a digitization process whereby the Super 8mm films are transferred to digital files. When Ellison pauses the projector to examine the face of the demon – an exposure of the apparatus and a veritable challenge to *see* – the film burns in the projector. A difference no longer denied, to use Baudry's terminology, the film frame and the stillness endemic to analogue cinematic projection is exposed; the demon is revealed, its face rendered visible, only to vanish in the filmstrip's penchant for fiery self-destruction.[122]

Ellison turns to Google to determine how to repair Super 8mm film. He dutifully follows the how-to guide's instructions, and splices the film together after removing the damaged frames, but he cannot salvage the image of the demon. In order to avoid such destruction, Ellison begins to project the Super 8mm films again, this time simultaneously recording the projector screen with a digital video camera. Having digitized the films, Ellison is able to adjust the lighting and contrast, thereby improving the image quality and illuminating the image. This helps him uncover some clues about the murders (he discovers that one film was shot in St. Louis, for example), and he is also able to spot the demonic face in the background of a shot. Zooming into the background of the image, exploiting the property of deep space proffered by linear perspective, Ellison adjusts the image to reveal a clear, crisp screengrab of the demon. Interestingly, Derrickson on the DVD commentary addresses a potential continuity error produced in the appearance of the demon in footage we have seen earlier in the narrative. To be sure, the demon is not present in the background of the Super 8mm films when Ellison first views them and is only visible when he watches the films again later in the narrative. Derrickson confirms that this is not really an error on the part of the filmmakers, since Bughuul, as the narrative makes clear toward the end of the film, has the demonic power of image manipulation and can therefore control the method and timing of his manifestation. That Bughuul is a living, demonic presence within the image itself is further confirmed when its head in the frozen screengrab turns to look out from the computer screen to Ellison. Evidently, the demonic presence has been transferred during the digitization process, "upgrading" to a new format.

When André Bazin discussed what he called the myth of total cinema in his 1946 essay, he argued that a desire for the complete representation of reality has always haunted the imagination of humankind. Defining the cinema as an idealistic phenomenon, Bazin writes that before any technology or any possibility for its development, the concept of cinema existed in the minds of men, "as if in some platonic heaven."[123] All previous forms of mechanical reproduction that dominated the nineteenth century were for Bazin efforts to realize this original desire, this foundational myth, of the total reproduction of reality in sound, colour, and three-dimensionality. Furthermore, Bazin argues that the origin of an art tells us something of its essence, "reveals something of its nature," such that silent and sound film are conceived to be steps toward the realization of this original myth.[124] Every development toward the realization of this goal is therefore a kind of paradoxical return to origin: "cinema has not yet been invented!"[125]

Importantly, Bazin does not credit those who made strides in the science of the moving image for the invention of cinema. Of Niépce, Muybridge, Demenÿ, and the Lumières, Bazin writes that they were "ingenious industrials" who lacked this originary idea of the cinema and did not intend to contribute to the realization of the total representation of reality.[126] Even Marey, whom Bazin singles out as an exceptional case, was interested in the analysis and science of motion and not in reanimating movement.[127] Bazin argues that the true inventors of the cinema, such as Charles-Émile Reynaud, intentionally sought to achieve the reproduction of the impression of reality – of pursuing this *idée fixe* – rather than producing commercial technologies out of which moving images would develop.[128]

Bazin's championing of the myth of total cinema is precisely what demonstrates cinema's place within the Frankensteinian ideology, according to Noël Burch. The reanimation of movement and the concerted effort to reproduce the impression of reality are indications that such developments are ideological in nature rather than strictly explorations of scientific principals. Although not in response to Bazin specifically, the incremental stages he describes as attempting to fulfill the desire for total cinema for Burch are "not just the achievement of captains of industry; [they are] also the pursuit of the fantasy of a class become the fantasy of a culture: to extend the 'conquest of nature' by triumphing over death through the ersatz of Life itself."[129] Here, technological development functions to correct the deficiencies in previous technologies that failed to achieve the bourgeois ideal of the illusion of reality. From ancient etchings to celluloid moving images, *Sinister* depicts this increasing verisimilitude as a "sinister" presence haunting the development of visual representation. For Bughuul's power lies in its ability to captivate and enthrall the spectator, to literally immerse its victim within the flesh of the icon, within the illusion of the real. For apparatus theorists and anti-illusionists, the cultivation and attempted perfection of total cinema, which today might find its corollary in virtual reality devices such as the Oculus Rift, should be challenged; the impression of reality must be revealed as an illusory technological construct, one that is inextricable from capitalist, industrial modes of production.

Laying bare the apparatus, *Sinister* confronts the demonic presence haunting mimetic representation. The photogram is exposed, the illusion of motion revealed, and the materiality and fragility of the medium remain at the forefront of the film. According to apparatus theorists, however, such a revelation would shatter the reality effect and thus safeguard the spectator against the threat of immersion and ideological interpellation. Yet Ellison and his family are not liberated from the tyranny of the image; they succumb to the destructive power of the demonic force. In this way, *Sinister* refuses the possibility of a non-ideological cinema. With the family murdered and Ashley having joined the spectres of children in the realm of the image, the box of Super 8mm reels returns to the attic to await discovery by the next victim. At the film's end, the cycle of haunting is set up for an inevitable and ceaseless return, reifying the threat expressed in the film's promotional tagline: once you see him, nothing can save you.

SPECTRAL VISIONS

What does it mean to see the spectral? To see the ghost? To see what haunts us? In classical film theory, spectral vision concerns the revelation of the invisible, illuminating the elusive fact of the soul, the universality of the human condition, the authenticity of the subject. In contemporary film theory and in apparatus theory in particular, to see the spectre is to acknowledge that which is ever present and inescapable, but that which refuses to show itself: ideology. Apparatus theorists compel us to look at the ghost, to see what has always been there yet has long remained imperceptible. In this way, both classical and contemporary film theory define the cinema as a spectral medium and command us to face, and be in the presence of, ghosts. In the former, this constitutes a celebration of the human spirit; in the latter, an acknowledgment that all is not what it seems, for what is too often taken for granted as an objective truth, an uncomplicated reality, a visual field conquered and mastered by the lens of the eye and the lens of the camera,[130] is contaminated by the sheen of ideology; a translucent sheet intervening between our actual conditions of existence and our perception of it. For apparatus theorists, to see the ghost, to become aware of its presence, to be awoken by its density is, like so many gothic and fantastic narratives, to banish it, to put an end to its cycle of return and reproduction. To thwart its continued, ineluctable return. In advocating for a self-reflexive cinema that gives up the ghost, lays bare the apparatus, and reveals to us what it is – machinic, economic, industrial – apparatus theorists hope that spectators may be empowered enough to counter the hegemony of capitalist exploitation. Yet, just as Althusser explains that there is no position that exists outside of ideology,[131] one cannot wholly escape the dominant regime of Cartesian perspectivalism and the power relations it subtends.

In reading the work of contemporary film theorists post-1968, one might ascribe to classical film theorists a naivety whereby the politics of representation and industrial modes of production are ignored. In fact, Bazin became a target of contemporary film theorists for just this reason, his poetic phenomenological approach to the cinema discarded as an uncritical celebration of the medium. However, the celebration of the preservative and evidentiary function of photographic media espoused by Bazin is more nuanced and melancholic than contemporary film theorists would have us believe.

Elsewhere in his work, Bazin explicitly celebrates the cinema, and its photographic base in particular, for defeating the inevitability of death, thereby linking the media with the "ersatz of life" so abhorred by Burch. In his seminal essay from 1945, "The Ontology of the Photographic Image,"[132] Bazin likens the practice of photography to historical practices of iconic preservation such as mummification and death masks. He argues that such practices evince a human psychological desire to overcome the linear progression of time and thus defeat death itself. Bazin identifies what he calls a "mummy complex" at the origin of the plastic arts of painting and sculpture, a foundational human desire to preserve our bodily appearance, to "snatch it from the flow of time."[133] This desire finds its fullest manifestation in the invention of photography: "For the first time, between the originating object and its reproduction" Bazin writes, "there intervenes only the instrumentality of a nonliving agent. For the first time an image of the world is formed automatically, without the creative intervention of man."[134] Unlike the arts of painting or sculpture, the automatic process of photography and its creation of an image via the registration of light on photosensitive emulsion defines it as an objective medium, one that satisfies, "once and for all and in its very essence, our obsession with realism."[135] This realism, however, acquires a haunting sensibility. In describing the charm of family photo albums, Bazin writes, "Those grey or sepia shadows, phantom-like and almost undecipherable, are no longer traditional family portraits but rather the disturbing presence of lives halted at a set moment in their duration, freed from their destiny."[136] In adding the dimension of duration to the stillness of the photograph, the cinema constitutes for Bazin an objective recording of time itself, a veritable image of duration, what he describes as "change mummified."[137]

As Philip Rosen has demonstrated, the authenticity the spectator ascribes to photographic images, according to Bazin, has just as much to do with the subject's understanding of how the image was produced and indeed with the subject's understanding of historicity.[138] But as Laura Mulvey has argued, both Barthes and Bazin locate the power of the photograph within the indexical ontology of the image. "For both Bazin and Barthes," Mulvey writes, "the photograph's beauty and emotional appeal lies in its 'thereness,' the fleeting presence of a shadow, which is captured and saved."[139] Significantly, both theorists articulate the profound realness of photographic images in terms of the supernatural and of illusion. For Barthes the indexicality of the image constitutes photography as a "magic" rather than an "art." Likewise in the case of Bazin, our experience of the photograph as an analogue of nature constitutes the medium as "an hallucination that is also a fact."[140] Or, as Timothy Barnard has translated it, "a photograph is a really existing hallucination."[141]

In associating the analogue celluloid image with the presence of death, *Sinister* resonates with theories of photographic media that render inextricable its association with death, loss, and mourning. In his meditation on the allure of photography, Roland Barthes crafts an analysis of the medium predicated upon its intimate relationship with death. In testifying to the irrefutable existence of a thing in the past, for Barthes, the evidential force of the photograph lies in time rather than the object: "The realists do not take the photograph for a 'copy' of reality, but for an emanation of *past reality*: a *magic* not an art."[142] This paradoxical magical realism of photography's ability to conjure the past within the present is shared by André Bazin; but unlike Barthes, Bazin argues that photography constitutes a triumph over death; its mechanical apparatus is able to defeat the ineluctable flow of time.

While espoused here as a laudable, if melancholic, characteristic of cinema that is central in defining its ontology and medium specificity, this indiscernibility of reality and illusion has elsewhere been articulated as cinema's penchant for evil. Jean Baudrillard argued as much when he wrote: "It is precisely when it appears most truthful, most faithful and most in conformity to reality that the image is most diabolical."[143] This confusion of reality and illusion, of the image and its referent, what Baudrillard describes as the diabolical seduction of the image, was also the target, as Tom Gunning has argued, of the apparatus theorists of the 1970s, who similarly regarded with suspicion the cinema's ability to masquerade as reality itself. As in Plato's cave wherein spectators shackled to the ground mistake for reality passing shadows cast by a flame on the cave wall, the cinema spectator is entranced by images, uncritically and unconsciously accepting their ideological interpellation. Gunning notes that the supposedly radical thought of apparatus theorists comes surprisingly close to the Manichean argument put forth by Baudrillard.[144] Believing the phenomenal universe to have been created by evil forces, the Manichean religion holds that the material world is a realm of darkness enslaving the human soul. Only in abstaining from the material pleasures of the world can the soul transcend this Earthly prison and return to the realm of light beyond the physical universe.[145] Jean-Louis Baudry fathomed himself such a shepherd in identifying the illusory power of the cinema and thus leading the entranced spectator out of the cave and into the light. But as Martin Jay has shown, the apparatus theorists are not alone, for such anti-illusionist critiques of ocularcentrism have persisted from ancient theologies through Western intellectual thought of the twentieth century. "The Evil Demon of Cinema," Gunning writes, "is not simply a duplicitous and complicit ideological swindle, but a banished deity of a nearly forgotten, but a once world wide, religion, a deity torn within by a cosmic struggle between Good and Evil, faced with a creation that is itself illusory, the product of demons rather than a beneficent creator."[146] The illusory power of the cinema, its diabolical potential, materializes in *Sinister* in the form of the iconic demon Bughuul, who succeeds in seducing the youngest member of the Oswalt family, ensuring their demise.

The intermittent motion of the Super 8mm projector bathing Ellison in periods of light and darkness enacts the Manichean crisis of Good and Evil, although here, the demonic, evil presence lies not in the gap between film frames, but resides in the image waiting to be seen. Fully realizing the iconophobic anxieties regarding the affective and illusory power of the image, analogue celluloid film returns in *Sinister* as a haunted object to be feared, its material base harbouring the demonic intent of seduction, absorption, and ultimately, the death of the subject.

The return of analogue celluloid film in *Sinister* thus stages a return to archaic suspicions of the illusory power of the image and of iconophobia that have remained latent, if not explicit, in Western religion and metaphysics. While *The Awakening* draws upon the historical practice of spirit photography that understood the spirit realm as natural, albeit invisible, elements of the material world and championed the scientific objectivity of photography as revelatory of this truth, *Sinister* emphasizes the danger and evil implicit in the illusory realism and objectivity of analogue film.

Within contemporary paranormal horror film, then, analogue film emerges as an ambivalent format that, on one hand, is represented as an archaic haunted object that poses a threat to protagonists. On the other hand, analogue film provides a verifiable, indexical trace of the real, thus acquiring the status of objective proof. This re-emergence at the turn of the twenty-first century is significant, as the ubiquity of digital media technologies today that dominate our visual culture has provoked a renewed interest in medium specificity and the relationship between analogue and digital ontologies. It is precisely this supposed loss of indexicality in relation to digital media that allows D.N. Rodowick to assert, "Digital media are neither visual, nor textual, nor musical – they are simulations."[147] Rather than forming an image by exposing photosensitive film to light, initiating a chemical reaction that imprints the referent onto the filmstrip, digital images are computational and are formed from the manipulation of numerical information. Rodowick continues, "Unlike analogical representations, which have as their basis a transformation of substance isomorphic with an originating image, virtual representations derive all of their powers from numerical manipulation."[148] Whether one agrees with Rodowick's position that digital technologies have removed all ties to reality, or that analogue photography and cinema have a privileged access to such a reality (which is certainly up for debate), what is clear is that the proliferation of digital technologies has produced a crisis of indexicality in both theory and practice that has beckoned the re-examination and theorization of the role of analogue in the age of digital technology and media convergence. As Mary Ann Doane notes, "within film theory, confronted with the threat and/or promise of the digital, indexicality as a category has attained a new centrality, as has the work of Bazin."[149] Analogue photography and film share an ambivalent relationship to referentiality and the real within contemporary paranormal horror films. The following chapter examines a format that has had a significant impact on the aesthetic form and function of paranormal investigation: television.

3

TELEVISUAL GHOSTS AND PARANORMAL INVESTIGATION

Eureka Springs, Arkansas, has the dubious distinction of being the location of one of the most allegedly haunted buildings in the United States: the Crescent Hotel. Built in 1886, the hotel/spa has since been recognized as a historically significant landmark by the Historic Hotels of America division of the National Trust for Historic Preservation.[1] In addition to its architectural splendour and the panoramic vistas offered by its location – perched on a mountainside overlooking the Ozarks – the Crescent Hotel is perhaps best known today for its spectral clientele, who failed to check out and remain indelibly present within its walls. While one might think tales of haunting and ghostly spirits would deter visitors wary of encountering such phenomena on their vacation stays, the hotel has promoted its haunted heritage and offers ghost tours for a fee.[2] It holds three tours per weekend in the evening and encourages guests to bring along their cameras for an "unforgettable, unrepeatable experience."[3] The hotel's promotion of paranormal investigation has proved to be lucrative; its tours highlight the unique architectural and historical features of the site as well as lurid tales of trauma and tragedy that befell its past inhabitants. The hotel's notoriety, and popularity, experienced significant growth after the 2005 airing of a *Ghost Hunters* episode that seemed to capture visual and aural evidence of ghosts. According to hotel spokesperson Bill Ott, after the episode's airing, the demand for ghost tours of the hotel grounds rose significantly. The hotel accommodated thirty to fifty tours per week with about twenty-five people participating in each tour.[4] Galvanized by the episode's display of evidence suggesting the existence of the supernatural, amateur ghost hunters flocked to the hotel, hoping to capture images and sounds of their own.

Paranormal investigation has become a ubiquitous presence on reality television, on networks with increasingly tenuous connections to the supernatural, such as SyFy, Travel Channel, A&E, E!, MTV, and the Weather Network.[5] The contemporary landscape of paranormal reality television was shaped by the legacies of the Society for Psychical Research (SPR), established in 1882 in the UK, and its American branch the American Society for Psychical Research, launched in 1884. As discussed in chapter 2, the SPR sought to accumulate testimony and evidence pertaining to paranormal experiences in an effort to ascertain scientifically not only the validity of the phenomena but also the forces that generate them. The SPR established a set of committees to examine specific paranormal phenomena: the Committee on Thought-Transference, the Committee on Mesmerism, the Committee on Reichenbach's Experiments,[6] the Committee on Haunted Houses, the Committee on Psychical Phenomena, and the Literary Committee.[7] By collecting as many testimonies, eyewitness accounts, and data as possible, the SPR intended to identify common, recurring characteristics of paranormal phenomena, ironically eschewing the sensational and anomalous in favour of commonalities out of which to derive a consensus. As this chapter will show, this approach stands in sharp contrast to contemporary paranormal reality television, which heavily favours visual spectacle and technological amusement rather than the careful articulation of statistical patterns.

The third issue of *Journal of the Society for Psychical Research*, published in April 1884, outlined the organization's investigative methodology. Of sixty-five case analyses conducted by the SPR, twenty-eight were categorized as "A" cases "because [the SPR] regard[s] the evidence as clear and strong, and the witnesses worthy of credence."[8] Visual perceptions accounted for twenty-four cases, while four accounts were of purely acoustic phenomena. The SPR eliminated the four cases based solely on sound as "it is generally impossible to prove that noises are not caused by rats, wind, or a dozen other things."[9] Additionally, the SPR chose to eliminate from consideration another five cases that it deemed to be "extraordinary" – that is, they fell outside common threads and continuities among the group.[10] The remaining nineteen cases shared, according to the SPR's analysis, an "apparently casual and objectless nature of the apparition."[11] The figures in the reported sightings lacked an "appearance of life" and looked like images "thrown by a magic lantern."[12] "Sometimes the appearance is described as life-like," the SPR continued, "sometimes it is recognised at once as a phantom. Sometimes it is shadowy, but more often the dress is seen distinctly, and is described as that worn by living persons in recent times."[13]

Despite these observations, the SPR refrained from using the term "ghost" to describe what the witnesses had seen. "We have not used the word 'ghost,'" they wrote, "because it might be thought to countenance the idea that these phenomena are due to the presence of departed spirits. We must repeat that for the present we absolutely decline to theorise."[14] Significantly, the SPR clarified that they were not convinced that ghostly perceptions were in fact the souls of dead people; instead, they described the visual manifestations reported by their witnesses as projected images, like "image[s] thrown by a magic lantern." This mediatized analogy of spectral figures was foregrounded in the journal's inaugural issue, in which Henry Sidgwick, the SPR's first president, defined apparitions of individuals seen just before or at the moment of their death as instances of telepathy. That is, the witness was actually perceiving the thoughts or emotions of another person in the moments leading up to that person's death. Like the words "telephone" and "telegraph," Sidgwick explained, "telepathy" indicated an experience of sympathy transmitted between two human beings at a distance.[15] What were commonly called apparitions were actually "feelings and ideas" that "under certain exceptional and as yet unknown conditions, are transmitted from one living human being to another, otherwise than through the recognised organs of sense."[16] At least for this category of paranormal phenomena, in which an individual perceived the visual presence of a loved one just before or at the moment of their death, the perceiver was not encountering a departed spirit, but an image of pain or sorrow transmitted across distances.

This conception of apparitions corresponds with Terry Castle's observations that the Enlightenment brought about an "internalization of the spectral" in which ghosts became reconceived as "*hallucinations*, or projections of the mind."[17] However, in addition to telepathy, Sidgwick's description of apparitions may also be understood as a form of *tele-vision*: seeing at a distance. Apparitions as manifestations of the transference of thoughts, feelings, and images shared properties with contemporaneous telecommunications technologies like the telephone and telegraph, as Sidgwick mentioned explicitly. By incorporating images, those technologies anticipated the medium of television, which similarly transmits images over great distances into the intimate space of the home. While the ardent dissenters of the paranormal-debunking magazine *Skeptical Inquirer* opine that "[t]here are a half dozen or so different definitions of ghosts" and "ghost hunters still don't know what ghosts are," ghost-hunting reality television expresses a decidedly televisual conception of the ghost, one that is heightened by its representation through the medium of TV.[18]

Within this spectral discourse, the medium of television accrues renewed significance as a technologized mode of vision and sound produced through Earth's airwaves. Building from the legacy of the SPR, paranormal reality television, I argue, posits a *geo-logical* explanation for ghosts, one that conceives of spirits as emanations and fluctuations of Earth's geothermal, electromagnetic, and atmospheric characteristics. This is most clearly demonstrated in the category "residual haunting" within the taxonomy of spiritual activity, a category that describes spirits of the dead as energies absorbed into and released from the bedrock of the Earth itself. The presence of ghosts is rationalized as the release of energy that has been stored in land and in certain rock formations such as limestone and quartz. The crust of the Earth, its topsoil, its landscapes, thus become indexical media that store the imprints and traces of dead individuals. In contradistinction with "intelligent haunting," a category of ghosts that are self-aware and actively communicate with the living, residual haunts consist of monotonous repetition wherein the spirit continues to perform the activities of its living self. Analogous with a tape player, such hauntings replay on loop the activities of the living spirit – children playing, maids cleaning, aristocrats smoking cigars. Incognizant of the living human beings who surround them, such spirits are unaware they are dead and thus occupy a spectral temporality distinct from linear, homogeneous, disenchanted time. Paranormal reality television presents us with a sedimented conception of haunting, the ghost fossilized as a present-pastness within landscapes. As such, the ghost hunter becomes a temporal archaeologist, mapping and mining the Earth's heterogeneous temporality, excavating its layers to reveal the presence of the spirits of the past.

Like nineteenth-century Spiritualism (see chapter 2), paranormal reality TV describes haunting in pseudoscientific terms, defining ghosts as the presence of spiritual energies. The materialization and movement of ghosts may therefore be tracked, these shows suggest, by measuring fluctuations in electromagnetic field readings and temperature. The technologies used in paranormal reality television, devices Matthew Bernico has called "apocryphal media" as they "only produce a belief that they work,"[19] bear out this conception of ghosts as physical properties of Earth's electromagnetic grid, materializing in waves, bursts, and flows of energy. Higher electromagnetic field (EMF) readings, for example, are interpreted as evidence of spectral presences, signifying a flurry of activity, the presence and surplus of energy for which there is no alternative explanation. Conversely, ghosts are also understood within the discourse of paranormal investigation to *consume* thermal energy; that is, ghosts require energy in order to manifest themselves. As a result, drops in temperature in certain spaces are presented as evidence of ghosts. Cold spots are registered with thermal imaging cameras that visually depict fluctuations in temperature through gradations of colour (red is hot, blue or black is cold). Moreover, investigators often articulate feeling cold in certain spaces, thereby suggesting the presence of a spirit. A cold spot localized within a specific section of an otherwise room-temperature space is thus presented as especially persuasive evidence of ghosts.

Another common device used in paranormal investigation is the EVP reader, a sound recorder that captures "electronic voice phenomena." EVPs are vocalizations of spirits either answering questions posed by investigators, often in monosyllabic terms, or other spectral articulations of speech. Central to the evidentiary status of the EVP is that they are not heard by investigators during the investigation itself but are only audible during playback. Because these ghostly vocalizations occur below the frequency threshold audible to the human ear, the presence of intelligible speech during playback on EVP recorders is interpreted as a spiritual event. A similar device known as the spirit box is used in *Ghost Adventures* and the web series *Buzzfeed Unsolved*.

FIGURE 3.1 | PROMO FOR *GHOST HUNTERS* SEASON 9, EPISODE 17, "ORPHANS OF GETTYSBURG," SHOWCASING NIGHT-VISION FOOTAGE THAT IS CHARACTERISTIC OF THE GENRE.

Instead of inaudible speech that is recorded and heard upon playback, the spirit box is said to manifest ghostly speech through the rapid shuffling of radio frequencies. The spirit box cycles through radio frequencies so quickly that it produces a buzzing white noise, which can then be manipulated by the spirit to communicate. Any words or sentences heard are deemed those of ghosts rather than simply a radio transmission due to the device's rapid rate of scanning. The clearer the utterance and the longer the phrase, then, the more conclusive the evidence for paranormal investigators.

But perhaps the most iconic, and ubiquitous, device in the subgenre is the night-vision camera. Paranormal investigations on reality television are almost always conducted in darkness overnight. While undoubtedly benefiting from horror film conventions in which limited visual fields produce suspense, shows like *Ghost Hunters* often claim that energy shifts or is somehow different at night, thus making nighttime investigations more conducive to spiritual contact. Thus, night-vision cameras are used to capture the movements and manifestations of ghosts that might otherwise be invisible to the eye in darkness. Full-spectrum cameras may also be used, resulting in a light pink image rather than the more common green and blue hues of night vision. As these devices demonstrate, ghosts are detected by measuring shifts and irregularities in the physical environment, rendering ghosts as geological phenomena.

In paranormal reality television, ghosts embody a distinctly televisual constitution. Both the apparatus of television and manifestations of haunting in ghost hunting amount to images and sounds transmitted through airwaves as electronic signals. The prefix "tele" in television refers to the collapse of *spatial* distance in that the production and reception of broadcast signals occur simultaneously in live programming; ghosts are similarly televisual in their collapse of *temporal* distance, a seeing at a distance through time. The ghost instantiates a temporal contiguity of past and present, a proximity marked by variations in temperature and electromagnetic signals measured by investigators with EMF readers, thermal cameras, EVP recorders, and other gadgets. Quite literally, ghosts are television.

TEMPORALITIES OF TELEVISUAL HAUNTING

Stefan Andriopoulos has demonstrated how the development of television was inextricable from the interactions among the fields of electrical engineering, physics, and occultism.[20] As Andriopoulos details, the mapping of the electromagnetic wave spectrum between 1887 and 1888 by Heinrich Hertz confirmed that Earth's atmosphere was not simply empty space, but, in Hertz's words, "filled with ether, a substance capable of propagating waves."[21] As Luis Hernan and Martyn Dade-Robinson note, the concept of "ether" was developed in the nineteenth century to reconcile the discovery of waves with the precepts of classical Newtonian physics.[22] Waves in this period were understood to be "periodic disturbances in the dimensions of space time" and required a medium through which to travel, spread, or broadcast. Terrestrially, air in the atmosphere functioned as a medium for the transmission of light, sound waves, and electromagnetic waves, but a problem emerged: how is it that light and energy from the Sun could travel to Earth through space without air as its medium?[23] It was deduced that there must be some medium to facilitate this transmission, and ether became the proposed solution. The concept of ether as an invisible medium was therefore highly amenable to Spiritualist discourses concerning the transmission of ghostly messages through space as well as the understanding of spirits as a category of waves themselves, as ruptures or vibrations within the continuum of space time that had been affirmed by scientific analysis. "The development of ether physics during the late nineteenth century," Hernan and Dade-Robinson write, "could merge discussions of the physical events of wave propagation and the discussion on the existence of the spirit world as special cases of vibration within the same medium."[24] This confluence of physical and spiritual transmission through the weightless yet material medium of ether greatly influenced the development of television; the transmission of electronic signals and spiritual messages shared the same medium in the form of ether.

Andriopoulos notes that, contemporaneous with texts exploring electrical television such as *Phototelegraphy and Electrical Television* (Benedict Schöffler, 1898) and *The Electrical Televisor* (Fritz Lux, 1903), theories of psychic communication were being published that used similar terms. Carl du Prel's *Television and Action at a Distance* (1895) and J. Körmann-Alzech's *Marvels and Secrets from throughout the Ages Revealed* (1904) advanced notions of psychic transmission in which a message would materialize in the form of an image in the mind of the receiver.[25] "Translating images into signals that can be relayed and reconverted into images," Andriopoulos writes, "this principle was outlined in comparable form in those spiritualist texts that formulated a theory of psychic television."[26] Just as with spirit photography (see the previous chapter), clairvoyance, telepathy, and telekinesis were regarded by their adherents not as *super*natural, but rather as natural and material powers of the human mind. As such, research and experimentation in the realm of psychic communication was understood to be an extension of the science of telegraphy and telephony. Central to both fields was the collapse of spatial and temporal distance and an emphasis on directness, simultaneity, and co-presence.

Andriopoulos has shown how Spiritualists seized upon this scientific research as confirmation of the existence and persistence of spiritual energy. Upon Guglielmo Marconi's successful experiments with wireless telegraphy, for example, the possibility of telepathy and thought transmission seemed closer to realization.[27] Moreover, the coalescence of electrical and psychic transmission is evidenced in the coinage of terms such as telepathy, telegraphy, telephony, telekinesis, teleplasty, and, of course, television.[28] Andriopoulos writes that "occultist studies on psychic 'clairvoyance' (*Hellsehen*) and 'television' (*Fernsehen*), carried out in the same period by spiritualists who emulated the rules and procedures of science, played a constitutive role for the technological inventions and developments of electrical television."[29] Indeed, the process of translating images into signals that are then transmitted and reconstituted as images was comparably explored within Spiritualist texts discussing psychic television.[30] Spiritualist research and investment in psychic television (or telesight), Andriopoulos argues, was therefore a necessary condition for the invention of electrical television.[31] For media theorists, temporal simultaneity and the promise of instantaneous transmission continued to define television as a unique medium distinct from cinema.

In describing the television coverage of a charity event, the *Bal des Petits Lits blanc*, André Bazin expresses a palpable sense of delight. Instead of having to attend such an event himself – a professional obligation with which he had complied in the past – the television transmission functioned as a substitute for his presence; it provided the visual pleasures of star gazing and the overall pomp and circumstance of the event with no need for him to physically attend. Beyond being entertained by the performances on display, Bazin was fascinated that he was able to watch the audience watch the performers. Specifically, he was amused by Charles Chaplin's incredulous laughter while viewing a clown act. Bazin muses: "while the guests were watching some poor music hall numbers, we were watching the guests."[32] Here, the object of Bazin's gaze from which he derives so much pleasure is the gaze of spectatorship itself; he is able to view the act of viewing. Because of this unique affordance ascribed to television, the home viewer occupies a position of superiority over the guests physically present at the event; not only does one witness the acts performed on stage, but one also witnesses the real-time reactions of those famous faces in attendance. The temporal simultaneity of the event and its televised transmission is championed as *the* criterion of uniqueness that distinguishes television from cinema.

Temporally present yet spatially absent, live televised transmission offers a novel viewing experience distinct from that of the cinema, a medium that is predicated on the projection of photograms and thus inextricable from the pastness of photography. While television shares the capacity of liveness endemic to radio broadcasting, the latter, of course, is purely a sonic experience and lacks the visual register of the image. Indeed, at a time when he was confined to a hospital bed, Bazin often relied on the radio for entertainment, and he complained that the medium demanded too much attention and exertion on the listener's part, an effort that was not rewarded.[33] In offering both sound and image, television promised an experience of temporal similitude and absent presence, for it transported the televisual world into the comfort of one's home. "Like those polarized glasses that let light pass in only one direction," Bazin writes, "the TV screen transmits presence one way, and always in our favour. The princess had 100,000 invisible guests in her salon."[34]

Referring to what he calls *télégenie*, a televisual adaptation of Jean Epstein's *photogenie*, which attempts to articulate how the cinematic image reveals the essence or the soul of those depicted, Bazin argues that the televisual image offers a unique sense of intimacy between the viewer and those on-screen. He is particularly intrigued by talk shows and interview programs where artists and intellectuals as well as ordinary workers are featured and rendered equivalent through the televisual image. "What counts most in television is no longer the social level, or the glory, or the intellectual value of the subject. It is primarily its human interest."[35] He continues, "The cinema will never film a biography of my concierge or my grocer, but on my TV set they can be admirable and astounding. Just as we stand equal before death, all men are equal before television."[36] The cinema, Bazin suggests, would never depict the actual individuals with whom one may interact daily, opting instead to employ actors portraying character types rather than specific people. Eschewing the artifice of performance – so Bazin would have us believe – television offers a veritable encounter with another person, whereby something of the individual's personality or essential humanity is exhibited. Bazin experiences this same sense of intimacy and familiarity with news anchors, reporters, and even TV actors, not just interview subjects. So much so that when he encountered television personalities in the streets, he found himself supressing the urge to shake their hands, as if they had developed a genuine camaraderie through rituals of daily TV viewing.[37] Because it offers both spatial intimacy in its location within the home and temporal simultaneity between the televised event and the act of viewing, television for Bazin is a uniquely personal medium, one that democratizes representation and one in which the revelation of the human spirit is inescapable.[38] For these reasons, Bazin suggests that television is perhaps "the most moral of the mechanical arts."[39]

It is interesting that Bazin likens the equalizing power of television to that of death. He repeats this claim in "The Aesthetic Future of Television," writing that "kings and shepherds, geniuses and simpletons are equal before television, in the same manner as we are all equal before death."[40] While both references to death attempt to convey the basic equality of all human beings regardless of social stature, it is a curious analogy to make given television's continued association with liveness and presence. As discussed in chapter 2, medium-specific relationships to death have often been identified with photography and celluloid film and have been attributed to Bazin's writings specifically. Dudley Andrew has pointed out, for example, that tucked away in his personal copy of Sartre's *L'Imaginaire*, Bazin articulated the specificity of the cinema as being derived from the uncanny realization that the image is both alive and dead, a reanimated still image.[41] Indeed, Bazin's argument concerning the photographic and celluloid image's intrinsic relationship to reality, as Philip Rosen has emphasized, is predicated upon the viewing subject's psychological investment in that realism, the subject's prior knowledge of how the photographic image is created, and its temporal dimension of pastness.[42] To further articulate this confluence of psychological desire and temporal deferral, Bazin enlists the metaphor of the "mummy complex," a metaphor that conveys a founding human desire to stave off the inevitability of death and decay. While the plastic arts from sculpture to painting are imbued with this preservative function, the cinema's material base as photographs projected at sixteen to twenty-four frames per second rather than a single, motionless object confers a unique temporal dimension to the medium. What is preserved in cinema is not simply an existential trace of the real, but duration itself; in this way, cinema constitutes a mummification of change, the preservation of duration.[43]

Bazin's conception of cinema's temporality firmly entrenches the medium within the realm of death, as the cinema initiates a present-tense unfolding of a past event, something that has already occurred but is reanimated in the present. Bazin takes this argument further in another essay in which he differentiates between photography and cinema's relationship to death. In "Death Every Afternoon," Bazin confers particular power upon the moving image, which, unlike a photograph, may represent the *process* of death in its duration rather than simply the still image of a corpse. The photograph, he writes, "does not have the power of film; it can only represent someone dying or a corpse, not the elusive passage from one state to the other."[44] The cinema, for Bazin, is therefore able to capture the existential transformation from living being to dead object through the duration of motion pictures. But if the cinema for Bazin is the medium that most fully epitomizes an existential relationship to death, how does this square with his comments concerning death in relation to television? While cinema metaphorizes the temporal dimensions of dying and decay, television, we are told, is analogous to death insofar as TV renders all subjects equal as in death. However, there is another sense in which one may find death operational within live TV that is implicit in Bazin's writing: the potential for accident, the contingent, and the spontaneous.

In a further distinction between the two media, Bazin argues that cinema's use of editing effectively "cheats with time" whereas television's "aesthetic morality is one of frankness and risk."[45] I have already addressed the issue of frankness and authenticity that Bazin attributes to TV. I now turn to this notion of risk, for it will serve as a key criterion for understanding live television. The prospect of the unexpected, of the sudden eruption of accident, error, and even violence has been a structuring condition of the appeal of live television. From the live broadcast of a sitcom, to a sporting event, to a newscast, the promise of contingency, I argue, haunts all live programming. Bazin reveals as much in relation to watching a live medical procedure being conducted on a diseased lung. The drama of the event is heightened by the risk that something may go wrong live before the audience, something that cannot be prevented or edited out as in a conventional film.[46] The central fascination, then, lies in the sense of being co-present with an unpredictable an unrepeatable occurrence, of bearing witness to the eruption of chance and error contemporaneous with its real-time occurrence.

This potential for catastrophe thus epitomizes television's promise of the unmediated temporal event, a "celebration of the instantaneous" that signifies a "*this-is-going-on*" rather than a "*that-has-been*."[47] Mary

Ann Doane has argued that television's temporal economy is constructed by three distinct, though not mutually exclusive, categories: information, crisis, and catastrophe. Information refers to the banal, everyday unfolding of news that, while interesting, is not especially gripping. We may here think of the nightly newscast that is defined by its regularity and predictability, rather than by shock or difference.[48] Crisis, however, refers to an attention-grabbing event that occurs over a specified amount of time. Doane uses the examples of political crises, such as hostage situations, hijackings, and coups that require a set duration, as well as the intervention of agents who are tasked with making decisions to resolve the crisis.[49] In contradistinction to these two categories, the catastrophe constitutes the temporal limit of live television as it embodies instantaneity, spontaneity, an "all-at-once-ness."[50] The potential to bear witness to such an unpredictable, unanticipated catastrophe that occurs in an instant informs the viewing pleasure of live broadcasting, a pleasure fuelled by suspenseful anticipation. Such a pleasure in risk and desire for accident is evident in Bazin's excitement in watching the medical surgery, but also serves to undercut his previous assertion of the essential aesthetic morality of television, for it does not operate to reveal an essential authenticity and equality of human beings, but instead relishes in the possibility of rupture, of chaos, of destruction. The pleasures of live television may therefore be summarized as being in time with the televised event – that is, of temporal simultaneity with the televisual field amidst spatial absence – as well as the anticipation of the spontaneous most fully manifested within the domain of catastrophe.

Live television, of course, is only one mode of broadcasting, with pre-taped programming accounting for a sizeable, if not majority, block of television's schedule.[51] Even pre-taped content, though, accrues a veneer of the live by virtue of its televisual broadcast and reception. Jacques Derrida articulates the uncanny sense of archived liveness, of inscribed presence, in what he calls the teletechnologies of the contemporary era, those of television and the nascent internet in particular. Referencing a televised interview in which he is participating with Bernard Steigler, Derrida says, "[N]ow, at this very instant, we are living a singular, unrepeatable moment, which took place only once, of something that was live, that is live, that we think is simply live, but that will be reproduced *as live*, with a reference to this present and this moment anywhere and anytime, weeks or years from now."[52] An experience of liveness is preserved in televisual recordings and experienced again as live upon future broadcasts. While this is also the case in recorded music, as in the playing of a vinyl record where the absent voice of a singer becomes a virtual presence, and indeed in any moving image or sound recording across media formats, what is unique for Derrida is the intensity, the *vividness* with which teletechnologies, here epitomized by television, reproduce liveness. Even when broadcasting what is acknowledged and understood to be a recording of the past, this "distance, lag, or delay" between the time and space of the recorded event and its reception by a viewer will nevertheless "continue to stay alive," producing a "living image of the living."[53] Once again referencing the recorded television interview he is conducting with Steigler, Derrida states that "the timbre of our voices, our appearance, our gaze, the movement of our hands" is preserved, archived, transported and (re)experienced in a future present.[54] As Mark Fisher has noted, there is a geographical *and* temporal displacement at work, signified by the prefix "tele" in television and in teletechnologies more broadly, a displacement that is masked by the intensity and vividness of its present-tense reception.[55]

Liveness is therefore an effect generated by the televisual apparatus at the point of reception, but also at the point of production. Even ostensibly live programming is carefully crafted aesthetically to produce and maintain a sense of immediacy and the temporal simultaneously. Jane Feuer offers a particularly persuasive analysis that demonstrates how television constructs an ideology of liveness despite its actual condition as fragmentary and discontinuous. She emphasizes that live TV should not be misconstrued as "real life" since this conception effaces all of the determinants between the actual event and the viewer's perception of it.[56] In her examination of *Good Morning, America*, Feuer notes that the program consists of an array of discrete segments and shifts effortlessly from pre-taped film, to video, to live segments.[57] These segments cover a wide range of discontinuous topics, which, at the time of Feuer's writing, included features on home maintenance, coverage of the Olympics and the Iranian crisis, celebrity tabloid news, film reviews, and more.[58] Equally discontinuous are the locations from which segments are transmitted – New York, Washington, and Chicago, among others – all anchored by the lead reporter. In this case, David Hartman functions as the patriarchal anchor of the *Good Morning, America* family.[59] Feuer's point is that despite the live television broadcast's claims of liveness, presence, and spatio-temporal continuity, it is, in fact, highly fragmented, constructed out of a series of disparate elements: "Network television never truly exploits its capacity for instantaneous and unmediated transmission. Only the ideological connotations of live television are exploited in order to overcome the contradiction between flow and fragmentation in television practice."[60] Feuer's critique of the uncritical association of television with an authentic reality "out there" is reiterated by James Friedman, who similarly argues that "television cannot bring 'reality' to viewers; it can only provide a representation of an event."[61] Despite such critiques, claims of live television's privileged access to an unmediated reality persist. While this understanding has been articulated in celebratory terms,[62] it has also been the source of anxiety. The perceived immediacy of access and omniscient vision have constructed television less as a window onto the world as in a photograph, and more as a medium of teleportation bringing the external world into the private realm of the home. It is precisely this characteristic of teleportation that has produced a sense of unease regarding television's presence in the home and contributed to its association with haunting and spectrality.

As Jeffrey Sconce has written, television's capacity to elide spatial distance has accrued uncanny and anxiety-producing effects. "With its illusion of fully formed realities of sound *and* vision adrift in the ether," Sconce writes, "television came to be conceived, not only as an electrical extension of human sight, but as an uncanny electronic space in and of itself."[63] The humming electronic presence of the television not only offered viewers a look into other worlds through the 4:3 cathode ray tube but also brought these other worlds into the home, generating a two-way portal that both transported and consumed. Sconce points out that films such as *Murder by Television* (Clifford Sanforth, 1935) and *International House* (A. Edward Sutherland, 1933) and TV shows like *The Twilight Zone* (CBS, 1959–64) and *The Outer Limits* (ABC, 1963–65) represented television as a medium of uncanny otherworldliness, its electronic presence intruding with uncomfortable proximity into the personal space of the viewer.[64] Here, the glass of the television monitor functions like the mirror in the occult and spiritualist practices of scrying and psychomanteum, wherein a mirror is used to facilitate the trans-dimensional communication with the spirit world.[65] Similarly, television's uncanny presence is attributable not only to its real-time views of distant locations and events but also, and perhaps more significantly, to the animated force of the electron that possesses the screen with a buzzing *élan vital.* Like the virtual image conjured through a mirror, the televisual image is (a)live due to the active spark of electronic scanning that brings the image into intelligibility. In other words, the electrical impulse is active, moving, and present *here* in your living room, in your monitor. Even when the set is turned off, as Sconce reiterates, television is always "on" and happening now.[66] This (a)liveness of electricity that is exploited ubiquitously throughout all paranormal reality TV shows as ghosts manipulate electronic signals to communicate with investigators as well as materialize as spiritual energies by and through electronic fields.

HUNTING GHOSTS

The rapid rise of paranormal reality TV is undoubtedly partly attributable to the surprise success of *The Blair Witch Project* (1999), which applied amateur film aesthetics in the context of documenting the supernatural.[67] But seven years earlier, in 1992, an infamous BBC broadcast was highly influential in the development of both found-footage horror and paranormal reality television. The broadcast consisted of a supposedly live investigation of a haunted home in Northolt, England, and featured well-known BBC personalities Sarah Greene, Mike Smith, Craig Charles, and Michael Parkinson. The BBC team encounters increasingly disturbing violent phenomena, and the broadcast culminates in the possession of lead anchor Parkinson by the malevolent entity known as "Pipes." The fate of the others is left unknown.

Although shot weeks in advance of its 31 October airing and advertised as a fictional performance, *Ghostwatch* (Leslie Manning, 1992) nevertheless succeeded in fooling some segments of the UK audience into believing that the broadcast was an authentic live news event. As Murray Leeder notes, the broadcast sparked a media firestorm; the BBC was flooded with hundreds of thousands of phone calls, children reportedly experienced symptoms of post-traumatic stress disorder, and even a suicide was blamed on the broadcast.[68] Like the *War of the Worlds* broadcast fifty years prior, *Ghostwatch* exploited the familiar conventions and protocols of broadcast news in order to portray the fictionalized events as a veritable catastrophe occurring in real time. In both cases, audiences tuning in mid-broadcast would have missed signifiers demonstrating the constructed nature of the performances and possibly mistaken the sensational programs for authentic news. The controversy surrounding both programs elicits questions regarding the role of network broadcasting in the public sphere, the responsibility of radio and television as informative and trustworthy sources in a liberal democracy, the problematic commingling of news and entertainment, and the appropriation of codes of authenticity to present fiction as if it were fact. As was the case with *War of the Worlds* in relation to radio, *Ghostwatch* was as much about the perils of live television broadcasting as it was about the haunted home.

The climax of *Ghostwatch* suggests that the live television feed itself functioned as a haunted conduit through which any television set could be infected. As such, any television tuned in to the *Ghostwatch* broadcast participated in a kind of national, televisual séance conjuring the evil spirit of Pipes.[69] Similarly, Jeffrey Sconce has argued that televisual liveness in the classical age of network broadcasting itself accrued associations with the uncanny, namely the television set's eerie predilection for transmitting spectral images of absent bodies into the intimate spaces of living rooms.[70] *Ghostwatch* represents as literal the invasive threat that television transmission poses to the sanctified domestic space of the home, as the evil ghost, the program suggests, is able to transcend the limitations of spatial distance and manifest itself through any conduit accessing public airwaves. As with the ghost, television's temporal simultaneity and collapse of spatial distance usher in a viewing experience that may strike viewers as *too* intimate and *too* close. This intimate proximity extends to the realm of reality television, which, although only occasionally live, presents itself as an up-close and personal document of real people in real situations.

The success and notoriety of *Ghostwatch* and *The Blair Witch Project* paved the way for reality TV programs concerned with documenting the supernatural. *Ghost Hunters*, to be sure, is but one example of the myriad programs within the subgenre, including its own spinoffs *Ghost Hunters International* (2008–12) and *Ghost Hunters Academy* (2009–10) as well as *MTV's Fear* (2000–02), *Scariest Places on Earth* (2000–6), *Most Haunted* (2002–present), *Ghost Adventures* (2008–present), *Paranormal State* (2007–11), *Celebrity Ghost Stories* (2008–14), *Ghost Lab* (2009–11), *Fact or Faked: Paranormal Files* (2010–12), *Paranormal Witness* (2011–present), *Haunted Collector* (2011–13), *Ghost Asylum* (2014–16), *Kindred Spirits* (2016–present), *Portals to Hell* (2019–present), and *Paranormal Lockdown* (2016–present), among others. According to Amy Lawrence, more than six dozen paranormal reality television shows aired in the United States between 2004 and 2019, attesting to the genre's widespread popularity.[71] Karen Williams situates paranormal reality TV within the broader history of fantastic media stretching back to the magic lantern performances and phantasmagoria shows of the eighteenth century as well as the classic stage trick "Pepper's Ghost" in the nineteenth century.[72] Williams sees paranormal reality television as a contemporary form of these earlier ghost shows, arguing that they share one of two central intentions of spectral performances: "earnest authenticating" on the one hand and "spectacle and effect" on the other.[73] *MTV's Fear*, for example, was a game show wherein contestants were "dared" to spend the night in haunted locations and perform specific tasks for cash prizes. Significantly, the program had no host, studio audience, or camera crew; each contestant was provided camera equipment and was fitted with a camera rig that filmed the contestants' frightened facial reactions. The show was therefore centrally organized around capturing the reactions and affective terror experienced by the contestants, rather than documenting or even investigating paranormal phenomena.[74] A program like *Ghost Hunters*, however, explicitly addresses the question of the existence of ghosts and the ability of various technologies to document and record evidence seeking to either prove or debunk claims of haunting.[75] Competition formats are therefore not interested in investigation as such, whereas *Ghost Hunters* and its ilk devote significant amounts of screen time to laying out their methodologies, explaining the function of each device and its accuracy in detecting spirits.

The Stanley Hotel in Estes Park, Colorado, remains one of the more notable locations to be investigated in *Ghost Hunters*. The hotel holds

FIGURE 3.2 | AN OMINOUS, WIDE-ANGLE SHOT OF THE STANLEY HOTEL, WHICH INSPIRED STEPHEN KING TO WRITE *THE SHINING*, FROM SEASON 2, EPISODE 22 OF *GHOST HUNTERS*.

cinematic significance as it inspired Stephen King to pen his famous novel *The Shining* on which the canonical horror film of the same name was based. "Wandering through its corridors," King stated in an interview, "I thought that it seemed the perfect – maybe the archetypal – setting for a ghost story."[76] King goes on to state that he experienced a nightmare during his stay in the hotel in which his son was being chased down a hallway by a fire hose. In a sweat, King woke up and immediately began to write the first pages of this novel.[77] While King provides a rather innocuous account of the inspiration for the book, Billy Ward, the concierge of the Stanley Hotel, tells the *Ghost Hunters* team and the television audience a decidedly more fantastic tale. In what follows, I provide an overview of that *Ghost Hunters* episode, which will serve as a model for how the show operates. I elaborate upon the premise of the show, the stated aims of the investigators, and the methodology employed. I will then analyze the show's representation of haunting, emphasizing its geological conception of spectral traces.

Ghost Hunters follows The Atlantic Paranormal Society (TAPS) headed by Grant Wilson and Jason Hawes. The pair was inspired to pursue paranormal investigation after having personal experiences of their own with the supernatural. As plumbers for Roto-Rooter,[78]

Hawes and Wilson emphasize their expert knowledge concerning plumbing, electrical wiring, and ventilation, thereby positioning themselves as uniquely able to distinguish authentic instances of haunting from banal domestic happenings. Rather than the ghostly footsteps of a departed loved one, for example, creaking floorboards may be identified as the expansion and compression of wood amid shifts in temperature and moisture content. Or, lights turning on and off on their own initially attributed to the spectral caress of a forlorn spirit may be the result of faulty wiring. Hawes and Wilson's professional affiliation therefore functions to provide an air of legitimacy to the TAPS team.

Because it emphasizes professional expertise and scientific verification, fans of the genre consider *Ghost Hunters* the most authentic of paranormal reality television shows.[79] This authenticity is generated in part by Hawes and Wilson's stated aim to *disprove* claims of haunting. As Lauro and Paul attest, "Hawes says that about '80 per cent' of cases can be dismissed, and they often are able to debunk phenomena such as strange sounds, and opening and closing doors as natural occurrences due to sloping floors, electrical lines and water pipes."[80] By including cases in the show in which claims of haunting are debunked, *Ghost Hunters* is able to manufacture a sense of legitimacy that renders any ghostly evidence more believable.

Unlike the affective and emotional approaches of *Ghost Adventures* and *Kindred Spirits* – programs that emphasize anger and empathy, respectively, as well as the subjective experiences of the investigators – *Ghost Hunters* presents a decidedly technophilic investigative enterprise. *Ghost Adventures* and *Kindred Spirits* certainly make use of spirit boxes, structured light sensor (SLS) cameras, EMF readers, and the like; however, these tools often serve to confirm or corroborate psychic, emotional, or historical information, content that is decidedly non-televisual on its own. Flashing lights and unintelligible sounds accrue evidentiary value by the extent to which they substantiate the visceral, affective, and psychical forms of spiritual communication. *Ghost Hunters*, in contrast, expresses skepticism concerning psychic mediumship and rarely incorporates the work of psychics in its investigations. Moreover, the *Ghost Hunters* team adopts a detached and dispassionate disposition when conducting their investigations, opting for a veneer of cool and unbiased observation. This admittedly makes for a more boring viewing experience, one that lacks the histri-

FIGURE 3.3 | SLS CAMERA FOOTAGE FROM SEASON 21, EPISODE 5 OF *GHOST ADVENTURES*. THE IMAGE DEPICTS AN INVESTIGATOR SEATED IN A CHAIR AND AN ANOMALY REPRESENTED AS A STICK FIGURE.

onics and camp quality of *Ghost Adventures*, in which lead investigator Zak Bagans regularly claims to be possessed by demonic entities and engages in angry, emotional outbursts. Boring, however, is part of the authenticating mission of *Ghost Hunters* and its attempts to construct credibility. For example, the presence of "orbs" in camera footage and photographs (small balls of light that represent the presence of spiritual energy) is often dismissed as evidence despite their ubiquity in paranormal reality TV. Instead, orbs are identified as bugs, dust, or rays of light picked up by cameras rather than as manifestations of concentrated spiritual energy. *Ghost Hunters* rejects these forms of evidence so typical of the genre in favour of technologies that chart and measure fluctuations in environmental conditions. As outlined in the introduction to this chapter, the preferred devices for supernatural detection include EMF readers, EVP recorders, thermal imaging, night vision, and full-spectrum cameras.

In emphasizing scientific inquiry and technological modes of evidence, *Ghost Hunters* attempts to distinguish itself from the traditionally feminine domain of Spiritualist communication. As chapter 2 discussed, Spiritualism was explicitly associated with feminine attributes of energy and sensitivity rather than the supposedly distanced, objective eye of male-dominated scientific inquiry. *Ghost Hunters* aims to embed the pursuit of ghosts and the supernatural in the traditionally masculine enterprise of scientific investigation, rejecting the historical association between Spiritualism and the feminine. The very title *Ghost Hunters* constructs the show as a militaristic pursuit of ghosts with all of the aggression, strength, and bravery signified by "the hunt." Karen Renner contends that in order to compensate for the feminine associations of Spiritualism, contemporary paranormal reality TV resorts to hyperbolic displays of masculinity, including "proclaiming and proving physical toughness; treating fear as 'girlish'; physically sacrificing themselves, soldier-like, for the greater good; declaring a desire to seek out truth and justice regardless of danger; substantiating emotion and intuition with evidence; heftily pronouncing their heterosexuality; expressing a need for 'extreme' experiences away from the staid norms of everyday life."[81]

Such hypermasculinity functions to shift the pursuit of the supernatural from the feminine attributes of sensitivity and affect to the more traditionally masculine domains of the investigative procedural and scientific evidence. To be sure, *Ghost Hunters* and *Ghost Adventures* sometimes utilize "provocation," a method wherein investigators challenge, berate, and/or insult the ghosts as a demonstrative show of strength and force in order to encourage paranormal activity. Renner notes that the television stations on which these programs typically air – Syfy, Discovery, Travel – are indicative of a shift in genre from the feminized gothic and occult to the masculine realms of science fiction, action-adventure, detective story, and western.[82]

Such methods stand in stark contrast to *Kindred Spirits*, led by Amy Bruni, the openly gay Adam Berry, and the queer psychic Chip Coffey, who approach the spirit world with a respect, empathy, and reverence akin to Spiritualism. Similarly, *Ghost Brothers*, the only show as of this writing to star Black investigators, approaches investigations with a mixture of humour and solemnity. When the team, composed of best friends Dalen Spratt, Marcus Harvey, and Juwan Mass, encounters the spirit of a slave in a former plantation in the first episode, they acknowledge the horrors of state-sanctioned violence suffered by the ghost and appreciate why the ghost may not want to communicate with the living. The team leaves the area as a sign of deference. Similarly, the YouTube web series *Queer Ghost Hunters* shows care and kindness towards the specifically queer ghosts the team aims to contact. Here, the Spiritualist tradition of the séance is performed as a queer historiographical method to (re)construct queer history and community across time.[83] *Ghost Hunters*, however, relies heavily on the data its investigators collect from their ghost-hunting equipment as well as on empirical observation. In *Ghost Hunters* in particular, the formal organization of the show as a detective procedural and its emphasis on the latest technological advancements reinforce its commitment to a masculine pursuit of the supernatural through science, logic, and reason.

Ghost Hunters episodes are organized into discrete segments punctuated by commercial breaks. The episodes begin with a preview in which narrator Mike Rowe, in an authoritative and dramatic manner, introduces the cases that will be covered in the week's episode. The preview includes clips from the investigation that are meant to build anticipation for the episode. Despite the show's concerted effort to present itself as methodical and scientific, the preview consists of emotional responses exhibited by the investigative team in order to suggest frightening and/or exciting encounters with the supernatural. The preview of the Stanley Hotel episode in Season Two, for example, includes Rowe posing rhetorical questions such as: "What will TAPS experience at the legendary Stanley Hotel?"; "What leaves [investigators] Brian and Steve all shook up?"; and "Who gets rattled by an unexpected encounter?" Each question is followed by footage from the upcoming episode that depicts the reactions of the TAPS team, such as gasps, vocal exclamations, and perplexed facial expressions, cueing the audience to wonder what could have caused these reactions from our stoic and professional ghost-hunting team.

The preview is followed by the opening credits sequence, which introduces each member of the TAPS team and their role within the group. Each member is given a title card including an action headshot accompanied by his name and role within the TAPS team.[84] Hawes and Wilson are identified as lead investigators, Steve Gonsalves as the tech manager, Donna LaCroix as the case manager, Brian Harnois and

Lisa Dowaliby as investigators, and, lastly, Dave Tango as investigator-in-training. Different people have served as the lower-level investigators throughout the show, but Hawes, Wilson, and Gonsalves have been largely constant throughout the series' run. Immediately following the opening credits, the case manager briefs Hawes and Wilson on the location and the specific claims of supernatural experiences associated with the property. Following this briefing, the investigation begins.

The investigation segment is introduced with a title card of its own. During this segment, the team is given a tour of the space, specific rooms are selected for scrutiny, and anecdotes of paranormal activity are relayed. In the Stanley Hotel episode, the concierge Billy Ward informs the team of various paranormal activities that have been reported. For example, the chefs working in the hotel's lounge space reported hearing sounds of a party while no one was present. On the hotel's fourth floor, we are told, it is often reported that children are heard playing and running down the hall. Ward informs the team that the fourth floor is the most active site for paranormal phenomena and that it was on this floor that Stephen King supposedly saw two ghost children playing with a ball. Ward describes other instances of paranormal activity: deceased housekeeper Ms Wilson dutifully continues handling guest luggage and tending to the rooms; furniture is mysteriously rearranged; books fall from shelves; the ghost of a homeless woman supposedly haunts the concert hall in which she tragically froze to death; and, most dramatically, a panic-stricken hotel guest claimed to be possessed by malevolent energy. This tale of possession is corroborated in the episode by interviews with two of the hotel's staff, who describe the woman as frantic and unnaturally strong.[85] Ward is careful to mention that upon inspection by paramedics, the woman was not intoxicated and had no drugs in her system, suggesting that the woman's claims were authentic. While the guided tour undoubtedly functions as an advertisement for the property, emphasizing the natural beauty of the location and its impressive architecture, the opening segments of *Ghost Hunters* forecast the findings of the investigations and often inflate or misrepresent the significance of evidence and the intensity of the reactions exhibited by the investigators.

Ward's anecdote concerning Stephen King's encounter with ghost children is particularly significant in that Ward incorporates an iconic image from *The Shining* as an instance of historical evidence. The fictional representation of haunting in the book and film is here appropriated as a veritable supernatural encounter, attesting to the blurred boundaries between event and representation. In what he describes as "mediated imaginary geographies," Tim Edensor has examined the ways in which the historical import and cultural value of places and spaces become entwined within, and inseparable from, their representations in film, television, and literature.[86] Edensor cites the film *Braveheart* (Mel Gibson, 1995) as a potent example. "Replete with images of 'romantic' highland rurality," he writes, "[*Braveheart*] has become embedded in the touristic promotion of the town of Stirling, newly labelled 'Braveheart Country.'"[87] For Edensor, then, media representations function as a kind of imaginary topography superimposed on the landscape wherein the fictionalized characteristics and history of particular spaces become accepted as authentic. Similarly, the ghost twin girls of *The Shining* are here entwined with the ghost children of the Stanley Hotel.

Paranormal reality television operates in much the same way as hotels, restaurants, prisons, mental asylums, and other notable sites that no longer exist independently from their association with tales of trauma, haunting, and possession. This conjunction of place with its popular representation in media is indicative of a broader politics of memory intrinsic to the act of ghost hunting, a politics that demonstrates how memory is "inscribed upon space."[88] In incorporating scenes and images from *The Shining* as events that took place in the hotel, Ward demonstrates the slippage between actual and imaginary history exemplified by mediated imaginary geographies. Like Jack Torrance (Jack Nicholson) in the film, the haunting of the fictional Overlook Hotel has been incorporated into the Stanley Hotel's actual history.[89]

Edensor argues that the industrial ruins of modernity are particularly potent examples of the spatialization of memory. He describes "derelict foundries, mills, workshops, and factories" as "haunted realms of industrial ruin" that continue to adorn the landscape of Western cities despite having been abandoned by the "flows of money, energy, people, and traffic within which they were once enfolded."[90] Like the former prisons and mental asylums investigated in *Ghost Hunters*, ruins constitute sites that "have not been exorcised" and consequently "seethe with memories."[91] Multiple temporalities and histories cohere within the ruin, a structure that, through decay, becomes a palimpsest revealing layers of memory and time. Like the Derridean conception of the spectre, ruins "begin at the ends of things," as Kathleen Stewart has written, thereby confounding a linear, progressive regime of time.[92] For this reason, Edensor considers ruins to be the perennial haunted sites of modernity, riven with indeterminacy. "The attempted erasure of the past is incomplete [in the ruin]," Edensor writes, "and the ghosts have not been consigned to dark corners, attics, and drawers, or been swept away, reinterpreted, and recontextualised."[93] Ghosts remain present as relics awaiting excavation.

Importantly, the ruin as haunted site for Edensor constitutes an alternative site of memory that not only resists a linear trajectory of temporal progress but also opposes attempts to fix and secure official histories in spaces such as museums and heritage sites.[94] "Heritage and museum spaces," Edensor argues, "seamlessly banish ambiguity and the multiplicity of the past to compile a series of potted stories, display boards, audiovisual presentations, and themed simulacra which attempt to capture the 'feel' of a historical period, performing a narrative and dramatic fixing, and which potentially limit the interpretative and performative scope of visitors."[95] *Ghost Hunters*, however, collapses this distinction between ruin and heritage site in that both are portrayed as harbouring layers of sedimented temporalities haunted by the ghosts of people who once frequented the location. Like Edensor, though, *Ghost Hunters* – like paranormal reality television generally – understands place as a contaminated site, one that is inflected with multiple pasts. Especially through the category of "residual haunting," a category that conceives of ghosts as absorbed energies stored within mineral deposits and rock formations, *Ghost Hunters* seeks to peel back the layers of sedimented history constitutive of contemporary geographies. In paranormal reality television, fissured landscapes retain the layered, folding, and colliding temporalities constitutive of haunting as such, thereby materializing the asynchronous temporal economy of the spectral.

The paranormal experiences described by the Stanley Hotel's concierge in the *Ghost Hunters* episode fall into two categories: intelligent and residual haunting. These categories define differing relationships between the ghost and its surrounding environment, articulating haunting as a geographical and geological condition. Julian Holloway and James Kneale have noted the increasing interest geographers have demonstrated in haunting and spectrality. Of particular interest to geographers, the authors write, is the estrangement and disruption wrought by the presence of ghosts in conventional spaces. "Arguably," Holloway and Kneale suggest, "what we are dealing with when a space becomes haunted is the disruption or dislocation of normalized configurations and affordances of materiality, embodiment and space."[96] In the context of a séance, for example, spirits manifest themselves by moving objects, altering temperatures, and manipulating or possessing the body of the medium. Haunted spaces are thus discernable in terms of reconfigured spatial relations, ones that render strange the ordinary and normalized operation of spaces and bodies.

In paranormal investigative parlance, the manipulation of objects in this manner would be indicative of an intelligent haunting, one in which the spirit is self-aware, acknowledges the presence of the living individuals around it, and seeks to garner attention through a variety of communicative means. As Dennis and Michele Waskul explain, "An intelligent haunting is defined as a ghostly presence that interacts with the environment, living people, or both. Those interactions are taken to signify that the ghost is aware of the living world, even self-aware, and hence 'intelligent.'"[97] The Waskuls note that being physically pushed or touched is also a sign of intelligent haunting, but more frequently such hauntings manifest themselves indirectly in the form of objects moving inexplicably: "doors open or close, electrical devices operate erratically, items move, something makes the sound of footsteps on floors or stairs or bangs or knocks on windows and doors."[98] Many such instances occur in the Stanley Hotel episode as various members of the TAPS crew react to creaks and knocks with unknown origins, phenomena that are ubiquitous in all *Ghost Hunters* episodes. But two incidents occur during their investigation that are of a more spectacular character than is typical for the show.

Wilson and two other investigators, Tango and Lisa, head into room 1302, and according to Wilson, they immediately feel that this room is different from the others. While they are sitting at a wooden side table and wielding night-vision cameras and flashlights, the table appears to jerk forward, startling Wilson. Importantly, it is not just the TAPS team that is startled by this event; so is the production's camera operator, Kendall Whelpton, who is interviewed to relay what he witnessed. This marks a rare moment when a member of the *Ghost Hunters* production crew is brought on camera to discuss a paranormal event. For the TV viewer, though, this manifestation of intelligent haunting is largely missed by the camera, as only a slight portion of the table is visible onscreen. In addition to the angle of the shot, the use of night vision obscures our view of the paranormal event. While ostensibly used to enhance vision and compensate for humans' poor capacity for seeing in the dark, night vision here produces a murky image awash in hues of green and black that serves as a barrier to our perception of the event. The testimony of those present in the room is meant to fill the gap left by the lack of evidentiary documentation and attest to the authenticity of the event; yet the TV audience is left with inconclusive evidence, unable to discern the authenticity of the haunted table.

The team also uses night-vision cameras to document the hotel rooms during the night while the team members are sleeping. Hawes opts to spend the night in room 401, a room that is often said to experience paranormal activity. Through grainy footage from a static camera set-up, we see Hawes sleeping (and hear him snoring) in bed. Off-camera, we hear creaking sounds followed by the clinking of glass. Hawes wakes up and picks up the camera, telling audiences that he heard the closet door open. He turns on the hotel room light and films the closet door, which is indeed open, and shows us a broken drinking glass on the nightstand. Hawes then sets the camera on the nightstand facing the closet door as he gets back into bed to sleep. While he is sleeping, the camera captures the closet door in the background slowly closing and latching shut. In the "findings" segment of the show, in which the team reviews all the footage they have recorded, Tango and Gonsalves replay the footage from Hawes's stay in room 401. This segment is intercut with interviews of Tango and Gonsalves contextualizing and interpreting the footage for the audience. In the interview, Tango describes the footage: "You just see this door start to move and close and latch. That's not normal, that's paranormal." Other evidence captured and reviewed in this segment includes banging sounds and thermal imagery of what appear to be ghostly legs walking down a hallway. Both examples are dismissed as natural, with Hawes and Wilson attributing the banging noises to pipes expanding and the hotel's heating system. The levitating table, the closing closet door, and the broken glass are presented as evidence without natural explanation, thus suggesting the possibility of haunting.

In another part of the hotel, Gonsalves and Harnois explore the billiards room, where guests have reported seeing and hearing ghostly parties and dancing spirits. Like the apparition of two children on the hotel's fourth floor, this tale of a spectral party is reminiscent of scenes from *The Shining*, yet again conjuring images from the film and appropriating them as instances of paranormal activity associated with the hotel. Nevertheless, Harnois proposes that this event might be explained by the hotel's geological foundation. "We're on a mountain," Harnois tells Gonsalves, "[there] could be a lot of limestone deposits and stuff like that. It could be a residual haunting they saw of a party back in the 30s or 40s." "Some kind of recording mineral," Gonsalves concurs. He continues, "These rocks do absorb and record history and things that have happened," and Harnois agrees that these rocks may be "play[ing] back a message." In the "findings" segment, the TAPS team gathers to go over the evidence they have compiled. Here, Harnois raises the possibility that the experiences reported in the hotel may be due to residual haunts and informs the team that the hotel sits atop a foundation containing granite and quartz. Wilson concurs that limestone, quartz, lead, and/or water tend to be present in instances of residual haunting, as they are absorbent of, and conducive to, spiritual energies. The team then accepts that some of the phenomena reported in the hotel – namely the sights and sounds of ghostly parties – may be due to the release of energy stored in these rock deposits, which literally replay the history they have absorbed.

If intelligent haunting describes ghosts that are self-aware and are actively attempting to gain the attention of the living, either by physically manipulating objects or by communicating vocally, then residual haunting describes the repetition of the past within the present. The Waskuls define residual hauntings as instances wherein spirits do not interact with their environment or living people around them. "A classic definition of residual haunting," they write, "involves people seeing or hearing a ghostly presence repeatedly in the exact same manner."[99]

Residual hauntings, then, describe patterns of repetition in which a ghost continues to perform the same actions in perpetuity. Such spirits do not exhibit conscious awareness and simply re-enact behaviours familiar to the spirit's routine while alive. The ghost of Ms Wilson, who continues to perform her duties as a housekeeper, is one example of residual haunting. The children spotted on the hotel's fourth floor playing with a ball is another. It is as if a historical moment remains present as a feedback loop, continuing to play itself out in contemporary time. Indeed, Hawes employs the analogy of a tape player to explain the phenomenon: "A residual haunting you can think of it like a tape player that keep on rewinding itself and playing itself over and over again. So when it comes down to it, a lot of quartz stone under the building, it really does fit into our theory."[100] Stone and minerals here function as recording devices that replay instances of the past within the present.

Like *The Stone Tape* (Peter Sasdy, 1972), a film in which an electronics team encounters a ghost trapped within the stone walls of a Victorian home, *Ghost Hunters* and paranormal reality television conceive of residual haunting as a form of spectral playback wherein stone functions as a medium of storage, containing and releasing spiritual energy. Stone and rock formations function as indexical storage media, registering and replaying traces of the past in the present, initiating a temporal and spatial superimposition. To witness a residual haunting, then, is to literally peer into the past, to transcend temporal distance, to look *tele-visually*. Aiming to capture visually these experiences of temporal superimposition, *Ghost Hunters* employs a variety of night-vision cameras. Because residual hauntings may produce apparitions, orbs, mists, and shadows, night vision is employed to enhance prospects of visual documentation.

In addition to night-vision cameras, the TAPS team frequently employs thermal imaging cameras as another technology of visual mapping. In the Stanley Hotel, Hawes and Wilson use thermal imaging in their investigation of the lounge. Wilson describes thermal imaging cameras as one of the most sought-after pieces of equipment for paranormal investigators. "A lot of paranormal investigation," he tells us, "deals with temperature changes and cold spots … When you have a thermal imaging camera, you can actually *see* cold spots, you can see drafts, you can see if someone's been in the room recently … It's a beautiful tool." Like night-vision cameras, thermal imaging devices serve a compensatory function in that they allow the investigator to see temperature. With this instrument, spaces are mapped in gradations of blue, yellow, green, and red, with abnormal temperature shifts understood to be evidence of a spectral presence. Because spirits require energy to manifest themselves, fluctuations in temperature are interpreted as the materialization and movement of spirits. The presence of ghosts is measured and defined quantitatively in relation to the temperature of the space, people, and objects around them. The use of thermal imaging cameras thus defines ghosts *geographically*, in relation to temperature relative to space, as well as *geologically*, in terms of energy produced and emitted by the landscape. Thus, thermal imaging cameras are more conducive to documenting evidence of residual haunts as opposed to intelligent hauntings.

Interestingly, the *Skeptical Inquirer* launched its own counter-investigation of the Stanley Hotel with the aim of debunking the claims made in the *Ghost Hunters* episode. The US Department of Agriculture (USDA) was enlisted to conduct a survey of the hotel's foundation. Karen Stollznow writes, "The USDA concluded formally that the soil is primarily metamorphic rock known as schist. This rock can contain minerals such as talc, graphite, *and* quartz, although the survey found that there were no 'large deposits of magnetite or quartz under the property.'"[101] Given the lack of the very materials *Ghost Hunters* foregrounds as spiritually conducive, Stollznow concludes that the TAPS investigation of the Stanley Hotel was "a load of schist."[102] The *Skeptical Inquirer* also critiques the use of night-vision photography to investigate spaces with the lights off, on the basis that signifiers of spirits – such as shadows and dark figures – would be better perceived in bright daylight. Benjamin Radford expresses frustration concerning this trope of paranormal reality television when he states, "Searching a dark room for a shadowy figure is an exercise in futility."[103] However, the logic of night-time investigations put forth by these shows is a geological one; it is often stated that energies shift at night, thereby increasing one's chances of encountering the supernatural. Night-vision cameras, moreover, serve a cartographic function for the investigation, mapping the terrain and illuminating objects. Trying to capture shadows and dark figures using night vision is certainly a dubious approach, but this convention succeeds in rendering the space of the investigation an uncanny one. Outlining the contours of rooms and landscapes in eerie shades of green, blue, or grey, night vision is well-suited to the task of recording intelligent hauntings, which primarily involve the manipulation and movement of objects rather than materialized darkness or spectral shadows.

Notwithstanding these valid critiques of paranormal investigation offered by the *Skeptical Inquirer*, the geo-logics of haunting exhibited in *Ghost Hunters* offer significant insights into the haunted constitution of space and place. Multiple temporalities exist as sedimented histories and memories within the palimpsest of haunted sites. In these fissured landscapes, time accrues in layers, mediating the past within the present and thereby initiating a televisual relationship between the realm of the living and the spirits of the dead. If electronic telecommunication holds ghostly potential in its collapsing of space and time through simultaneity and instantaneous transmission, haunting in paranormal reality television offers a temporal transmission, a seeing *through* time. Space itself functions televisually in paranormal reality TV as haunting is the manifestation of time stored within the materiality of space. As such, landscapes and certain geological formations in *Ghost Hunters* harbour alternative temporalities that counter rationalized linear time. As Jeffrey Jerome Cohen contends, "thinking geologically" brings the past and the present "into unaccustomed proximity."[104]

Stone, for Cohen, challenges conceptions of temporal order in ways I have argued are implicit in *Ghost Hunters*' conception of haunted presence. Moreover, Cohen advances a theory of stone that epitomizes the spectral. "Because of its density, extensiveness, tempo, and force," Cohen asserts, "there is something in rock that is actively unknowable, something that will not surrender itself to stabilities, a truth behind the trope that stone rebukes epistemology."[105] Like the ghost, rock refuses easy categorization and recuperation into the realm of knowledge. Furthermore, ghosts and stone offer what Cohen describes as a certain vivacity, a liveness that is "pulsing, radiant, and thrumming with possibility."[106] Stone offers temporality on an "inhuman scale," one that upends measurement and comprehension.[107] "Stone challenges small, linear divisions of human history through its aeonic insistence," Cohen argues. He continues, "The lithic thickens time into multiple, densely sedimented, and combustively coincident temporalities."[108] Residual haunting epitomizes the weight of time metastasized in stone, raising the spectre of an aeonic temporality that diminishes and even erases the human. "The allure of stone," Cohen writes, "the lithic sublime, is primal."[109] This helps explain the horrific affect associated with paranormal reality television and haunted spaces more generally: an encounter with a time sufficiently great and expansive as to subsume the human within its accumulation.

Cohen emphasizes that stone is the pre-eminent medium of story and narrative, for it endures through time, accumulating traces and cataloguing time into the future. The lithic trace, he argues, is therefore a testament to both erasure and endurance, "a 'material connection' to spur narrative."[110] The story told by stone is one that spans millennia. To touch stone, to hold it in one's hand, is to "press flesh against the first moments of time," to encounter an "alien duration."[111] *Ghost Hunters* and paranormal reality television are parts of this enduring story, one that dislodges the finite temporality of the human through the aeonic time of spirits, energy, and stone.

Ghost Hunters revisited the Stanley Hotel in a Season Three live special on 31 October 2006. Over the span of six hours, viewers monitored camera footage of the hotel and communicated with the TAPS team live via the internet. Viewers could notify the team of any ghostly phenomena or sightings while the investigation was in progress. The footage captured during the live investigation was then edited into a traditional episode titled "The Best of the Stanley Hotel," which aired on 8 November 2006. The team pores over the typical forms of evidence from mysterious sounds, electromagnetic fluctuations, and cold spots; they even seem to capture the voice of the spirit of a young girl.[112] Hawes concludes upon reviewing the evidence that the Stanley Hotel is "definitely haunted." Despite his assertion, the technologized forms of evidence produced in the show cannot elicit a definitive judgment regarding the existence of ghosts on the part of the television viewer. As Sarah Juliet Lauro and Catherine Paul argue, *Ghost Hunters* and paranormal reality TV operate within what they call the "postmodern fantastic," a realm in which contemporary technology functions as a barrier to knowledge rather than a revelation of incontrovertible evidence.

Borrowing Tzvetan Todorov's concept of the fantastic,[113] Lauro and Paul argue that the use of technology in paranormal reality TV elicits a hesitation concerning contemporary technology's ability to register that which eludes our corporeal senses. They couple Todorov's "fantastic" with the aesthetic and sociopolitical condition of the "postmodern," a term they use to denote the collapse of reality into representation such that the boundaries delineating reality and simulation, truth and fiction, become blurred. This sense of the postmodern utilized by Lauro and Paul is perhaps best expressed in the paradoxical phrase "Reality TV," a term describing a genre that purports to re-present the real but is highly contrived and carefully constructed. Of the postmodern fantastic, they write: "this is the hinge between that which can be and cannot be perceived (and therefore, believed), which relies on non-natural, human-made inventions to try to make visible, audible and tangible phenomena that lie outside the purview of human understanding, though not, potentially, outside of the natural world."[114] Like nineteenth-century Spiritualists and the revelationist tradition of classical film theory, Lauro and Paul point to how paranormal reality television shows evince a faith that man-made technologies can penetrate the realm of the invisible and document the paranormal. But these very technologies as well as the mediation of television, they argue, also function as obstacles to belief, for the the television viewer is unable to trust that the ghostly evidence is authentic. When presented with supposed evidence of the supernatural, the television viewer is confronted with choices: "she might accept that the technology has captured something ranging from inexplicable to proof of spirits, *or* she might find the technological medium of the show itself an obstacle to acceptance."[115] Paranormal reality television exists in this realm of the fantastic, oscillating between documentation of spirits and the documentation of forgery.

Similarly, Karen Williams concludes, "Rather than 'claiming the real,' these shows are claiming the *possibly* real, and they do so by generating and recording specific affective responses in their subjects."[116] Williams therefore disputes claims by Hawes and Wilson that *Ghost Hunters* is a scientific enterprise aiming to disprove claims of haunting. Williams argues that, more than the evidence accumulated in the investigation, it is the documentation of the personal experiences of the investigators and their reactions to phenomena that convey the perception that the supernatural may possibly exist, despite the lack of clear proof. "There is a reason no 'real' ghost is represented in these reality shows," Williams writes. "Neither the medium of television nor its forms of reality TV could ever represent its 'reality': death and disconnection."[117] Williams suggests, however, that ghost-hunting shows and reality television share an essential affinity: "each being at once a medium for the revelation of an unseen real and a sensational form of entertainment."[118] In this way, paranormal reality television in its portrayal of haunting most fully expresses the promise of televisuality: seeing across time and space through instantaneous transmission.

The geo-logic of residual haunting considers the Earth itself to be an indexical recording medium *par excellence*, and technologies used in the show function to map the topography of space and fluctuations in the Earth's electromagnetic spectrum. The medium of television becomes significant in this formulation of haunting as its mode of telecommunication is predicated upon the transmission and reception of messages via airwaves, through the ether. As the next chapter will outline, television has experienced a shift from the traditional broadcast model to cable installation, satellite feed, and digital transmission. Between the passage of the US Telecommunications Act in 1934, at which time airwaves as a public resource were ceded to the corporate control of media conglomerates, and the conversion to digital transmission in 2009, analogue TV depended on a geological infrastructure, one that expressed the condition of spectrality as tele-visual projection.[119] *Ghost Hunters* and paranormal reality TV exploit television's ethereality: its association with liveness and presence; its superimposition of past and present, time and space; and its condition as a medium conjuring images through air. Television and spectrality share an essential ethereality, one that is embedded in the materiality of Earth as medium.

4

TAPE: VIDEOGRAPHIC RUIN AND THE LURE OF THE TANGIBLE

Despite the contemporary surge of internet streaming sites such as Netflix, Hulu, Amazon Prime, Criterion Channel, Mubi, Shudder, Tubi, and more, a handful of distributors have remained steadfast in their devotion to videotape. "Since 2009," Daniel Herbert writes, "about ten companies have released over twenty different movie titles, both old and new, on magnetic tape."[1] Significantly, horror and cult films have been instrumental in initiating this resurgence. Herbert credits MPI and its subsidiary Gorgon video, who had already experienced a video hit with the release of *Faces of Death* (John Alan Schwartz, 1978), for the current revival.[2] MPI released *House of the Devil* (Ti West, 2009), itself a throw-back to classic 1980s horror films, in limited edition VHS copies in a highly successful promotion for the film's home video release. So successful, in fact, that the initial release of fifteen-hundred VHS tapes went through two printings and exhausted the inventory of three separate box cover suppliers.[3] Following suit, Magnet Releasing distributed VHS copies of the horror anthologies *V/H/S* (Joe Swanberg et al., 2012) and *V/H/S/2* (Simon Barrett et al., 2013) while cult film distributor Severin Films launched a VHS video subsidiary specializing in the release of controversial cult fare.[4] More recently, the season one collector's edition of *Stranger Things* was released on DVD and Blu-ray in packaging masquerading as a VHS tape, complete with worn box corners, retro box art, and "VHS Hi-Fi" labelling.[5]

These VHS releases, however, are not earnest attempts to restore the lost dominance of the format in the now defunct video rental and retail market; rather, they function as collectible objects one displays on a shelf and not strictly, or even primarily, as viewable content. *House of the Devil* and the *V/H/S* anthologies were also released on DVD in far greater numbers, clearly signifying DVD as the films' intended viewing format. Moreover, it is standard practice for distributors to include the DVD or digital download code along with the purchase of the VHS version, suggesting that these tapes are intended to be collectible objects with paracinematic value rather than as strictly viewable media.[6] The return of VHS is therefore explicitly a veneration of the objecthood of video in contradistinction to what Herbert calls the cultural logic of intangible media: a desire for the physicality of video, its protocols of use, its unique aesthetic of degeneration, and the tactility of the videographic apparatus that has been largely replaced by the rise of digital video formats. Often aligned with the *sobriquet* "trash cinema," horror, exploitation, and cult films are particularly well-suited for the revival of VHS, a format relegated to the garbage heap of outmoded technologies.

The resurgence of videotape is more than just nostalgia. Its resurgence, and its prevalence in found-footage horror films, have reinscribed the format with the uncanny characteristics of lost history, of memories in the process of disappearance. The discovery of lost footage, its very *foundness*, triggers such affective resonances. I contend that through processes of discovery and excavation, videotape in found-footage horror becomes what I call a *videographic ruin*, accruing an aura of archaeological significance. Videotape's status as ruin lies not only in its positioning as an historical artifact, one that records and preserves traces of the past through time, but also in its convergence of multiple media forms. Video exudes the heterogeneity of the ruin, composed as it is from elements of television, cinema, and computer. Contaminated by layers of time and technological change, video occupies the historical-technological juncture between our analogue past and our digital present. The *V/H/S* franchise is the most explicit in this regard due to its remediation of video aesthetics (despite having been shot digitally), its emphasis on finding and excavating videotapes, and the affective relationship it represents between viewer and videographic apparatus. Through the act of discovery, videotape is transformed from mere storage format into a highly cathected relic. The status of tape as ruin is ever greater given the senescence and imminent obsolescence of videotape as a format, having been superseded by DVDs and digital files, and the proclamation of the death of VHS in 2006.[7] As we move deeper into the realm of digital saturation, analogue media and the lure of the tangible remain a spectral presence, perpetually returning to haunt today's media landscape.

VIDEO RUINS

While a variety of moving image and sound formats have served the function of found documents in found-footage horror, it is videotape that often occupies the locus of fascination and investigation. As Alexandra Heller-Nicholas notes, videotape has been a privileged object in found-footage horror, with many such films featuring "tape" or referencing video in their titles: *The Poughkeepsie Tapes* (John Erick Dowdle, 2007), *[REC]* (Jaume Balagueró and Paco Plaza, 2007), *The Mitchell Tapes* (Thomas S. Nicol, 2010), *Anneliese: The Exorcist Tapes* (Jude Gerard Prest, 2011), *The Tapes* (Lee Alliston and Scott Bates, 2011), the *V/H/S* franchise, *The Lost Tape* (Rakshit Dahiya, 2012), and so on.[8] Significant precursors of found-footage horror include *Cannibal Holocaust* (Ruggero Deodato, 1980) and *Man Bites Dog* (Rémy Belvaux, André Bonzel, and Benoît Poelvoorde, 1992), but it is *The Blair Witch Project* (Daniel Myrick and Eduardo Sánchez, 1999) that is typically credited with inaugurating the cycle and establishing the discovery of onscreen footage as historical evidence.

The Blair Witch Project premiered at the Sundance Film Festival in January 1999 where it garnered significant word-of-mouth and publicity for its *cinema vérité* realism, use of unknown actors, improvisational dialogue, and its intriguing premise: the film we are watching consists of discovered footage recovered from the depths of the woods near Burkittsville, Maryland. The opening title card informs us that in 1994, three student filmmakers set out to investigate the potential existence of a witch aiming to document any evidence that might give credence to the local legend. After embarking on this investigative mission, however, the students were never seen again. Their whereabouts and their survival remaining a mystery, the students' footage, the title card reads, was found a year later, presumably documenting the last several days of the students' lives. The film garnered critical praise for its ingenuity and restraint, opting to forgo onscreen spectacles of violence and gore in favour of a decidedly psychological approach to horror, one that emphasized isolation and confinement rather than bodily mutilation. While the jittery hand-held cinematography compensates for this lack of corporeal violence through its vertiginous decomposition of diegetic space (so intense, in fact, that some audience members experienced nausea),[9] much of the suspense is achieved through *invisibility*. Despite the revelatory desire expressed by the three filmmakers, the witch is never captured onscreen; instead, her haunting omnipresence is suggested through the mythic density of the decaying woods over which she exercises dominion.

The film and video footage recovered from the woods attains the status of ruin, material relics that compose a fragmentary and incomplete picture of a past event. The film presents as evidence various reels of 16mm film and Hi-8 video that are then composited into a single documentary work. As Caetlin Benson-Allott and Kimberly Jackson have noted,[10] *The Blair Witch Project* contains two distinct documentaries emblematized by different formats: 1) the official film being shot by the three students employing 16mm film; and 2) the behind-the-scenes footage using Hi-8 video recording the making of the official documentary. The beginning of the film maintains a sharp distinction between the "official" documentary shot on film and the amateur video footage, establishing a medium-specific hierarchy of artistic value. As the film progresses, this distinction between professional and amateur footage and their respective value as archival documents gradually breaks down until both formats are employed interchangeably. By the film's end, the film and video formats are fully enmeshed, subsumed into one another in a contaminated intermedial mix. This contamination is fully expressed in the closing of the film's last sequence in which the colour video camera operated by Mike (Michael C. Williams) is destroyed, but continues to record sound. We therefore hear the sound picked up by Mike's video camera while seeing the silent black-and-white 16mm footage being recorded by Heather (Heather Donahue). As they investigate a dilapidated house in the woods, Heather's screams for Mike are rendered eerily distant, despite the viewer being aligned with Heather's perspective through her camera. In portraying the breakdown of boundaries separating these medial systems simultaneously with the disembodiment of the characters within a collapsing structure, *The Blair Witch Project* evinces the collapse of the hierarchical value traditionally assigned, both culturally and institutionally, to the analogue celluloid image while revealing the contaminated status of the video medium.

The success of *The Blair Witch Project*, *Cloverfield* (Matt Reeves, 2008), and *Paranormal Activity* (Oren Peli, 2009) introduced mainstream audiences to the unique aesthetics and narrative conceit of found-footage horror: first, that the footage we are seeing was previously shot in the course of the events it depicts; second, the footage became lost or was discarded; and third, the material was subsequently discovered and is now being exhibited for the first time. The footage typically documents the traumatic, horrific events that befall the protagonists, events the characters are compelled to capture on film or video as evidence. As such, found-footage horror is characterized as much by its formal attributes as by its narrative premise, through the extended use of first-person point-of-view shots, shaky hand-held cinematography, jump cuts, discontinuous editing techniques, and poor image and sound quality. Found-footage horror taps into the mystique of the found object while re-inscribing videotape with characteristics of uniqueness, scarcity, and affectivity. The *V/H/S* franchise foregrounds the discovery and acquisition of videotapes while emphasizing an embodied spectatorship engendered through the videographic apparatus that proves both pleasurably transfixing and destructive.

The *V/H/S* franchise consists of six feature films, two spin-offs, and a limited series on the Snapchat social media platform. With the exception of the spin-off film *SiREN* (Gregg Bishop, 2016), the films are anthologies comprised of distinct vignettes written and directed by different filmmakers and linked together by a frame narrative. *V/H/S* and *V/H/S/2* are chiefly concerned with the eponymous format while the third entry in the franchise, *V/H/S: Viral*, turns its attention to digital video uploads and file sharing. While it largely abandons the specificity of videotape in its exploration of digital viral videos (although it does include some instances of analogue video damage), *V/H/S: Viral* remains an anthology film; as such, it formally reproduces an interest in collections and collecting that shapes the *V/H/S* franchise as a whole, despite the relative absence of the VHS video format. The franchise contributes to the legacy of horror anthologies such as *The House*

That Dripped Blood (Peter Duffell, 1971), *Trilogy of Terror* (Dan Curtis, 1975), *Creepshow* (George A. Romero, 1982), and *Night Train to Terror* (Jay Schlossberg-Cohen, 1985), thereby constituting a nostalgic re-emergence of a bygone narrative format popular as B-movie theatrical exhibition and direct-to-video rental fare. Unlike more recent examples of the horror anthology form including *The ABCs of Death* (Simon Barrett, et al., 2012), *XX* (Annie Clark et al., 2017), and *Nightmare Cinema* (Joe Dante, et al., 2018), the *V/H/S* franchise explicitly establishes its films as found-footage situating the collection and circulation of videotapes as central to its narratives.

V/H/S opens with a blue screen featuring static distortion and text reading "play" on the top left-hand corner, a familiar sight for those of us accustomed to VHS playback. An establishing shot of sorts, the image features distortion and wear endemic to the materiality of videotape, indicating that our screen is, in fact, a video monitor displaying analogue video footage. The tape begins to play and we are presented with a static shot of a bedroom as a man and woman enter the frame, presumably with the intention of recording themselves having sex. This footage is interrupted with several instances of video damage including rainbow flares and lines of distortion. The video then abruptly shifts to footage of a group of criminals stealing, sexually assaulting a woman, and vandalizing property. In a motif that recurs throughout the film, such disruption suggests that the tape has been erased and taped over in certain sections. The group is tasked by an unknown patron to break into a home and search for a specific videotape to collect and return to the patron in exchange for a cash payment. The group gleefully accepts this arrangement and breaks into the home. Once there, they discover a man, seemingly unconscious, sitting in a chair facing several television monitors displaying static and white noise.[11] The group searches the home and finds a cache of hundreds of unlabelled VHS tapes and are unable to identify the specific tape requested by the mysterious patron. Undeterred, the group agrees to gather all tapes present in the home. Several tapes are played by various members of the group during the film, and it is these diegetic tapes that comprise the film's vignettes.

The re-emergence of videotape and its afterlife as collectible object embodies the spatial and temporal sedimentation of the ruin, the crumbling and deteriorating remnants of lost time. Videotapes and VCRs "linger on" as "'residual' technologies" haunting a contemporary media landscape increasingly characterized by digital media formats.[12] The physical decay and weathering of videotape manifests itself through visual and audio damage during playback, materially inscribing fading history in unique forms of audiovisual disturbance such as video moiré, skew error, dropout, noise bars, tracking errors, and a muffled soundtrack.[13] This damage and deterioration constitutes what Lucas Hilderbrand has called video's "inherent vice," the inevitable materialization of wear and breakdown that reveals video's status as a degenerative format. "The specificity of videotape," Hilderbrand writes, "becomes most apparent through repeated duplication, wear, and technical failure: that is, we recognize videotape as tape through its inherent properties of degeneration."[14] Videotape indexically inscribes its history of use, duplication, and endurance through time in the form of visual and audio damage. Videotape as crumbling ruin therefore acquires value precisely through these signifiers of damage that not only confer uniqueness and specificity to a given tape, but also facilitates an affective encounter with history. In this way, videotape has accrued a Benjaminian aura, despite its status as a mechanically reproducible format.[15]

While Benjamin attributed the withering of aura in an artwork to technological reproducibility, "substituting," as he wrote, "a plurality of copies for a unique existence," in videotape, each copy accrues its own unique existence through its individual history of recording, duplication, circulation, and use.[16] While many others may possess a VHS copy of a particular film, no one possesses *this* copy, *my* copy, with its unique markers of damage and image loss that testify to my own practices of repeated viewing, pausing, and rewinding. When away from his collection, for example, Charles Tashiro laments that while he has access to the same films elsewhere, "they are not *mine* as a figurative extension of my body and personality, physical projections of my desires and fears."[17] Like the ruin, videotapes "seethe with memories" accumulating visual and audio debris amidst the successive fading of its content.[18] Videotape harbours audiovisual remnants and artifacts from multiple layers of time, congealing multiple temporalities within a singular object. We see this in operation within the first minutes of *V/H/S* when recordings from different times seep into one another, entwined in an unstable and corrupted storage format. Increasingly defined through contamination and anachronism, videotape has thus returned as ruin, promising an alluring haptic experience of history while conferring the pleasures of ownership and possession associated with the acquisition of an archival document. Found-footage horror films literalize this conception of videographic ruin by centering their narratives around the discovery of lost or discarded videotapes.

A violent encounter with a succubus, an ill-fated honeymoon, a supernatural slasher in the woods, a live-streamed haunting-turned-alien abduction viewed through a couple's online video chat, and a Halloween haunted house that is quite literally possessed by a malevolent entity, each of these segments is intercut with the increasingly sinister environment in which the protagonists of the frame story find themselves. Members go missing while others inexplicably carry on the task of watching the tapes while the man previously laying unconscious in a chair disappears. The man roams the house, threatening the safety and security of the amateur sleuths and, in the frame narrative's climactic moment, attacks and presumably kills the last remaining perp in the house. Throughout the film, our protagonists are drawn to the incessant glow and hum of the video monitors, compelled to continue viewing the tapes despite the clear danger of the situation. Of all the segments, however, one deserves special attention for its unique use of video error and damage.

Entitled "Tuesday the 17th," a humorous allusion to the *Friday the 13th* slasher franchise, the segment features a group of friends heading to the woods for a camping trip. Upon entering the woods, one of the friends, Wendy (Norma C. Quinones) makes repeated cryptic references to events that occurred there a year prior. As the vignette unfolds, we learn that Wendy had survived a murder spree in these woods one year ago; in leading her friends to the site, Wendy hopes to confront the killer and exact her revenge. The killer, though, is not a flesh and blood human, but rather manifests within the diegesis as video tracking errors forming the outline of a human figure. The materialized error proceeds to slash its way through the group of friends and succeeds in vanquishing Wendy. The tracking error slasher introduces anachronism and rupture into the segment, at once producing jump scares proper to the horror genre as well as visual tearing, static,

FIGURE 4.1 | THE GLITCH KILLER VISUALIZED AS VIDEOGRAPHIC RUIN IN *V/H/S*, 2012.

and decay proper to analogue video damage. The image breaks down and crumbles, producing a violent instance of video ruin that pierces the screen. Such graphic disintegration and video error has been likened to the degraded settings of gothic fiction, with Marc Olivier writing, "The jarring spectacle of data ruins is becoming to the twenty-first century what the crumbling mansion was to gothic literature of the nineteenth century: the privileged space for confrontations with incompatible systems, nostalgic remnants, and restless revenants."[19] The tracking error slasher is quite literally ruinous, persisting in its contaminated and anachronistic form within the present as its media architecture withers and decays. As Olivier notes, Wendy's diegetic camera is a digital video camera, making the appearance of analogue video tracking errors (errors produced by a misaligned videotape and tape head in a VCR) an impossible incursion of the analogue into the realm of the digital. Moreover, the tracking error is itself a digital effect created by the filmmakers and inserted into the segment.[20] "Tuesday the 17th" therefore emblematizes the contamination and anachronism of the videographic ruin that defines the *V/H/S* franchise more broadly.

The powerful affective and cultural resonance of the ruin is derived in part from its fusing, commingling, and contaminating of disparate materialities and temporalities. A stubborn emblem of a past long receded, the ruin is both a site of preservation and loss, a structure that endures through time while simultaneously gesturing toward its future obsolescence. To be in the presence of the ruin is to encounter an anachronistic collection of traces haunted by the people, events, and memories to which it bore witness. "Ruins are thus in a state of indeterminacy," Tim Edensor argues, "the attempted erasure of the past is incomplete and the ghosts have not been consigned to dark corners, attics, and drawers, or been swept away, reinterpreted, and recontextualized."[21] The past endures in video ruins not only through the audiovisual damage it accumulates through time, but also in its historical relationship to television and cinema, medial spheres from which video has failed to fully disentangle.

The diegetic tapes in *V/H/S* integrate digital image production and analogue storage, collapsing the facile binary opposition between analogue and digital. Here, analogue mildew grows atop the crumbling infrastructure of digital video; not only are digitally-generated analogue video effects inserted into digitally recorded images, those images are then stored and viewed through an analogue videographic apparatus. Multiple instances of contamination and layers of mediation coexist within the diegetic videotapes; as Olivier writes, "we see laptops running Skype, video spyglasses, smartphones, a nanny cam, VHS, Hi8, HD, digital SLR, GoPro video cameras, and security cameras."[22] This contamination of digital video with analogue remnants points to the instability of video as a medium, one that lies uneasily between analogue and digital, and between the medial spheres of television, cinema, and computer. To be sure, the term "video" is today used to describe all manner of moving images from VHS cassettes to YouTube "video" clips, regardless of how those images are captured.[23] In this way, video resists medium specificity and lacks a cohesive theory specific to its unique characteristics. As Lili Berko has written, the videographic apparatus represents a convergence of cybernetics, communications, and aesthetics, encompassing the histories of radio, cinema, television, electronic media, and computer technologies.[24]

The development of video grew out of the television broadcasting industry in response to a need to archive live programs for posterity as well as for re-broadcast in different time zones. Attempts to record television signals date back to 1927, when John Baird's "phonovision" process recorded TV signals as grooves on phonograph records.[25] David Sarnoff, the head of RCA, also wanted to develop a video playback unit using magnetic tape - what he called the videograph – during the Second World War; however, it was not until 1956 that Ampex, RCA's rival, achieved this goal.[26] Beginning in the 1950s, it became increasingly important financially for television broadcasts to reach primetime audiences on both the East and West coasts, a geographical and temporal limitation previously overcome through the production of "hot kines" whereby a kinescope camera filmed a television broadcast from a monitor. With hot kines, a broadcast in New York could be filmed, processed, and re-broadcast on the West coast within a span of three hours to meet primetime markets.[27] The Ampex magnetized tape and videotape recorder (VTR) simplified this process, making the documentation of broadcasts more cost-effective and efficient. During this period, video was understood as the visual channel of broadcast transmission, a supplement to the audio transmission of radio.[28]

Beginning in the late 1960s and culminating in the late 1970s, video's relation to television would undergo a significant shift with the introduction of videocassette formats, first adopted by local and national television stations, and eventually the first commercially available Videocassette Recorders (VCRs) and videotapes for home use. In 1965, Sony released the first portable VTR onto the American market, principally for use by television stations using three-quarter inch tape.[29] Sony's VTRs would not be made available to the general public until their development of half-inch tape,[30] a technical modification that allowed for the compact size of cassettes and recorders as well as increased playback time. The development of the cassette cartridge proved especially important for user-friendliness and shifting videotape from a cumbersome and costly format available only to television stations to an accessible consumer product. Central to the successful adoption of Sony's U-matic videocassette format by television stations in the early 1970s was in placing the tape and reels *inside* the plastic case which would then be unspooled and threaded by the internal mechanisms of the accompanying VTR.[31] This system eliminated the time-consuming, and potentially complex, requirement of manually threading 16mm film, thereby constituting a significant modification that would prove essential in the creation of a home video consumer market.[32] While several formats and designs were experimented with in the early days of cassette cartridges, Betamax and VHS would prove to be the most successful, initiating a format war that would result in the creation of a home video standard.[33]

Sony's Betamax format, introduced in Japan in 1975 and in North America in 1976, was marketed as a time-shifting technology that allowed one to record programming from television, thereby freeing one from network schedules and allowing one to watch "whatever, whenever," as the Betamax tagline claimed.[34] Here, the dominant function of video became one of delayed viewing, of deferred time,[35] while also initiating new cultures of circulation and exchange. Betamax faced competition with JVC's Video Home System (VHS) that similarly produced cassette cartridges to record television programs. Despite their identical designs and tape decks, the two formats were incompatible and differed in image quality and tape length. Betamax, though generally agreed to have had superior image quality, only contained an hour's length of recordable content. At fifteen to thirty dollars per cartridge, the one-hour limit proved a nuisance when attempting to record movies aired on television or longer form programs, each regularly interrupted by advertisements.[36] The ability of VHS tapes to record two hours of content, and going so far as to release a four hour cassette tape so consumers could record a football game in its entirety, contributed to its successful adoption as an industry standard.[37] Moreover, feature films in the public domain had already been made available in the VHS format as well as pornographic content. Indeed, the robust market for pornography on VHS was a strong propellant to the emergence of a home video market.[38] From its origins in television broadcasting, then, magnetic tape shifts to become a consumer product principally associated with time-shifted television viewing, and subsequently becomes an extension of cinema as film studios embrace the VHS format as a source of revenue from the sell-through and rental of pre-recorded videocassettes.[39] Historically, videotape occupies a liminal position between television and cinema, incorporating aspects of both media systems while refusing easy assimilation to either. This is also true technologically as video depends upon televisual, cinematic, and computational technologies to function.

Consisting of a videotape recorder and playback deck, a video camera, a television monitor, a videocassette, computer interfaces, and software, the videographic apparatus collapses the borders of medium specificity, occupying a position that is neither wholly cinematic nor televisual, analogic nor digital. Television screen, video monitor, and computer interface, Berko writes, are screen technologies predicated upon the "phantom electron,"[40] invisible processes of electronic writing wherein a scanning beam in constant motion brings the image into view. As such, the image produced on TV monitors occupies a perpetual state of becoming-present as electronic signals are transmitted, stored as written information, and read by a scanning beam. In the following passage, Yvonne Spielmann details the technical operation of electronic video images:

> In a simple technical assembly with a camera and monitor, information carried by light is registered by the cathode ray and translated into video signals that are transmitted to a screen radiating the electronic signal. In these two processes of registering and reproducing, the electronic signal, which contains the video information, is continuously written in scan lines. This process of writing the video information in lines from left to right requires a horizontal line shift at the end of every line and a vertical line shift from the first to the last line. The ongoing process of writing generates television and video images, respectively, by bringing the flow of electronic information into a form (a horizontally and vertically established structure of lines) and by broadcasting in standardized formats (like PAL and NTSC).[41]

Unlike the photogram of a celluloid film strip, the video image is not stored as viewable content on film but is continually constructed through dual processes of writing and transcription, processes that remain invisibly enacted by the "phantom electron." That is to say, one cannot hold a strip of magnetized videotape to a light source and view an image that bears any resemblance to profilmic reality; rather, magnetized videotape does not contain an image at all, but the written information of the electronic signal. Video and television, then, share these processes of writing and reading that both distinguish them from the cinema as electronic formats as well as demonstrate the intimate relation between television and video.

V/H/S foregrounds this invisible process of electronic writing from its opening shots, which figure erasure and reinscription as an important property of videotape. The footage from the frame narrative segment, titled "Tape 56," is periodically interrupted with footage from a (failed) sexual encounter. The emergence of the previously recorded content bleeding through the footage reveals what was once stored on the tape, content that was subsequently marked for erasure. The sex scene's appearance is marked by visual and auditory static, setting it apart as footage recorded at a different time. Although similar in form and function to intercutting, such interruptions lack the intentionality of an editor, instead suggesting a failure to copy successfully or the extent of damage extant on the tape itself. Videotape is here a palimpsest, containing the traces of previous recordings and content that periodically rupture the continuity of playback.

In this sense, Hilderbrand's characterization of damage as the "inherent vice" of video takes on a revelatory function. Inherent vice in this context refers not to the Thomas Pynchon novel, but to the term librarians use to describe the "acidity of chemically-produced wood pulp paper" that eats through the pages of books, turning them yellow and leaving them crisp and fragile.[42] "Inherent vice" thus articulates a significant feature of written material texts: the very manufacturing of the paper on which words are printed, that brings the text to light, that renders it readable, is simultaneously what guarantees the text's inevitable destruction. In a similar fashion, videotape reveals itself as tape – as material, tangible, magnetized tape – through its own unique properties of degeneration and decay brought about by the format's propensity for copying and duplication.[43] The veneer of the image is gradually stripped of its vitality upon each instance of inscription. In bearing the scars of its own duplication, age, and circulation, videotape becomes a highly cathected object imbued with memory, historicity, nostalgia, and, in the case of horror film, trauma. It is precisely this conjuring of historicity that videotape emblematizes in found-footage horror more broadly and the *V/H/S* franchise in particular. The electronic signals are written in scan lines and read by the VCR's helical scan process (analogous to processes of reading and writing); they are then made even more visible throughout the *V/H/S* franchise as material glitch and error, signifying ruptures produced by reinscription. Rather than purity, this electronic form of writing is bristling with contamination in the form of audible static, visual tearing, and discoloration. The spectres of memory and historicity are materially stored as traces in videotape, written in electronic impulse and magnetic oxide. Such is the allure of video as ruin: a crumbling and degenerative object, a fragment of the past.

The processes of discovery and excavation of videotape in found-footage horror thus contribute to the reification of video as ruin. Central to the production of an affective encounter with history – what Jaimie Baron has called the archive effect – is the relative temporal and intentional disparity between the original context of the document's production and its presentation as a historical artifact. The present-tense exhibition of film footage in a documentary, for example, contrasts with the historical period to which the footage properly belongs. This temporal disparity between the "now" and the "then" in a documentary film employing historical documents constructs the latter as archival.[44] The archive effect is therefore, in part, a product of the relationship between textual elements, the "nowness" of the work's address and the "thenness" of its historical artifacts.[45] Intentional disparity is an equally important feature of the archive effect, a juxtaposition that emerges between the original purpose of the historical document and how it is being used in another work as documentary evidence. When one experiences the archive effect, one is confronted with a document that one recognizes to be from another time and created for a different purpose than one for which it is now presented. This generates historicity, an affective encounter with the historical, an experience of "historicalness" and the attendant sense of profundity that accompanies engagement with a living remnant. The archive effect inheres most acutely within the *found* document since the pretence of discovery contributes an additional attribute of wonder: the wonder of the find. "Foundness," Baron states, "is one of the perceived qualities through which certain documents produce the archive effect and attain both their 'aura' and their evidentiary function."[46] This sense of discovery associated with the found document aids in its positioning as archival.

The wonder of the find has been exploited by video stores to attract and retain clientele by appealing to their devotion to videotape and sense of curiosity. At Spudic's Movie Empire in California, for example, one could purchase a mystery box consisting of "fifteen VHS tapes, one DVD, two video games, and five buttons for twenty dollars."[47] The appeal of acquiring tapes with unknown contents in a mystery box elicits a desire on the part of the purchaser for the possession of tape itself regardless of its content. Jeff Scheible articulates this phenomenon as an "inversion of cinephilia" in which the love of film becomes a love for the "audiovisual data *of* the film."[48] The mystery box reproduces VHS as found document, enacting both the archive effect and a cinephilic desire for the possession of film as object. Similarly, the archive effect and the thrall of video images materialize in the *V/H/S* franchise as a lure of the tangible, a desire for the haptic and embodied relationality between video and spectator.

THE LURE OF THE TANGIBLE

V/H/S/2 opens just like the first instalment: a blue screen accompanied by audio and visual static indicates that we are watching the contents of a videotape, thus emphasizing at the outset the resurgence of an outmoded video format. Visual error and image tearing transition us to footage of a sexual dalliance at a motel surreptitiously shot by a seedy private investigator. Having been chased away by the couple he was filming, Larry (Lawrence Michael Levine) joins his investigator partner Ayesha (Kelsy Abbott) in their getaway car as they speed away. Another instance of buzzing static and image damage interrupts the continuity of the scene before we return to the investigators in the car. Given videotape's propensity for copying and re-recording, it is unclear if this footage follows directly from the previous footage or if it takes place in other time and space. In the car, the investigators receive a new assignment – to track down a missing college student. The mother of the student provides her son's home address, and Larry and Ayesha head to the location, breaking into the home.

As in *V/H/S*, the investigators discover a stack of TV monitors displaying static as well as piles of VHS tapes. Unlike in the first film, this ominous display of video architecture is joined by a MacBook laptop,

FIGURE 4.2 | A STACK OF TELEVISION MONITORS WELCOMES THE PROTAGONISTS WITH ITS OMINOUS STATIC AND ETHEREAL GLOW IN *V/H/S/2*, 2013.

contributing its digital glow to the darkened room awash in the radiant light produced by the television monitors. Ayesha clicks around on the laptop and opens a recorded video message, presumably from the missing student, that relays his excitement about acquiring a VHS tape. "I found a new one," the student says, directly to camera. "It's third or fourth generation from the quality. I got it from some guy down in Little Armenia with a pawn shop. He's definitely not the type of guy you usually see on here trading with us, but I think he's somebody who's worth checking in on again. Most of his collection, I would say, was snuff and CP, but he had at least one that was the real thing." The student holds up a VHS cassette suggesting that the tape he holds in his hand is "the real thing." Ayesha locates the tape, labelled with an "X" in black sharpie, amidst the pile of VHS tapes in the room. Just as Ayesha inserts the tape into the VCR, a menacing figure is seen lurking in the background of the home, posing a threat to the investigators. Just as with its predecessor, the content of the diegetic tapes will function as the segments of this anthology.

The student's recording suggests that not only is there an underground network of trading and sharing videotapes, but also that certain tapes are coveted as authentic. Later in the film, Ayesha plays the student's recording for Larry in which the student says, "[This] tape is the final link for me. I know a lot of you have posted that it only affects you if you play it in a correct sequence." With this statement, what remained vague and opaque in the first *V/H/S* is made explicit: the videotapes produce and emit some kind of force that promises to physically and mentally affect the viewer. The allure and intoxicating thrall of the videographic apparatus is precisely what is sought in the *V/H/S* films as the tactility of videotape and the magnetic-electronic constitution of images produces an embodied form of spectatorship akin to a trance. The frame narrative of *V/H/S/2* depicts Ayesha becoming increasing affected by the video images, getting nose bleeds, a migraine, and becoming somewhat hypnotized by the video screens. Toward the end of the film, when Larry returns to check on her, Ayesha is lying on the floor with blood running from her head. The two films therefore suggest that the VHS tapes themselves have the power to physically affect the viewer, leaving one in a hypnotic catatonic state potentially resulting in death.

The physical and psychical effects experienced by viewers of these VHS tapes are attributed to the materiality of the videographic apparatus itself, the electrical pulsation of the monitor, the buzzing aural and visual hum of static, and the magnetic charge produced by playback. These conditions of viewing, the relationality of viewer to video screen, affect the bodily composition of the viewer, transforming the magnetic charge of the body and producing pleasurable hypnotic effects. As Simon Barrett clarifies in the audio commentary on the *V/H/S/2* Bluray, the materiality of VHS and the videographic apparatus becomes a desired, sought-after object for a subculture of collectors aiming to achieve this hypnotic experience of bodily transcendence. Given this, the format of recording does not matter to the characters in the film; it is the storage and playback of videotape and its electrical and magnetic characteristics that produce the conditions of transcendence into which the body is enfolded. As is often the case in horror film, these conditions of embodied pleasure risk injury and death, a fate that befalls the diegetic viewers in the *V/H/S* franchise.

The physical embodiment of the videographic apparatus is not new to the horror genre; *Ringu* (Hideo Nakata, 1998) and its American remake *The Ring* (Gore Verbinski, 2002) famously portrayed the viral threat of a haunted videotape, and 1982's *Poltergeist* (Tobe Hooper) remains the paradigmatic text of the haunted television monitor. But perhaps most emblematic of the visceral affective power of video is David Cronenberg's *Videodrome* (1983). As in the *V/H/S* series, a video signal and videotape – a Betamax tape, to be precise – begin to alter the mental and physical constitution of the protagonist Max Renn (James Woods). He experiences hallucinations brought about by his exposure to the video signal in which his body becomes entwined and enmeshed with various technologies, most significantly that of video. In one scene, Renn sees his television set throbbing with desire as the video image of Nicki Brand (Debbie Harry) beckons him to kiss her lips, which occupy the entirety of the TV screen in close-up. Renn approaches the TV monitor, whose screen has protruded outward into a malleable film, enjoining his lips (and face) with that of the video image in an erotized amalgamation of body and technology. Similarly, another scene depicts Renn with a vaginal slit in his abdomen that becomes a receptacle for a Betamax tape containing the videodrome signal, a literalized erotic incorporation of embodied video. In *Videodrome*, videotape functions as an erotic object promising bodily transcendence while simultaneously threatening its destruction.

The lure of the tangible has been part of video cultures since videotape cartridges were first introduced to the consumer market. Beginning with Betamax, videophiles, aided by the hallowed pages of *TV Guide*, set out to record video copies of television programs and feature films, thereby initiating a robust network of circulation and collecting.[49] The activities of this community were documented in *The Videophile's Newsletter*, which informed readers of the most recently acquired recordings, the growing collections of notable individuals, and mailing information for trading tapes. The newsletter also organized dubbing gatherings in which individuals would connect their respective VCRs and dub (i.e., copy) their tapes from one machine to the other.[50] In a statement that evokes the eroticized fetishization of videocassettes, Hilderbrand describes such gatherings as "orgies of dubbing," wherein individuals would "daisy chain" their tape decks together, sharing and swapping hardware in a hedonistic and exuberant celebration of access and excess.[51] Because Betamax tape decks were only outfitted with simple input and output jacks, however, the practice of dubbing required technical expertise on the part of the videophile, who would be required to open the tape deck and modify its circuitry. Instructions for such tasks were published in *The Videophile's Newsletter*, which encouraged people to experiment with video hardware, communicate directly with VCR manufacturers, and discover novel tricks and uses for the videographic apparatus, novelties that would surely be shared in *The Videophile's Newsletter*.[52] With the development of video rental stores and the shift from video as a time-shifting format to the rental and sale of pre-recorded tapes of feature films, the expertise generated through the interaction, circulation, and experimentation of the videophiles was no longer necessary. The labour-of-love enthusiasm that once animated this subculture of copying and sharing evaporated as pre-recorded content reached the mass consumer market through the video store.[53]

While advanced knowledge and technical skill is no longer strictly necessary to participate in video copying and circulation, collecting as an activity betrays an affective investment in video as a cherished object. Charles Tashiro describes the visual and tactile pleasures of acquiring additions to one's video collection. "It is more than the excitement of possession," Tashiro writes, "it is the thrill of tuning body and mind to similar desires, the run of the finger along the edge of the cover like a run of the mind along the imagined, unending shelf [of the collection]."[54] The embodied pleasures experienced by the collectors in the *V/H/S* films allegorize this desire for physical media, for the intimacy inscribed in the unique instances of damage and decay, for a remnant that serves as a material link to the historical. In video collecting, the pleasures gained by this excavation of technological detritus in search of valued treasures is intensified when the video is obscure, limited, and difficult to obtain. Popular titles that are readily available are less attractive to collectors in video trade circles; the more obscure, idiosyncratic, and outside the mainstream the title, the more valuable it becomes as a collectible.[55] The pleasures of the physical media object becomes a pleasure of the *rare* object, its value located precisely in its scarcity and uniqueness.[56] The collectors in *V/H/S* and *V/H/S/2* are indeed seeking the rarest of experiences: a specific sequence of tapes that, when played in the correct order, generates intoxicating electrical-magnetic sensations produced by the relationship between the viewer and the videographic apparatus. As the missing student articulates in the second film, this underground network of collectors is interminably seeking "the real thing."

The eroticized representation of video underscores the haptic allure of video as found object in found-footage horror. In the *V/H/S* franchise, the videographic apparatus produces unique fields of electrical energy and magnetism that promise a pleasurable bodily sensation transcending the limits of consciousness. And like in *Videodrome*, the cassette cartridge itself harbours erotic potential in its plastic armature and protocols of use. Enclosed within the cassette cartridge is the desired content – the information stored on magnetized tape – concealed behind the threshold of a plastic flap. Once inserted into a VCR, the flap opens, allowing the spools and sprockets to properly thread the tape and expose its contents. The materiality of videotape, its tactility, and its status as ruin brought about by the rise of digital video formats have together renewed the VHS tape as an object of *passion* facilitating the pleasures of circulation and collection.[57] Benson-Allott similarly notes the association between videotape and female genitalia, but she aligns the mysterious promise of videotape with Freud's uncanny, linking the simultaneous experiences of desire and anxiety pertaining to the strangely familiar.[58] This is emphasized in the *V/H/S* franchise in particular and in found-footage horror more broadly: the content concealed within the videocassette's cartridge elicits a desire and erotic fantasy of exposure even while threatening to destroy the viewer. To be sure, the allure of the ruin lies in its evocation of temporal proximity, in the materialized contact it engenders across time, in an exposure of a history that is simultaneously concealed and made present. Videographic ruin, the videotape as relic, as evidentiary artifact in found-footage horror, produces just such a desire.

UNPACKING MY VIDEO LIBRARY

The resurgence of videotape in recent years is indicative of a broader interest and desire for the unique aesthetic and experiential affordances of physical analogue media. Like Walter Benjamin unpacking his library, the VHS collector is awash in memories and the "thrill of acquisition" upon perusing their collection of videotapes.[59] For Benjamin, the pleasure of collecting books lies principally in the history of circulation inscribed in the materiality of the text. He writes, "The period, the region, the craftsmanship, the former ownership – for a true collector the whole background of an item adds up to a magic encyclopedia whose quintessence is the fate of his object."[60] Videotape's inscription of its own history of circulation and playback, the degeneration and decay of sound and image that signify its value, is materially preserved on the shelf of the VHS collector. More than just the film's content, then, a video collector is intent on the preservation of a cultural moment in which the reproduction and circulation of tape reigned supreme. A cinephilic passion for film is collapsed within a technophilic passion for hardware, the videographic apparatus.[61]

In 2015, Yale University Library acquired 2,700 VHS tapes mostly comprised of 1970s and 1980s horror and cult films, making Yale "the only U.S. institution that deliberately collects these horror and exploitation movies in magnetic tape format."[62] Even while many organizations have attempted to divest their collections of videotape, Yale's collection aims to preserve videotapes that were never transferred to any subsequent format as well as to document the unique moment in film history between classical Hollywood of the 1950s and the corporate conglomeration that defined the 1980s and 1990s.[63] Author David Gary espouses a Benjaminian rationale in justifying the collection of VHS by comparing them to books, the treasured objects of library archives. "Much like a book's physical features (paper, binding, dust jackets, the bite of the metal type into the page), and the seemingly secondary aspects of the text (the preface, acknowledgement page, table of contents, index)," Gary writes, "VHS tapes have tangible qualities that have defined the medium's uniqueness and its legacy."[64] This logic is similarly expressed by private collectors and cult cinema fans, who fetishize the uniqueness of individual videotapes in addition to their investment in its content. The more obscure, the more bizarre, the more trashy, and, crucially, the least accessible tapes are those that accrue the most value as collectibles.[65] No two tapes are exactly identical, whether a recording of an off-air vintage TV episode or an original release copy of *Manos: The Hands of Fate* (Harold P. Warren, 1966).

Benjamin further expresses the joyful excitement of acquiring a book with unknown contents. "One of the finest memories of a collector," he writes, "is the moment when he rescued a book to which he might never have given a thought, much less a wishful look, because he found it lonely and abandoned on the market place and bought it to give it its freedom."[66] While the acquisition of media with unknown content always poses a risk since the object may be too damaged or outside the interest of the collector, it nevertheless holds the promise and pleasure of an unanticipated find. That is, the mystery of acquiring unknown objects is part of the appeal and allure of collecting. The resurgence of VHS videotapes in found-footage horror expresses this allure of discovery and, as we have seen, the lure of the tangible through fetishized tactile, embodied spectatorship. The content of videotape concealed behind the plastic flap of the cassette cartridge and hidden until playback evokes the eroticized thrill associated with revelation. The *V/H/S* series emphasizes the embodied pleasures of viewing magnetic tape and the erotically charged tactility of the videographic apparatus.

Today, videotape endures as ruin, as a relic of a bygone media landscape. Multiple temporalities inhere within the videographic ruin, materializing the entwined histories of television, cinema, and computer. The error, damage, and degeneration endemic to video playback exudes the ruin's sedimented temporal logic, storing and reproducing traces of the past. As palimpsest, what is etched within the videographic ruin is not only increments of time, but also the affective intensities generated through repeated impassioned viewing. The fetishization of VHS tapes in the *V/H/S* franchise and found-footage horror articulates a contemporary investment in videotapes as "technologies of memory" that facilitate affective encounters with history.[67] Amidst increasingly ephemeral experiences of media consumption that reject physical possession and ownership in favour of streaming, videotape emerges as a cathected ruinous object, beckoning us to press play.

5 HYPERLINKED HAUNTINGS: DIGITAL HORROR AND NETWORKED SPECTRALITY

In 2014, a bizarre crime rocked the small town of Waukesha, Wisconsin, one that initiated a moral panic within the town and went on to garner international media attention. During a birthday slumber party, two twelve-year-old girls coaxed one of their peers to leave their home and follow them into the adjacent woods. There, the girls proceeded to stab the victim nineteen times with a blade, carrying out a premeditated plan to murder the young girl. Thankfully, the victim survived. Perhaps more disturbing than the young age of those involved was the motive given to the police for the heinous act of brutality: the girls confessed they had plotted the attempted murder in an effort to please something they called the "Slender Man." This sinister moniker, however, did not belong to any existing individual preying upon the youth of Waukesha; rather, the Slender Man referred to a fictional character developed on internet message boards through the circulation of horror fan fiction.

The character was first introduced on the web forums of Something Awful.com, a site dedicated to user-generated content. Accompanied by the tagline "The Internet Makes You Stupid," the site employs an irreverent and satirical tone as users gather to mock popular culture. One feature of the site is a photo-editing contest dubbed "Photoshop Phriday" in which users challenge forum members to create Photoshopped images relating to a specified theme. On 8 June 2009, a user with the screen name "Gerogerigegege" challenged the community to submit Photoshopped images of the paranormal; the doctored photos would then be submitted to websites dedicated to the collection of supernatural photographs. In keeping with the derisive and incendiary tone of the website, this challenge was posted with the intention of trolling other sites that expressed a genuine interest in aggregating paranormal evidence, tricking them into posting fake images. On 10 June of that year, user Victor Surge, real name Eric Knudsen, uploaded two black-and-white images to the forum that drew immediate attention. The first was a black-and-white photograph of a children's playground with a watermark reading "City of Stirling Libraries Local Studies Collection" in the top-right corner. Ostensibly depicting an innocuous scene of children playing, the background of the image hides a mysterious figure among the trees. Unnaturally tall and sporting tentacled limbs, the figure looms over the playground in malevolent vigil of the children. The posted image was accompanied by the following text: "One of two recovered photographs from the Stirling City Library blaze. Notable for being taken the day [on] which fourteen children vanished and for what is referred to as 'The Slender Man.' Deformities cited as film defects by officials. Fire at library occurred one week later. Actual photograph confiscated as evidence (1986, photographer: Mary Thomas, missing since 13 June 1986)."

The image and text are thus presented as evidentiary documents in the posts, initiating what Jaimie Baron has called the archive effect triggered by temporal and intentional disparity.[1] We are told that the image is a historical document recovered from a fire in the library archive that was subsequently seized, presumably by local police. The same post suggests that the missing children, the missing photographer, and the library fire are all connected to the figure in the photo identified as the "Slender Man," although authorities dismiss his odd appearance as a photographic defect. The second image, also in black and white, similarly depicts a group of children. This time, the children appear distressed, apprehensive, and afraid, walking along what appears to be a dirt road in the woods. Once again, a tall figure is present in the background of the image, seemingly leading the children. The text accompanying this image is at once more opaque and more ominous than the first: "'We didn't want to go, we didn't want to kill them, but its persistent silence and outstretched arms horrified and comforted us at the same time ...' 1983, photographer unknown, presumed dead." The mythology of the Slender Man began to grow almost immediately upon the posting of these first images, with users adding

FIGURES 5.1 AND 5.2 | THE FIRST AND SECOND OF TWO SLENDER MAN IMAGES POSTED TO THE SOMETHING AWFUL FORUM.

their own characteristics, history, and stories, thereby contributing to a communal fictional narrative surrounding the character. Over time, the Slender Man spread from the forums of Something Awful to become a popular subcultural internet meme, replicated and developed through message boards, creepypastas,[2] online storytelling forums, and alternate reality games. The Slender Man stabbing, as it came to be known, thrust mainstream attention upon the fictional character and inspired debates concerning the relationship between youth audiences and the internet.

The attempted murder renewed media-effects arguments that have targeted a variety of media in years past, from the penny dreadfuls of the nineteenth century to film serials of the 1930s and 1940s, horror comic books of the 1950s, the "vast wasteland" of television programming, and violent video games, to name a few. The Slender Man as an internet phenomenon similarly focused attention on the potential negative effects of the internet and particularly the harm it can pose to youth audiences. The message boards on which the character was developed were branded "sick" and "twisted" by concerned members of the public.[3] CNN commentator Miguel Marquez placed blame on the internet itself, stating in an interview with Nancy Grace, "If you push your kid in a room with the internet and you close the door, it's the same thing as letting a stranger, a grown man, into your 12-year-old's room with them. Why would parents do that?"[4] For its part, Something Awful posted a response to the stabbing in its typical sardonic fashion:

> We are 15 years post-*Blair Witch*. These girls were 12. Found footage Youtubes, shaking cameras and bad Photoshops of people with socks on their head standing in the woods should not be fooling anyone. Especially not 12 year olds who should be better at the Internet and media culture than actual adults. But maybe all these chemtrails and Art Bells are actually making people dumber. Maybe there is a lot of lead paint being used in Waukesha. Maybe the Internet makes you stupid.[5]

The moral outrage expressed by Marquez and the contemptuous response from Something Awful reveals a tension concerning the role of the internet in contemporary culture, one that rests on the degree to which the internet blurs the boundaries separating reality and fiction. From the perspective of Something Awful, the twelve-year-old millennials ought to have been more adept and media-savvy than adults in their navigation of the internet. The site insists that youth audiences, having grown up amidst the ubiquity of found-footage horror films and YouTube videos, (should) have adopted a disposition of suspicion and cynicism toward online truth claims. Understandably, Something Awful would view such a disposition as encouraged by the myriad social media platforms that display curated representations of ourselves without making any claims of objective authenticity. In sum, Something Awful argues that the digital internet age is an epoch of unbridled and instantaneous circulation of content, the truth-value of which is often unverifiable. As such, the generation for whom the internet has always been present ought to be more proficient and sophisticated in navigating its virtual spaces than generations past, and able to deftly differentiate between fictional stories and veritable news or archival documents.

While Something Awful envisions a sophisticated youth audience able to critically engage with, and actively participate in, the circulation of online content, the Slender Man stabbing confirms for Marquez the need for parental protection and corporate control, as the internet constitutes a portal transmitting infinite amounts of potentially dangerous material into the homes and bedrooms of children. Implicit in Marquez's statement is a dual anxiety concerning invasion and illusion – that the computer screen functions as a gateway through which the "dark side" of the internet enters the hallowed space of the home, and that online content may potentially deceive, manipulate, and inculcate audiences with false impressions, encouraging behaviour detrimental to the self and to society. Like the 1915 Supreme Court ruling authored by Justice Joseph McKenna that demonized cinema (see chapter 2), statements such as those by Marquez single out the internet as a dangerously influential and manipulative medium, one that affects the psychological stability of the user and one's grasp of reality.

Several authors, such as Shira Chess and Eric Newsom, Tina Marie Boyer, and Andrew Peck, have conceptualized the Slender Man phenomenon as a manifestation of contemporary folklore borne out of the "digital campfire" of internet message boards.[6] Chess and Newsom identify the communal construction of the Slender Man as central to its folkloric status, its characteristics having been developed over time through the mutual participation of message board users. In each telling of a Slender Man tale, in each new iteration of the myth offered by users, the aesthetics, conventions, and backstory of the Slender Man were revised by the Something Awful community until a consensus was reached. While there are innumerable competing storylines and *modi operandi* associated with the Slender Man, the essential attributes of an unnaturally tall, faceless, white, male figure with elongated limbs, sometimes sporting tentacles, were established through this communal process of telling and retelling stories on message boards. As such, it is the sharing, modification, and adaptability of the Slender Man through processes of communal storytelling that mark it as a folkloric figure, in that it is the product of negotiation by a community through time.

Andrew Peck similarly attributes the popularity of the Slender Man phenomenon to the unique participatory environment afforded by the networked communication model constitutive of the internet. "Through social interaction," Peck argues, "users collaborated in an ongoing process of performance, interpretation, and negotiation that constructed the details, motifs, and shared expectations of the Slender Man legend cycle."[7] In his analysis of posts on Something Awful's message boards, Peck observes that the Slender Man's characteristics became standardized through a process of acceptance and rejection within the community amidst the sharing of stories featuring the character. Once the initial images were posted to the Something Awful site, for example, it was not directly mandated that such images be accompanied by text or story; yet by the second page of the message board, nearly all Slender Man images included text, thereby establishing the expectation that written text would accompany an image as evidence of its spooky premise.[8] Furthermore, stories that featured the Slender Man in realistic contemporary settings were deemed scarier and more unsettling than those that situated the figure within fantastical story worlds.[9] As a result, stories that included the Slender Man within realistic settings garnered praise and shares while those that did not were critiqued and fell out of view. The narrative convention of placing the Slender Man within realistic scenarios was thereby standardized not through explicit decree, but through positive reinforcement in the interactive message board community. In fact, Peck points out that when users attempted to explicitly list the conventions of the Slender Man in an effort to define and canonize the character, other users rejected such attempts with derision. Users indicated that the mystery surrounding the Slender Man, its ambiguity, and its lack of clear and defined motives all contributed to its effectiveness as a frightening monster.[10] Central to the Slender Man's appeal and to its success as a growing internet legend was its status as a communal creation developed through community participation and shared storytelling. As a "crowd-sourced monster" that benefited from a sense of communal ownership as a "shared public resource,"[11] the Slender Man epitomizes key ideas about the internet and digitality while extending the ancient form of storytelling into contemporary networked culture.

Like Peck and Chess and Newsom, Tina Marie Boyer identifies the Slender Man as a transmedial figure whose success as legend depends upon its spread across a variety of platforms and in multiple media. The Slender Man's haunting presence in photographs and stories shared on the forums of Something Awful eventually migrated outward onto other website forums, generating further creepypastas, blog posts, and YouTube videos.[12] The Slender Man continued to be recycled, reused, and repurposed on the forums of Reddit, 4Chan, and Tumblr, even developing its own parodic incarnations such as the Trender Man, alternatively described as the sassy brother or cousin of the Slender Man, with a keen interest in fashion.[13] The website KnowYourMeme.com, which charts the historical development and evolution of contemporary internet memes, traced the spread of the Slender Man from its origin on SomethingAwful.com and the /x/paranormal 4Chan message board to sites like Tumblr, Fangoria, TVTropes, DeviantArt, Mythical Creatures Guide, and Unfiction Forums, to name a few.[14] Although the Slender Man continued to gain popularity within discrete online communities, the figure remained a subcultural one, circulating among fans "in the know" rather than garnering mainstream attention. This began to change with the production of the YouTube Web series *Marble Hornets*, which ran from 2009 until 2014.

Through *Marble Hornets* as its principal case study, this chapter explores the emergence of digital spectrality in contemporary horror through a dichotomy of contagion and erasure wherein the ghost functions as a hyperlinked haunting. In works as varied as *Pulse* (Kiyoshi Kurosawa, 2001), *Feardotcom* (William Malone, 2002), *Halloween: Resurrection* (Rick Rosenthal, 2002), *The Den* (Zachary Donohue, 2013), *Unfriended* (Levan Gabriadze, 2014), and *Host* (Rob Savage, 2020), the internet is figured as a malevolent force of interconnection, a web in which one is ensnared and from which one cannot escape. The expanding network of digitized communication, our access to heretofore inaccessible archives of information, and the ways in which we are increasingly connected to one another through a variety of devices and platforms generate the conditions of possibility for viral contagion and supernatural infection. If the pseudo-live television broadcast *Ghostwatch* produced a national séance in which all TVs tuned to the channel functioned to conjure and transmit an evil ghost (see chapter 3), the internet and the World Wide Web exacerbate the threat of unmitigated and unrestrained supernatural contamination.

Because every network connection access point serves as a potential conduit, a portal that facilitates paranormal border crossings between the material and metaphysical worlds, digital horror foregrounds the danger of unbridled access to the internet conjuring machine and the particular threats posed by amateurs toying with supernatural forces they are ill-equipped to handle. Indeed, within the dichotomy of contagion and erasure as outlined in this chapter, one finds a secondary dichotomy animating digital horror, that of the amateur and the professional. Oftentimes, untrained, unskilled, and uninformed characters seek to interact with supernatural forces for pleasure and thrills; in so doing, they inadvertently unleash ghosts and demons that enter our realm through the digital doorway and proceed to infect other devices, terrorizing unsuspecting users who are connected to the network. Implicit in digital horror is a critique of the amateur who lacks sophistication and foresight and who fails to appreciate the complex and powerful digital tools and their occult instrumentalization. Within a broader poetics of the paranormal, then, the ghost in digital horror performs the work of the hyperlink: a figure with which interaction elicits a temporal and spatial transition, a figure whose presence points to, and is embedded from, another time and another space. The ghost-as-hyperlink destabilizes the present as well as the binary of materiality and immateriality through its "paradoxical incorporation,"[15] a dynamic that also characterizes digitality as a seemingly immaterial media sphere that nevertheless depends upon a physical infrastructure and a host of material hardware. Lisa Blackman has discussed what she calls the afterlives of data in decidedly spectral terms, articulating how data points and bits of digital information become unmoored from their original contexts and are decontextualized, recontextualized, and discovered anew on digital platforms. "The afterlives of data," Blackman writes, "attract, collect, and channel fragments, gaps, anomalies, puzzles, and parallel temporalities," thereby demonstrating the potentially destabilizing effects, and affects, of the recombinatory nature of hyperlinked networks.[16] Digital horror portrays the hyperlinked internet as a perpetual séance on a mass scale unequalled by earlier technologies of electronic connection and mass communication. The effects of this mass, hyperlinked digital séance in horror are invariably contagion, infection, and (mortal) erasure.

In Kurosawa's *Pulse*, the internet functions as a conduit through which ghosts of the dead access the world of living. As a consequence, those who encounter ghosts through computer interfaces or in physical spaces become isolated, paranoid, and depressed, eventually killing themselves and becoming their own ghosts. Significantly, ghosts in Kurosawa's film travel through internet and computer networks, subjecting unsuspecting individuals to their haunting presence while spreading psychological anomie and malaise. Furthermore, the ghosts themselves are subject to decay and erasure; they materialize throughout the film as spectral doubles of their human forms but also ossify into ash before crumbling away, leaving behind only a blackened stain to mark their presence. *Pulse*, then, depicts the consequences of networked communication through its ghostly allegory of isolation, loneliness, and decay, suggesting that the interconnection facilitated by internet networks and digital communications paradoxically produces communal isolation.

Feardotcom tells a similar tale. A generic mix of neo-noir detective thriller and slasher horror film, *Feardotcom* follows detective Mike Reilly (Stephen Dorff), who is tasked with investigating mysterious deaths that are possibly linked to a notorious serial killer who has thus far eluded police. When several people are discovered dead with similar symptoms (bleeding eyes are particularly noteworthy here), Centers for Disease Control researcher Terry Huston (Natasha McElhone) joins the case in order to determine whether the deaths may have been caused by a viral contagion. Working closely with Reilly, the pair discover that each victim had logged onto the website feardotcom.com and died forty-eight hours later. The site features disturbing images and seemingly authentic footage of death and murder, which subsequently haunt those who visit the site. Victims suffer from increasingly intense hallucinations until they eventually kill themselves or are killed by an accident brought about by a hallucination. By the film's conclusion, we learn that the website is indeed haunted by a vengeful spirit who was murdered on a live-camera show streamed over the internet. Like *Pulse*, the ghost of *Feardotcom* utilizes a website in order to spread its haunting presence as a viral agent, killing those who access the webpage. In addition to the threat posed by its viral spread, the film emphasizes the hallucinatory effects of this spectral encounter, in which one's sense of reality collapses. As such, digital spectrality not only threatens to spread exponentially along digital networks but also threatens to collapse one's sense of reality, as the viewer mistakes an artificial simulation for reality itself. The duality of contagion and erasure manifests itself here through the hyperlinked virality of the ghost and the collapse of reality and simulation, respectively.

Marble Hornets, for its part, crystallizes the concerns of this chapter and unites the themes that have animated the preceding chapters of this book. While *Unfriended*, its sequel *Unfriended: Dark Web* (Stephen Susco, 2018), and *Host* have inaugurated a new digital horror subgenre dubbed "desktop horror," wherein the films' action is depicted entirely on computer interfaces thereby making them prime case studies for examining networked digital horror, *Marble Hornets* adopts a complex transmediality that represents digital horror not only in terms of real-time communication and participation, but also an archive of asynchronous materials across physical and digital formats. As such, the transmediality of *Marble Hornets* connects the electromagnetic constitution of videotape, the instantaneous transmission of television, and the present-pastness of the cinema with a dichotomy of contagion and erasure through its alluring tale of the Slender Man and its serialized distribution via YouTube.

Comprised of eighty-seven videos varying in length from a brief thirty seconds to fourteen minutes, *Marble Hornets* exploited integrated social media platforms in order to generate substantial interest in and spread of its Slender Man narrative. While much of the narrative is accessed through YouTube videos posted on the *Marble Hornets* channel, its narrative unfolds over several social media platforms simultaneously, including Twitter, Instagram, and Something Awful forums. In fact, the series began not with a YouTube video, but with a post on Something Awful by user "ce gars," the screen name for the man who would become the central protagonist of the web series. The post, written on 18 June 2009, describes the central premise of the show: Jay (Troy Wagner), the writer of the forum post, tells us that he and his fellow film school student Alex (Joseph DeLage) had been working together on a film project titled *Marble Hornets* in the summer of 2006. Alex's behaviour grew increasingly erratic and strange, the post alleges, culminating in the cancellation of the film project and Alex's request for the footage to be burned. Jay instead requested to keep the footage in his apartment. Alex reluctantly agreed on the condition that Jay never speak about the footage with him. Shortly thereafter, the post continues, Alex transferred to another school and was not heard from by Jay again. Having forgotten about the footage, Jay rediscovered the boxes of tapes in his apartment three years later in 2009. He decided to comb through the footage in an effort to uncover an explanation for Alex's bizarre behaviour and sudden relocation. Jay informs us the tapes are not stored in any logical order and do not have timestamps indicating when they were shot. So, Jay tells the forum that he will examine the footage looking for any evidence, which he will then upload onto the YouTube channel as well as post on his Twitter and Instagram accounts.

The first video, which was uploaded to the YouTube channel on 20 June 2009, consists of a travelling shot from a car window of an industrial landscape. On-screen text embedded by Jay repeats the premise of the series, informing viewers of the narrative set-up for those unfamiliar with the initial forum post. This introductory entry is followed by "Entry #1," in which Jay claims to have found something

FIGURE 5.3 | FIRST SIGHTING OF THE SLENDER MAN IN ENTRY #1 OF *MARBLE HORNETS*.

strange: we are presented with shaky hand-held camera footage presumably shot by Alex inside his home. In the brief clip, we see window curtains being opened to reveal a thin, tall, faceless, white figure standing on the front porch outside, blurred in the periphery of the frame. The video lacks recorded sound, with Jay suggesting the camera's microphone either malfunctioned or the soundtrack was purposefully deleted by Alex. Lasting only forty-eight seconds, "Entry #1" establishes the found-footage aesthetic of the series, the convention of the Slender Man occupying the periphery or background of the image, and technological interference as a result of the paranormal presence of the Slender Man. Although the posts do not seem to adhere to any discernible release schedule, Jay continues to post YouTube entries that he claims are intriguing or evidential in an effort to unravel the mystery surrounding Alex.

Entries uploaded to YouTube are supplemented by Jay's ongoing Twitter posts, which document his research progress, his mood, and his thoughts regarding the unfolding mystery. On 6 July 2009, for example, Jay tweeted from the *Marble Hornets* account, "Found something unexpectedly." The following day, Jay tweeted that he would upload the seventh entry to YouTube shortly; on 8 July, "Entry #7" was uploaded with the ominous caption "Patterns emerging." The entry depicts footage shot by Alex in which he and Brian, an actor from the *Marble Hornets* project, rehearse lines for the film. The footage is shot from the inside of a car, with Brian occupying the passenger seat. Behind Brian, who is shot in a medium close-up, we see an alleyway outside the passenger window in the background of the frame. When Brian lays his head back against the car seat headrest, the Slender Man appears almost imperceptibly in the background of the frame, his presence disguised by the brick wall, metal staircase, and white-washed background. Given the tight framing and composition of the shot, one may not notice the Slender Man's presence at all; however, Jay's tweet and video caption prime the viewer to scan the image for evidence. Moreover, it is clear that Alex notices the Slender Man in the background as he abruptly pans the video camera away from him, loses focus of the shot, and stops filming. Continuing his narration, Jay concludes through embedded on-screen text, "someone was following Alex." The narrative of *Marble Hornets*, therefore, unfolds not only on YouTube but also in the social media accounts associated with the central protagonist. This transmedial organization of the series encourages fans to interact directly with the content producers through Twitter replies and direct messages. Because of the interactive structure of the series, audiences become enfolded within its fictional diegesis, as Jay responds to fan inquiries regarding clues and his own state of mind. Importantly, the degree of narrative immersion afforded by its transmedial approach to storytelling constitutes a central appeal of the series as a whole.

As the series continues, several important developments occur. On 22 July 2009, a separate YouTube channel called "totheark" is created. The channel posts direct video responses to the *Marble Hornets* channel that challenge, question, and mock Jay's narration of events. The videos from this channel differ radically in form and style from the handheld cinematography of the main channel. Totheark's videos adopt a decidedly avant-garde aesthetic, favouring abstract and surreal imagery that heavily accentuates digital datamoshing as an artistic choice. Like structuralist filmmaking practices of the 1960s and 1970s, totheark's videos foreground the technologies of their making, heightening their status as constructed works through both visual and sonic digital distortion. The channel continues to post obscure yet vaguely threatening responses to the *Marble Hornets* main channel, providing alternative clues, messages, and camera perspectives of specific events. Significantly, totheark's channel is referenced only in Jay's uploaded videos and Twitter feed, rather than being integrated into the series proper. Except for the few instances in which totheark evidently hacks the *Marble Hornets* channel and posts videos to the main channel, audiences must search for the channel themselves, prompted by the references made by Jay in his videos and tweets. Thus, totheark is an ancillary source of narrative information that expands on the story without being essential viewing.

The beginning of the series consists largely of found footage, as Jay uploads previously recorded clips from the *Marble Hornets* tapes, but then, in "Entry #15," he shifts the temporal register of the series. On 2 October 2009, Jay tweeted that he had arranged a meeting with Tim, a former actor on the *Marble Hornets* project, that he planned to film and upload to the channel. Jay's tweets indicate that the meeting took place on 3 October and that the fifteenth entry was posted later the same day. *Marble Hornets*, then, shifts from a found-footage work to one that occurs more fully in the present, as Jay begins to film himself, documenting his experiences in real time. Like Alex before him, Jay begins to experience paranoia, sickness, and memory loss as he becomes more obsessed with the case. While Jay continues to upload footage from the *Marble Hornets* tapes, the series becomes more rooted in the present from its fifteenth entry onwards, thus creating a complex chronology that alternates between a distant and a more immediate past, that is, between the 2006 footage shot by Alex and the current ongoing investigation conducted by Jay. The present-tense temporal register of the series is further accentuated by the ongoing participation of audiences providing their own commentary online in real time.

By "Entry #18," Jay not only shares the same afflictions suffered by Alex but also becomes a target of the Slender Man and his proxies, masked individuals who have succumbed to the thrall of the Slender Man. In pursuing the mystery and in viewing the Slender Man in Alex's footage, Jay is exposed to the haunting presence of the figure, thereby establishing the Slender Man as an agent of viral contagion. In "Entry #26," posted to YouTube on 18 April 2010, Jay decides to quit his mission as his memory loss, physical sickness, and the overall danger posed by the Slender Man and his proxies become too great. However, having discovered evidence of Alex's recent whereabouts, Jay vows to find Alex and continue to uncover answers concerning the Slender Man's origins and motives. The next entry, "Entry #27," is uploaded seven months later, on 23 November 2010, and depicts Jay waking up in a hotel room having no memory of the preceding seven months. This marks the beginning of the series' second season, which continues to follow Jay and Alex as they attempt to evade the omnipresent haunting of the Slender Man.

As of this writing, the *Marble Hornets* YouTube channel boasts 630,000 subscribers with total views in excess of 115 million.[17] Although the first entries consistently generated millions of views with a peak of 7.8 million for "Entry #1," the series experienced a notable drop in viewership as it progressed. Nevertheless, *Marble Hornets* continued to attract hundreds of thousands of views over the course of its five-year run. The growing narrative complexity of the series inspired an internet following of its own, with fans discussing the developing mystery at its heart, pinpointing clues, and providing their own theories concerning the story on the forums of Something Awful, Buzzfeed, Reddit, and a series-specific Wikidot page consisting of comprehensive fan-generated content, including a chronological timeline of videos and posts, filming locations, and theories explaining events of the series. Additionally, the series' narrative grew to encompass the video games *Slender: The Eight Pages* (2012) and *Slender: The Arrival* (2013) as well as the feature film *Always Watching: A Marble Hornets Story* (James Moran, 2015). While the most recent feature film adaptation, *Slender Man* (Sylvain White, 2018), establishes its own story world distinct from that of *Marble Hornets*, the film nevertheless incorporates conventions, motifs, and themes that were developed through *Marble Hornets* and subsequently recycled in other Slender Man works, including memory loss, "slender sickness," somnambulism, and the aesthetic predominance of the glitch. The Slender Man's hyperlinked haunting and transmission across platforms express a sinister quality of contemporary networked culture in which viral contagion undermines the autonomy of users through increasingly complex circuits of connection.

Since the 1980s, the dual processes of digitization and corporate conglomeration have produced a media environment defined by what Henry Jenkins has called "convergence culture." In describing convergence, Jenkins borrows from MIT political scientist Ithiel de Sola Pool, whom Jenkins calls the "prophet of media convergence,"[18] and whose 1983 book *Technologies of Freedom* broadly defined the process of convergence as a blurring of distinctions between previously distinct media. While in the past, Pool argued, a given medium was concerned with a particular function and operated within a particular market, regulated by regimes specific to that medium, the emergence of "new media" has collapsed the boundaries separating these distinct modes of production and distribution.[19] The conversion of media content into numerical digital code allows content to be transcoded and accessed through a variety of platforms and delivery technologies. A feature film may be viewed in theatres on a 35mm celluloid projection, often having gone through a digital intermediary, or it may be projected via digital DCP technology. Beyond theatrical exhibition, the same feature film may be accessed on home video on DVD, as a legal digital download file, as an illegal DVD rip or torrent file download, and viewed on devices as varied as televisions, laptops, iPads, and smartphones. While the rise of new media and digitization are not solely responsible for contemporary media convergence since analogue media were already contaminated medial spheres, digitization has exacerbated the convergence process, exponentially increasing the possibilities of content sharing and viral spreading. Importantly for Jenkins, convergence culture describes not only the ways in which content is circulated among multiple media platforms but also how this dispersed distribution is facilitated by the cooperation of multiple media industries as well as the mobility of media consumers.[20] Convergence, Jenkins writes, "represents a cultural shift as consumers are encouraged to seek out new information and make connections among dispersed media content."[21] Here, the active participation of the consumer is a precondition for the spread of a media text and its subsequent success.

Given the importance of consumer activity and participation, Jenkins identifies convergence as both a top-down corporate-driven process motivated by the acquisition of multiple avenues of profit generation and a bottom-up grassroots mobilization of consumer action.

Marble Hornets and the Slender Man mythos demonstrate the productive tension between the promise of unrestricted sharing engendered by the internet and digitality and the opposing forces of corporate control. When drafting the iconography of the Slender Man for the Photoshop Phriday contest, for example, Victor Surge stated that he took inspiration from existing horror villains such as the "tall man" (Angus Scrimm) in the *Phantasm* franchise (1979–2016).[22] The Slender Man also bears a resemblance to Kane (Julian Beck) in *Poltergeist II: The Other Side* (Brian Gibson, 1986), a similarly menacing tall man in a suit, as well as the silent troupe of demons dubbed "the gentlemen" in a third-season episode of *Buffy the Vampire Slayer* (1997–2003). Although potentially unintentional and indirect, this process of adaptation from earlier examples of menacing men in suits is indicative of the sharing and remixing of existing cultural figures that commonly occurs in networked online spaces.

Within a week of the original posting on Something Awful, forum users were appropriating the Slender Man character, refiguring, remixing, and adapting the character for distinct purposes. Despite being the creation of Eric Knudsen, users did not seek permission to reuse and repurpose the Slender Man in their own fictionalized versions. As Chess and Newsom state, the Slender Man was treated as communal property; as such, experimentation and appropriation by forum users was encouraged without Knudsen claiming exclusive rights to the character or its likeness.[23] Knudsen did eventually copyright the Slender Man as a unique artistic creation in 2010, although he stated that he did so not to maintain creative control or to secure financial gain from its use; rather, he sought copyright in order to keep the Slender Man growing within web forums and among independent content creators rather than at the behest of a centralized copyright holder. "The move [to copyright the Slender Man]," write Chess and Newsom, "prevented mass media versions of the character, meaning that primarily, the Slender Man has been developed in digital subcultures."[24] The evolution of the Slender Man as a horror icon, then, evinces the entanglement of the corporate logics of artistic production with amateur content creation at the heart of convergence culture, in that it was inspired in part by pre-existing franchise entities, subsequently repurposed in online fan adaptations, and further adapted as a feature film distributed by Sony Pictures. The transmedial storytelling model of *Marble Hornets*, wherein the series' narrative unfolds through a variety of media platforms, demonstrates the centrality of audience participation in the viral spreading of media content, and, thus, the successful diffusion of the Slender Man myth within popular culture.

"Our message is simple," write Jenkins and co-authors Sam Ford and Joshua Green in *Spreadable Media*. "If it doesn't spread, it's dead."[25] Yet in the works discussed in this chapter, it is *precisely* the dead that spread through networked platforms of mass transmission and circulation, threatening to haunt, possess, and destroy the viewer who happens to access an infected digital interface such as a website or digital file. As in *Sinister*, *The Ring*, and *Ghostwatch* (see previous chapters), haunting is here portrayed as a contagious enterprise, one that is facilitated by contemporary media of reproduction and transmission. The Slender Man spread from the forums of Something Awful into multiple media forms and narrative cycles, its influence ultimately spreading from niche web forums to mainstream international news. Contemporary forms of digital web-based circulation have increased the speed and scope of content spreading as relationships among people have become increasingly linked technologically; at the same time, sharing has become a cultural imperative in networked spaces. For Jenkins, Ford, and Green, this confluence of sociocultural practices and emergent technological developments is what constitutes "networked culture."[26] "The participating public is more collectively and individually literate about social networking online," the authors write, "because people are more frequently and more broadly in contact with their networks of friends, family, and acquaintances; and because people increasingly interact through sharing meaningful bits of media content."[27] In contemporary networked culture, then, relationships among people are increasingly mediated through digital interfaces. Moreover, information is shared through online spaces, creating the conditions of possibility for the rapid viral spreading of content.

Jenkins, Ford, and Green contend that networked culture has increased the speed and scope of content circulation, emphasizing that spreadability is essential to the success of any media venture today; yet they oppose the use of the term "viral" to describe digital circulation. To be sure, "going viral" has become a common turn of phrase, describing videos, photos, and articles that quickly garner thousands or millions of views and shares. While virality accurately conveys the speed of content circulation, the authors contend that the term misrepresents and undervalues the contribution of users' active participation. Implicit in the term "viral" is the suggestion that content is circulated without the consent or agency of the user, or even in the face of the user's active resistance.[28] After all, one catches a virus against their will, it occurs *to* one, one is not a willing participant in its distribution. Similarly, the authors object to virality as a biological metaphor because it suggests that media content is autonomous and self-replicating.[29] Accounts of viral media such as Richard Dawkins's *The Selfish Gene*, the authors contend, undervalue the activity of users and the choices users make in the diffusion of content online. The metaphor of the viral vis-à-vis media circulation, then, fails to adequately address the ways in which users assess a given text and decide how and with whom to share content.[30] As the authors argue, it is the users' "choices, investments, agendas, and actions that determine what gets valued." These avenues of inquiry are occluded by the concept of virality.[31]

To overcome such problems with the concept of virality, Jenkins, Ford, and Green propose the term "spreadable media." Unlike virality, the authors write, spreadable media "avoids the metaphors of 'infection' and 'contamination,' which overestimate the power of media companies and underestimate the agency of audiences."[32] Although the authors oppose virality as a term delimiting the movement of content in online spaces, horror films explicitly reinforce the insidious connotations of the viral as an infectious and contagious process. Ghosts and malevolent entities travel through digitized networks of circulation only to haunt, possess, or even kill the user who happens to encounter the infected digital content. In *Marble Hornets*, the Slender Man's contagious countenance is spread from Alex to Jay via the interface of digital video footage. Once Jay becomes aware of the stalking presence of the Slender Man and views his menacing presence in the footage, he becomes a target of the Slender Man's attention. As with *The Ring*, *Sinister*, *Ghostwatch*, and *Unfriended*, the platform of transmission becomes a conduit of spectral contagion, infecting the viewer.

Unlike *Sinister* and *Ghostwatch*, though, *Marble Hornets* replicates the theme of contagious spreading through its networked distribution online. As I have outlined, the series' narrative unfolds concurrently across a variety of social media platforms, including message boards, YouTube videos, Twitter accounts, and Instagram posts. For Jenkins, Ford, and Green, this tendency toward transmedial storytelling is a constitutive feature of convergence culture as content not only must be accessible via a variety of platforms in order to succeed but also must build an expanded story world that can be explored by dedicated viewers. Such "immersive story worlds" consist of serialized narrative structures, ensemble casts of characters both past and present, rich backstories, and an emphasis on narrative and historical continuity within the diegesis.[33] The Wikidot page dedicated to *Marble Hornets* is an apt illustration of the immersive characteristics of contemporary transmedial content, as it maps the series' story world both geographically and temporally. The web page fills in narrative gaps in the YouTube postings through the assembly of peripheral narrative information, contextualizing such tidbits within the broader unfolding story of the Slender Man's haunting presence. For example, "Entry #37" of the series consists of VHS tape footage dated 4 April 1991 and appears to depict a birthday party for a young boy. The image and soundtrack are distorted, generating eerie, mechanical intonations of the dialogue, and the image is obscured through bursts of static and vertical roll. Friends and family of the boy sing "Happy Birthday" and identify the young birthday boy as Alex, presumably the same Alex who is currently being stalked by the Slender Man. Moreover, a brief single-framed image of a symbol – a circle with an "X" drawn through it – is superimposed over the face of the young Alex, indicating that he has been a target of the Slender Man since childhood. Such an observation expands the narrative world far beyond the filming of the *Marble Hornets* student project, generating another narrative avenue of exploration for viewers and fans of the series to explore.

As a transmedial series that expands its narrative over a variety of platforms in unpredictably scheduled instalments over the course of five years, *Marble Hornets* thereby demands a degree of viewer dedication and investment that is unlike more traditional television and web series. It is precisely the narrative complexity of transmedial texts such as *Marble Hornets* that secures their popularity. However, they also initiate what Jason Mittell has called "forensic fandom," the tendency of viewers to delve deeper into a series' story world in an effort to discover new information regarding the characters and the diegetic world in which they live.[34] Like soap operas that have created expansive story worlds far greater than the central narratives included in the program,[35] transmedial texts such as *Marble Hornets* are intended to be ongoing and continuously explored, dissected, and discovered by viewers.

Marble Hornets and the Slender Man mythos more generally are not meant to conclude; they are designed to continually unspool and diverge along a variety of narrative pathways for dedicated viewers to explore, thereby cementing their status as important transmedial works borne out of the unique conditions of networked convergence culture. The Slender Man's method of haunting as a contagion that spreads through its digital capture is analogous with contemporary modes of content circulation in which texts are disseminated through sharing across interconnected networks of users rather than the centralized distribution model of traditional media. For this reason, it is perhaps only logical that a new folkloric icon has developed during the first decades of the twenty-first century, a media environment defined in part by interconnected media circulation.

Like traditional folklore, which develops amidst the participation of communities over time, digital new media – and the internet in particular – facilitate renewed conditions of diffusion for crowd-sourced and community-based storytelling. "Perhaps nothing is more human than storytelling," Jenkins, Ford, and Green write, "whether by fire or by 'cloud.'"[36] Chess and Newsom echo this statement in linking internet communities with the idyllic cultural imaginary of community-based storytelling situated around a fire. They write, "though the storytelling has moved from traditional storytelling places to online spaces, the folkloric qualities remain when stories are told around digital campfires."[37] The analogy of the digital campfire evoked by Chess and Newsom and the "cloud" metaphor evoked by Jenkins, Ford, and Green both evince a conception of the internet in terms of panoptic visuality, the flicker of the campfire giving way to the cloud as a transcendent, immaterial repository of folktales. The breadth and speed of transmission afforded by online digital circulation seems to fulfil the promise of the internet as pure vision and unlimited access. While *Marble Hornets* and the Slender Man mythology attest to the hybrid participatory conditions of convergence culture, they also stand as warnings against the threat of such interconnection and the attendant contagion of networked digitality. Most significantly, Marble Hornet's emphasis on amnesia, altered perception, and the ubiquity of the digital glitch that obscures the intelligibility of the image all suggest the precarity and uncertainty regarding the authenticity not only of the recorded document but also of reality itself. The central threat of *Marble Hornets*, then, concerns the uncontrollable spread of doubt, misinformation, and disorientation through vast networks of interconnected platforms.

ERASURE

Unlimited access and pure visibility are central to the governing conceptions concerning the revolutionary power of the internet and its political potency. Wendy Hui Kyong Chun has written that discourses surrounding the internet in the 1990s were replete with a renewed sense of promise for democracy, the public sphere, deconstruction, and commerce.[38] Similarly, Alexander Galloway has suggested that early internet culture harboured a revolutionary belief in the new medium's ability to collapse hierarchies of political and economic power while liberating the masses through unprecedented access to information.[39] Such celebratory rhetoric regarding the promise of the internet, however, ignores the extent to which the internet is constituted by absence, darkness, and erasure rather than visibility and illumination.

As Mirzoeff reminds us, much of the internet is comprised of "dark matter," that is, websites that are not hyperlinked and cannot be accessed through any network of links.[40] Dark matter in this sense raises questions concerning our conceptions of the digital archive as permanent and accessible; like a ghost, dark matter haunts the visible surface of the internet as an imperceptible presence. Mirzoeff extends this ghostly quality of the internet further, writing, "It has been estimated that only five per cent of the fiber-optic cable in the United States is 'lit,' that is to say actively carrying information. The rest is the ghost net. The ghost net surfaces in everyday surfing as ghost sites, pages that are no longer updated or maintained but are still there, lurking."[41] Abandoned pages, dead links, and dark matter are therefore constitutive of a far greater amount of the digital space that comprises the internet than the "live" pages we access every day. It is this ghost net that is frequently explored in networked horror films; the dark corners of the internet and the potentially dangerous content that lies therein are the sources of horror. In films such as *Feardotcom*, *Pulse*, and *Unfriended: Dark Web*, characters veer too far away from the illuminated surface of the internet into its darker depths, sowing the seeds of their own destruction. Characters in these films function as inverse-Icarian figures, drawn too far into darkness and away from the safety of light, thereby bringing about their deaths. So too in the case of the Slender Man stabbing and its subsequent news coverage. The Something Awful message boards were portrayed as a dark corner of the internet in which nefarious content was circulated among a network of deplorables. As Andrew Peck summarizes, "the relative obscurity of the character and its de-contextualized association with the stabbing served to kindle a classic moral panic narrative. Headlines and sound bites focused on the dangers of unsupervised tween media use and the corrupting allure of the dark corners of the internet."[42] Like the tween girls involved in the stabbing, Jay in *Marble Hornets* ventures too deep into the digital archive amassed by Alex and, as a result, becomes a target of the Slender Man. The internet is constituted by and through darkness, absence, and erasure; in much the same way, Jay's immersion in the Slender Man mythology produces gaps and absences of its own.

Throughout *Marble Hornets*, the status of the image as a verifiable document is undermined both by the diegetic narrator, Jay, and by the totheark response channel. From the earliest entry, Jay establishes that because the tapes are being reviewed without any discernible chronology applied, a coherent timeline of events is difficult to establish. For example, "Entry #2," Jay tells us, appears to have happened before "Entry #1." Similarly, "Entry #6" appears to be a continuation of footage from "Entry #1," as Alex documents the presence of the Slender Man outside his window. This discontinuity not only encourages Mittell's conception of forensic fandom, wherein viewers are tasked with piecing together narrative clues, but also foregrounds temporal discontinuity as a central feature of the series. Such discontinuity suggests that the footage presented to us cannot effectively testify to a logical order of events, putting its status as evidence into question. This pattern of discontinuity continues throughout the series as more footage is discovered, prompting re-evaluation of previously held knowledge.

This becomes most apparent beginning in "Entry #18," when Jay confesses that he is taping himself in addition to reviewing the previously recorded tapes by Alex. Here, Jay exhibits the same symptoms of paranoia suffered by Alex; however, his acts of self-surveillance aid Jay's investigation as a supplement to his increasingly weakened memory. In "Entry #18," Jay breaks into to a home at night in search of former *Marble Hornets* cast member Brian. The home is in disarray, suggesting that it has been ransacked by unknown entities. Inside the house, Jay is attacked by a man in a mask. Jay tells us through embedded text that he does not remember what happened after this encounter and that he woke up in another location – inside his car in a wooded area. "Entry #19" takes place during Jay's memory lapse between his encounter in the home and waking up in his car. The footage depicts Jay sleeping in his bedroom while a masked man ominously looks over him from the corner of the room. The footage contains image and sound distortion, contributing to the disturbing effect of the entry. The footage ends with a static shot of an empty bed, suggesting that Jay has either left or was taken by the masked individual. In his embedded textual narration, Jay states that his room remains empty in the surveillance footage for three hours until he returns to his bed and falls asleep. Without any memory of this event taking place, Jay becomes justifiably concerned, opting to continue to record himself as a means to preserve a record of events amidst his failing memory. Digital video footage is employed, then, to compensate for the memory loss suffered by the series' protagonist; however, the status of this digital video footage as trustworthy and authentic comes into question as visual and audio distortion routinely occurs throughout the footage and the events it depicts are impossible. Perhaps this is no more evident than in "Entry #24."

This entry consists of a four-camera surveillance set-up in Jay's home. The footage is accompanied with a time code on the right side of the screen, indicating that cuts among the four camera set-ups are continuous in time and contiguous in space. Jay moves from his living room into his bedroom and lies on his bed to go to sleep. One camera then depicts Jay getting up from his bed and exiting from his bedroom door. The next camera set-up, though, is placed in the living room facing Jay's bedroom door and does not show the door opening or Jay exiting. The time code in the footage confirms that the two cameras are indeed recording the same space at the same time, yet the separate footages from the cameras are incompatible in what they depict. The discrepancy between the two shots is emphasized in the YouTube entry as Jay places the two shots in split-screen with the time codes, demonstrating that Jay impossibly opens the door and exits his bedroom in shot one while the door remains unopened in shot two. Given Jay's lost memory of the event, the viewer is left with two possibilities: the footage either has been tampered with or it depicts a veritable supernatural occurrence. The spatio-temporal integrity of the scene has clearly been breached, leaving either a technological or supernatural explanation. The authenticity of the footage and its status as a document of events is therefore undecidable from the perspective of the viewer, and this only increases the obscurity and inscrutability of the event without illuminating the mystery. Even though employed to compensate for Jay's fragile mental state and intended to provide an omnipresent visual record, the digital surveillance generates more questions than it answers, occluding any possible reasonable conclusion behind a fog of ambiguity.

Jay's amnesia, the indeterminacy of the video evidence, and the gaps in the archival record of digital tapes accumulated throughout *Marble Hornets* mirror the absences that structure the internet as a digital archive. The evidential status of the footage is compromised not only because there are chronological gaps within the footage but also because the footage is itself infected by the Slender Man and his acolytes. As previously discussed, totheark's response channel counters the narrative set forth by Jay as he conducts his investigation, challenging Jay's conclusions and the veracity of the evidence he collects. Moreover, the images themselves are frequently corrupted by glitches, producing visual and sonic distortion that renders the images illegible. These glitches occur most often when the Slender Man or his proxies are nearby, suggesting that the supernatural presence of the Slender Man himself overwhelms the camera's ability to register a coherent image. These absences and image corruption subvert the supposed objectivity of surveillance, since the images are internally compromised by tothearkʼs hacking abilities and by the incompatibility of recording technologies with the supernatural countenance of the Slender Man. In other words, the freedom and access commonly associated with digital technology and the internet are here controlled by the insidious presence of the Slender Man, who, it should be noted, is identified within the *Marble Hornets* universe as "The Operator." Despite Jay's efforts, then, the Slender Man – The Operator – exercises control over the investigation, altering, corrupting, and deleting the digital footage. Like Jay's memory and perception of events, the digital footage and the YouTube interface to which it is uploaded are compromised and controlled by the Slender Man, thereby challenging the precepts of access and freedom generally associated with the internet as the ultimate public sphere.

The revelation that the Slender Man is the operator behind the unfolding mystery and the *de facto* curator of Jay's investigation reflexively highlights the invisible sets of standards and controls that govern our navigation of the internet. Alexander Galloway has identified the various ways in which the internet, from its inception, has been highly structured and regulated despite our perception of it as an open digital space within which users are freely mobile. "The founding principle of the net is control, not freedom," Galloway writes, "*Control has existed from the beginning*."[43] As Galloway makes clear, control over the internet and our experience of it are both determined by the Unix-based systems on which most computers operate, the C or C++ language in which most computer programming is written, the corporate ownership of hardware and software, and other technical standards set out by the Institute of Electrical and Electronics Engineers (IEEE).[44] The history of computing, Galloway argues, is one of standardization and protocological strategy, whereby an elite group of scientists, professors, and industry leaders – a group Galloway refers to as a technocratic ruling class – determine how computers and the internet can be used.[45] The decisions made by this technocratic ruling class, much like those of the faceless Slender Man in his business suit, determine and delimit the internet's operational protocols. So much so, in fact, that control has been *the* outcome of the past several decades of developments of networked communications, according to Galloway.[46] Standards and protocols, of course, only become such when they are perceived to be the natural operations and uses of a technology. Given this, the successful adoption of standards and protocols is signified by their invisibility, that is, by the extent to which they are not noticed or perceived. In this way, the aesthetic convention of the glitch in *Marble Hornets*, and in networked horror films more broadly, becomes particularly significant. It is through the glitch that the invisibility of an orderly system of controls becomes jarringly visible.

Quoting the *Oxford English Dictionary*, Hugh S. Manon and Daniel Temkin define the glitch as a "surge," "'a sudden short-lived irregularity in behavior,' whose aftereffects are at once shocking and effusive."[47] Similarly, Iman Moradi defines the glitch as the visual manifestation of an error resulting from the unexpected or imperfect execution of a program due to a mistranslation, loss, or breakdown in communication signals.[48] A glitch, then, is a deviation from the intended and expected outcome of a system whereby software is unable to read corrupt data and unable to execute commands. As Mark Nunes writes, glitches constitute aberrant signals in otherwise orderly systems of communication.[49] Such failures in communication result in visual distortion and datamoshing, as the mimetic qualities of the image break down into abstract formations of coloured lines and pixels, what Manon and Temkin refer to as "blockiness" and "crystalline fragmentation."[50] As such, the glitch visualizes the internal operations of digital computational processes through failure, revealing the limits and fragility of digital media. The glitch, then, exists at the intersection of order and chaos, control and accident, predictability and uncertainty. Nunes contends that our contemporary networked society is governed by what Jean-François Lyotard has described as a "logic of maximum performance," one that privileges efficiency, accuracy, and the elimination of error.[51]

In initiating the cessation of a process, in failing to execute an intended order, the glitch disrupts such aims of orderly and efficient communication within a delimited system. Yet several authors have articulated the productive potential of the glitch and its revelatory function. Benjamin Mako Hill, for example, celebrates glitches as reminders of the fragility of digital media and the dangers of our reliance on precarious technologies. "When technology works smoothly," Hill writes, "its nature and effects are invisible."[52] The glitch, however, destroys the veneer of smoothly operating technological systems and brings into view the fact of mediation, and its vulnerability. For Hill, "errors can help reveal these hidden constraints and the power that technology imposes."[53] Manon and Temkin similarly state that the glitch reveals the fact of mediation such that "its simulation of analog can no longer remain covert."[54] Through breakdown and failure, the glitch reveals that mediation is indeed taking place through a constructed system of protocols and control, thereby demystifying the perceived naturalness of networked communication. Part of the productive potential of the glitch, then, is to disrupt the habitual manner in which we engage contemporary technologies, so as to remind us that our menu screens, icons, and interfaces are not file folders, pieces of paper, or desktops, but simulations. "We cannot help but misperceive skeuomorphic user interfaces such as buttons, drop-down menus and browser windows as bearing a real physicality," Manon and Temkin write. "A glitch ruptures this immersive environment, undercutting the sovereignty of the digital by revealing its pervasiveness."[55] While frustrating and, at times, terrifying, glitches reveal an ideology of efficiency, productivity, order, and information control underlying the supposed freedom and accessibility of networked culture.

Nunes, however, argues that glitches, as visual representations, serve the ideological function of order and control through their recuperation within a system of communication. For Nunes, the presence of an error message paradoxically indicates the successful operation of a system since error messages are *predictive*: they anticipate problems before they occur and terminate the operation of a command. Such error messages indicate that the system is working properly in that it accurately predicts potential errors and stops programs from running before such errors take place. "While the error notice signals failure," Nunes writes, "it does so within the successful, efficient operation of the system."[56] These errors, such as the common 404 error message, are "systematically contained within a program of control" and ultimately signify the need for greater control within the dominant ideology of networked society.[57] Manon and Temkin suggest a similar effect when they point out that when an error is aestheticized through the glitch, it is contained and domesticated; in their words, the glitch "render[s] the prospect of real collapse familiar and somehow less scary."[58] As manifestations of system breakdown and signifiers of its containment, the glitch and digital error reside at the intersection of success and failure, control and disorder, predictability and contingency. This is perhaps no more evident than in the intentional production of glitches in visual art and in fictional films, a paradoxical instance of planned disorder that explores the creative possibilities of the glitch.

Manon and Temkin provide the following list, which outlines several ways in which glitch art has been explored by artists through both software and hardware manipulation:

> Photos altered in sound editors, music edited in Photoshop, an album made of data files recorded as sound (*Wrong Application*, 2001), video files edited in text editors, Microsoft Word de- and re-constructed, glitched operating systems (*Satromizer OS* by Ben Syverson and Jon Satrom), glitched fonts (Antonio Roberts's *Dataface*), a glitch programming language (Daniel Temkin's *Entropy*), glitched wikis, as well as a host of tools, from the hands-on *notepad* (Jeff Donaldson and Daniel Temkin) to the automated tools written by Anton Marini, which produce glitch-like visuals for live performance.[59]

In such works, the artist generates the conditions for glitches to occur without having control over the final result or the final image. The artist, that is, sets a computational process into motion with the aim of producing an error that will generate the geometrically fragmented abstractions of a glitch. "One *triggers* a glitch, one does not create a glitch," Manon and Temkin assert.[60] Because such glitches are the desired effect of these artists' processes, they can seem too manipulated, too purposeful, and too overly constructed to be regarded as "authentic" glitches. This serves to subjugate some intentional works of glitch art to the "glitch-alike" (i.e., as not genuine instants of creative destruction).[61] The appropriation of glitch aesthetics in popular film and television further problematizes the relationship between the glitch and authenticity, for unlike glitch art, which aims to reveal the materiality of mediation, such works merely employ glitches as markers of authenticity, as indexical signifiers that testify to the existential relationship between the digital image and a profilmic real. The use of glitches as indexical markers achieves additional purchase given the transition from analogue celluloid film to digital image production, a transition that has often been viewed as spelling the death of film as an art form based on indexical referentiality.

Discussions of the index and cinema often begin with André Bazin, who, in his seminal essay written in 1945, outlined his theory of the photographic image (see chapter 2). "For the first time, between the originating object and its reproduction," wrote Bazin, "there intervenes only the instrumentality of a nonliving agent. For the first time an image of the world is formed automatically, without the creative intervention of man."[62] Unlike the arts of painting or sculpture, the automatic process of photography and its creation of an image via the registration of light on photosensitive emulsion defines it as an objective medium, one that satisfies, "once and for all and in its very essence, our obsession with realism."[63] Bazin therefore argued that the essence of photography lies in its unique capacity to capture a physical imprint, or trace, of reality on the filmstrip through a chemical reaction of light and without the influence of an artist.[64] In "The Myth of Total Cinema" (1946), Bazin elaborated on his theory concerning the relationship between photographic media and reality by asserting that humankind has always held a vision and desire for the perfect replication of reality. As such, the emergence of the cinema and subsequent developments in film sound and colour constitute asymptotic advances toward the realization of the total reproduction of reality.[65]

Bazin's insistence on the realism and objectivity of the automatically reproduced photographic image resonates with Walter Benjamin's earlier essay from 1936, which similarly interrogates the influence of mechanical technology in the arts. In "The Work of Art in the Age of Mechanical Reproduction," Benjamin shares Bazin's sentiment that the invention of photography constituted a definitive break from the history of art because it was able to reproduce images without the intervention of an artist. However, unlike Bazin, Benjamin is more interested in the production of facsimiles of images and their dissemination rather than in the relationship between a representation and reality. For Benjamin, what is lost in the process of mechanical reproduction is the uniqueness and singularity of the art object, for it "substitutes a plurality of copies for a unique existence."[66] He describes this tendency as the "decay of the aura,"[67] a process for which cinema is an exemplar.[68] Importantly, Benjamin does not regard this decay of aura – that is, the loss of the unique, singular experience of the art object – as something to be lamented. To the contrary, the loss of the aura emancipates the work of art: individuals may now access the work without having to travel to a venerated institution, and moreover, the religiosity of ritual and the blind sense of worship that accompany such pilgrimages are done away with. This eradication of aura thus opens up the work of art to political critique and scrutiny.[69]

With André Bazin and Walter Benjamin, we have two distinct yet related theories concerning the specificity of mechanically (re)produced art. Although these are not the only theorists who wrote on the subject,[70] the digital turn in technology and media has generated renewed fascination with these seminal texts. Mary Ann Doane argues that the transition to digital cinema incited a re-examination of the semiotic character of the index within film theory in light of the promise and/or threat digitality posed to the medium of cinema (see chapter 2).[71] Indeed, because of the increasing use of digital technology in photography and cinema and its perceived lack of existential referentiality – that is, its absence of an external trace of the real – what was once heralded as the ontology, the very essence, of the photographic medium has been lost. The erasure of this existential bond between the photographic image and its referent, it has been argued, has fundamentally transformed the ontology of the photographic image. In *The Virtual Life of Film*, for example, D.N. Rodowick writes that "digital media are neither visual, nor textual, nor musical – they are simulations."[72] "Unlike analogical representations, which have as their basis a transformation of substance isomorphic with an originating image," he continues, "virtual representations derive all of their powers from numerical manipulation."[73] For Rodowick, then, digital images lack this fundamental imprint of the real that was once central in defining photography and cinema's specificity as media.

Similarly, Barry Keith Grant locates what he calls a "postmodern anxiety" regarding the truth-status of the digital image in contemporary horror and science fiction films that employ documentary conventions. Focusing on found-footage horror films like *Cloverfield* (Matt Reeves, 2008) and *Paranormal Activity* (Oren Peli, 2009), or what he calls *verité* horror and sci-fi, Grant argues that the combination of explicitly fantastic elements such as ghosts and computer-generated monsters and the realist aesthetics of documentary convention challenge the truth-claims of all documentary footage more broadly. "The monsters of verité horror and sf films," Grant writes, "exist in physical environments that are common public spaces, looking like footage we might take on our cell phones or our own digital cameras and share on the Internet."[74] As such, the presentation of fictional material through a cinematic mode usually associated with documentary authenticity uncomfortably blurs the boundaries between fact and fiction. While Grant does not argue that viewers are tricked into believing that the giant monster at the centre of *Cloverfield* is an existing entity caught on camera, he suggests that our knowledge of *Cloverfield*'s artifice reflexively encourages us to question the truth-claims of *all* documentary footage. The ambiguous authenticity of documentary footage is exacerbated, Grant contends, within the realm of digital cinema production due to the lack of indexicality – that an image can be generated without any reference point in reality and is susceptible to an infinite amount of manipulation. "Verité horror and sf films," therefore, "express a postmodern vacillation between our simultaneous faith in and fear of the truth claims of documentary images today."[75]

Like Jay in *Marble Hornets*, the veracity of the digital image is under suspicion, not only because of the gaps and absences the tapes reveal but also due to the predominance of glitches and material manipulations evident in the footage itself. While glitches signify the failure and breakdown of processes of digital image production, it is precisely this failure that functions to secure the authenticity of the digital document. Here, the glitch serves an indexical function in testifying to the relationship between the digital image and the real. It is therefore through breakdown, obscurity, failure, and *erasure* that networked horror and *Marble Hornets* in particular aim to convey authenticity. In order to demonstrate how the glitch can function indexically, a brief return to Charles Sanders Peirce and his theory of signs is necessary.

Unlike the conventional arbitrariness of the symbol and the mimetic resemblance of the icon, the index is the privileged sign category vis-à-vis reality as it is the sign directly caused by the referent and therefore cannot exist with having been generated by the referent itself. Peirce defines the uniqueness of the indexical sign by referencing photography as an example: "Photographs, especially instantaneous photographs, are very instructive, because we know that they are in certain respects exactly like the objects they represent. But this resemblance is due to the photographs having been produced under such circumstances that they were physically forced to correspond point by point to nature. In that aspect, then, they belong to the second class of signs, those by physical connection [indices]."[76]

Because digital images lack a photochemical relationship to profilmic reality, they are often said to lack this indexical criterion that guarantees the image a degree of authenticity. A digital image, it is claimed, corresponds to a sequence of 1s and 0s, the binary code that is translated and transcoded into pixels of colour gradations that produce the image. As Braxton Soderman explains, "a digital camera uses a sensor containing an array of picture elements (pixels) that sense light, changing photons into analog electric voltages (similar to a video camera) that are then processed through an analog-to-digital converter and stored as an organized set of binary digits."[77] Tom Gunning, however, argues that the index and the digital are not mutually exclusive terms. Gunning reminds us that the indexical quality of photography does not lie in its resemblance to the referent but in the chemical reaction generated by the exposure of emulsion to a light source.[78] Like traditional analogue photography, the 1s and 0s produced in digital photography are caused by light that exists in profilmic space and are stored as numerical data. Therefore, the binary code of a digital image is indexically determined by external reality.[79] Gunning goes on to demonstrate that the storage of numerical data has historically been understood as indexical; he highlights measurement devices such as thermometers, speedometers, and barometers, as well as medical devices measuring pulse and heart rate, as registering numerical data that we nevertheless understand to be indexical even though they involve the conversion of information into numbers.[80]

This conception of numerical data as indexically determined by external reality coheres with Peirce's broader philosophy of mathematics as with his semiology. Here, conceptions of the glitch and error become especially significant because it is through error and failure that an external reality – an absolute truth in Peirce's theorization –

becomes indirectly observable. For Peirce, the production of errors through an equation and the presence of deviation functions to reveal the fallibility of the equation. That an error is present, therefore, *points to* the existence of truth, an actual pattern that has yet to be defined by an accurate equation. "Rather than treating error as a deviant instance in need of correction," Nunes summarizes, "Peirce maintained that the *equation* (and *not* the instance) contained the potential to reveal truth, a kind of real, yet unactualized pattern that transcended the missteps of error in actual human execution."[81] In other words, error and deviation confirm that there is truth to be discovered, thereby raising the status of error to an indexical marker of reality. Errors and deviation demonstrate the possibility of accurate and authentic numerical representations of external reality that are indexically caused.

In arguing that numerical data and algorithmic code constitute the referent of the digital image, Soderman takes the indexicality of the digital image further. Although the indexical sign may involve physical touch, Soderman focuses on the criterion of *causation*, maintaining that an algorithm forces a program to follow a set of instructions, thereby directly causing the resulting digital image. Given this understanding, Soderman contends, digital images are "physically compelled to correspond to a symbolic algorithm."[82] The digital image is thus forced to appear according to the precepts and execution of a program.[83] It is this forced connection that for Soderman secures the digital's indexical status. As Gunning and Soderman demonstrate, then, the digital image may still be indexical if it is caused by the conversion of light external to the camera lens and in the execution of algorithmic code. Furthermore, the eruption of a glitch testifies to the fallibility of the recording technology, the fact of mediation, and the materiality of digital images. The inscrutability of the glitch, its "crystalline fragmentation" that renders the image illegible, paradoxically reveals its indexical status. Indeed, it is precisely the non-representational, the formlessness, the unrecognizability of the index that gives it authenticity. As Didi-Huberman has written, "the effacement of all figuration in this trace is itself the guarantee of a link, of *authenticity*."[84] The erasure of the legibility of the image inherent to the eruption of a glitch thus testifies to its indexicality and, therefore, its authenticity. This cultivation of authenticity is precisely how the glitch is employed in networked horror films and throughout *Marble Hornets*.

There are innumerable instances in *Marble Hornets* in which the eruption of a glitch testifies to the presence of the Slender Man. In "Entry #13," Alex is filming in a wooded area when the sound suddenly breaks, becoming sharp with static until it ultimately cuts out altogether. Alex runs away from the area in an apparent attempt to flee something when his camera captures a split-second glimpse of the Slender Man in close proximity. In "Entry #26," Jay uploads footage from a tape he has recently found. The tape depicts a woman – presumably Alex's girlfriend – filming Alex in a living room asking where the camera had come from. When Alex tells her to put the camera away, the woman turns to face the hallway, revealing the Slender Man standing in front of the camera. Once again, the sound quality deteriorates, producing screeching tones as Alex and the woman scream. The image contains visual tearing and falls out of focus, obscuring our view of the Slender Man. More dramatically, "Entry #40" depicts Jay walking through the woods, a location of central importance throughout the series. A static hissing sound plagues the soundtrack, growing in intensity until the Slender Man appears. Jay drops to the ground as the image exhibits datamoshing and black-and-white pixellation, visual evidence of the corrupting influence of the Slender Man's presence. Similarly, the ending of "Entry #43" finds Jay encountering the Slender Man in the woods; here, the image repeatedly cuts to black as the camera struggles to remain filming. As in other entries, high-pitched static screeches erupt on the soundtrack and the image crumbles into pixelated datamoshing. The image ultimately succumbs to the overwhelming interference generated by the supernatural presence of the Slender Man and reverts to a digital negative before collapsing into black.

Finally, "Entry #44" contains one of the more violent instances of glitching and image corruption. This footage functions as a flashback of indeterminate origin and depicts Alex setting up a surveillance camera in his bedroom as he prepares for bed. Once Alex is in bed, the Slender Man appears in the corner of the bedroom, his unnatural height emphasized by the low-angle camera position showing his head at ceiling level. The room is bathed in an orange hue as the shot is lit with only one light source, a lamp on the nightstand next to Alex's bed. As in previous entries, the image begins to degrade as the colours are desaturated until the image becomes unintelligible. Suddenly, the footage erupts into a rapid and jarring vertical roll as the Slender Man appears to grow in size while the soundtrack buzzes with static intensity. The footage then cuts back to the stable image of the bedroom with which the shot began, only to depict Alex missing from the bed. All of these examples demonstrate how the Slender Man functions as a corrupting force whose presence causes digital glitches in the image and soundtrack. As such, the glitches function as indexical markers of the presence of the Slender Man, whose supernatural countenance overwhelms the digital camera's ability to register a coherent image.

The jarring eruptions of glitches have become a convention in networked horror films, in which the integrity of the image gives way to digital ruination. Marc Olivier observes that in found-footage horror films, the glitch adopts the function of a musical score, since many found-footage films eschew non-diegetic music in an effort to maintain a sense of authenticity.[85] Without a musical soundtrack, static and sonic distortion produce tension and suspense within audiences, ratcheting up anticipation and anxiety regarding the potential for horrific shock. Moreover, the sudden bursts of sonic and visual errors serve much the same purpose as jump scares, resulting in visceral jolts that are conventionally the province of loud musical stings in traditional horror films. More than this, though, the glitch in supernatural horror films functions much like the crumbling castles and abbeys that adorn the landscape of gothic literature, Olivier contends. "The jarring spectacle of data ruins is becoming to the twenty-first century what the crumbling mansion was to gothic literature of the nineteenth century," he argues, "the privileged space for confrontations with incompatible systems, nostalgic remnants, and restless revenants."[86] The Slender Man in *Marble Hornets* and the ghosts that haunt networked horror films are thus irreconcilable with digital modes of image production, their spectral ontologies unable to be wholly transcoded. In *Marble Hornets* specifically, this incompatibility marks the footage as contaminated, obscuring and erasing footage by paradoxically revealing its digital materiality. As a viral contagion, the digital glitch the Slender Man betokens spreads to the consciousness and perception of protagonists Alex and Jay, wiping their memories and damaging their comprehension of reality. Through glitch, erasure, and failure, the spectral is registered as an indexical trace, an absent presence haunting the ruination of digital materiality.

In its promise of unlimited access, the internet ostensibly achieved the goal of pure vision, of *clairvoyance*, that had undergirded modern visual culture since the illumination of the Enlightenment. Mirzoeff writes that the development of electricity in the nineteenth century, with the subsequent emergence of networks of visibility, mirrors contemporary discourses concerning the power and promise of digital media. "Electricity was at the same time the light source of clairvoyant panopticism and was the subject of interminable comment in the period," Mirzoeff writes, "just like today's obsession with the digital."[87] Then as now, there persists a cultural investment in the ability of technologies to compensate for our deficient bodily vision through automated sight, granting clarity, precision, and perspective that lies beyond our corporeal visual faculty. "Clairvoyance was," Mirzoeff continues, "a desire for unlimited sight that the new technologies of the period seemed all but ready to deliver, just as new media today promise access to all manner of visualized knowledges."[88] The contemporary networked horror films examined here, however, demonstrate an unease concerning the access and excess of the internet as digital archive. The discourse concerning the internet as a limitless archive belies the centrality of erasure and loss constitutive of the internet as such, and moreover, the webs of connectivity initiated by digital networks are represented as dangerous avenues of contagion. As the case study of *Marble Hornets* demonstrates, the promise of access afforded by the ubiquity of the internet threatens to lead unwitting viewers into treacherous territory, exposing them to the haunting presence of the malevolent Slender Man. Indeed, the Slender Man's threat inheres in his exposure; those who seek him out suffer mentally and physically from the spectral toxicity embodied in him. *Marble Hornets* and networked horror film more broadly thus function as warnings concerning the overabundance of the internet archive, cautioning viewers to stay away from the far reaches and dark corners of the web lest they suffer psychic and bodily injury.

As with new media of the past, then, contemporary digital new media exhibit the promise of utopian visions of knowledge, communication, democracy, and the potentiality of a renewed public sphere,[89] but also anxieties concerning loss, manipulation, and the vanishing of the real. The "new" in new media is therefore a red herring; as Wendy Chun asserts, the internet was not new in 1995, the year it arguably became new.[90] Rather, the internet became new through its representation as wondrous, strange, exotic, and dangerous in films, television, novels, advertising, and political discourse.[91] The designation "new" in relation to media, Chun asserts, has less to do with a radical alterity proper to the present than with a recycling of familiar although forgotten elements. Citing the *Oxford English Dictionary*, Chun writes that "the new is 'fresh, further, additional,' 'restored after demolition, decay, disappearance, etc.'"[92] Essential to the new is therefore a repetition of the old, a perpetual return. Given this conception, new media are essentially ghostly phenomena, and the ghost is a new medium *par excellence.* As a revenant that will continue to return in the future, the spectral is new media, the ghost a pure medium of return and renewal.

SÉANCE CINEMA 6

In 2010, Canadian experimental filmmaker Guy Maddin was commissioned to produce a project to celebrate the opening of the TIFF Bell Lightbox, the pre-eminent *cinemathèque* associated with the Toronto International Film Festival. Remarking on the newness of the state-of-the-art facility, Maddin lamented the building's lack of history and its absence of ghosts. "[TIFF artistic director] Noah Cowan and I talked about how brand spankin' new the place is," Maddin stated, "and how it wasn't haunted by any film history or any ghosts yet. So I volunteered to haunt the joint."[1] To remedy the building's radical contemporaneity and lack of historical referents, Maddin offered to conjure cinematic ghosts, thereby infusing the building with the spirits of film history. Inspired by his desire to see the lost works of his favourite auteurs,[2] Maddin shot a series of short films, speculations, in effect, based solely upon titles and available information regarding the inaccessible works. The project, titled *Hauntings*, consisted of an eleven-channel Super 8 and digital video installation exhibiting adaptations of the lost or unproduced works on loop in the gallery space of the Lightbox. "From Hitchcock to Murnau to Ophuls," the exhibition website reads, "these 'lost, unrealized and aborted' films were shown both in the main gallery space and projecting out from the fifth floor of the building every night during the festival."[3] *Hauntings* transformed the resounding newness of the Lightbox into a ciné-mausoleum bathed in the shimmering projections of cinema's imagined past.

Maddin and co-directors Evan and Galen Johnson further developed the project into a sprawling multimedia work that included installation, live performance, a feature film, and an interactive website. The film shoot itself doubled as both a live performance and an installation

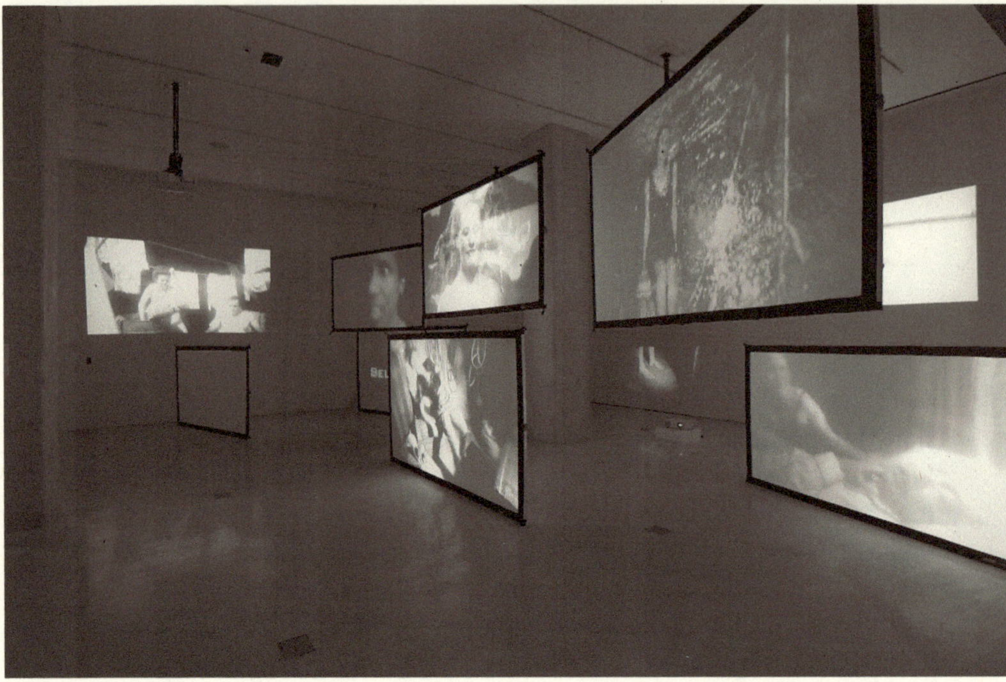

FIGURE 6.1 | GUY MADDIN'S *HAUNTINGS* INSTALLATION AT THE TIFF BELL LIGHTBOX.

piece, as filming was done in full view of gallery attendees at the Centre Pompidou in Paris and the Centre Phi in Montréal. From the pool of short films, a feature-length film was composed and released theatrically as *The Forbidden Room* (2015). Significantly, the release of the feature film was a contractual obligation in order for the filmmakers to secure funding for the subsequent interactive website that constituted the cornerstone of the *Séances* project. In collaboration with the filmmakers, the Halifax-based internet development firm Nickel Media segmented each produced film into discrete scenes. Stylistic techniques such as a zoom-in and fade-to-black were identified as "connector shots," and an enigmatic central tableau – what the filmmakers call a "chewy centre" – was identified in each film. From there, an algorithm was devised to shuffle each element, thereby generating a unique arrangement of scenes joined together through connector shots. The compiled database of scenes and shots was then made available on the National Film Board of Canada website, with the intention

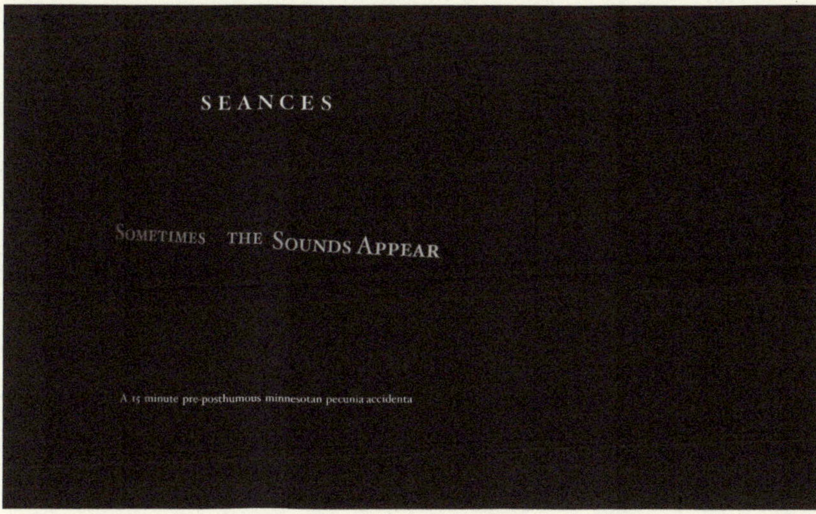

FIGURE 6.2 | SCREENGRAB OF THE *SÉANCES* HOMEPAGE.

of producing unique and unrepeatable film experiences for viewers to encounter.[4]

The site instructs users to click and hold the mouse in order to conjure the spirit of a lost film. From the compiled database, three films are randomly selected by the algorithm and are shuffled within one another according to a randomized pattern of scenes, connector shots, and "chewy centres." Once the film is complete, the particular configuration of shots identified by a unique film title is destroyed, ensuring that it cannot be repeated in the same exact form. The film's unique title is then added to a growing necrology (a list of viewed and subsequently destroyed films), and the viewer is offered the opportunity to tweet the film's title on their Twitter account with the caption "I just watched [film title] and you can't #seances #threestars." The viewer is free to continue generating/conjuring unique films that, as the NFB has stated, have never been seen before and will never be seen again.[5] In crafting a speculative adaptation of lost or otherwise inaccessible films from the early years of cinema history and promptly deleting the unique permutations of these adaptations, Maddin and the Johnsons effectively manufacture experiences of loss and ephemerality endemic to the cinema within the digital space of an interactive web installation. *Séances* thus crystallizes central ideas concerning spectrality and

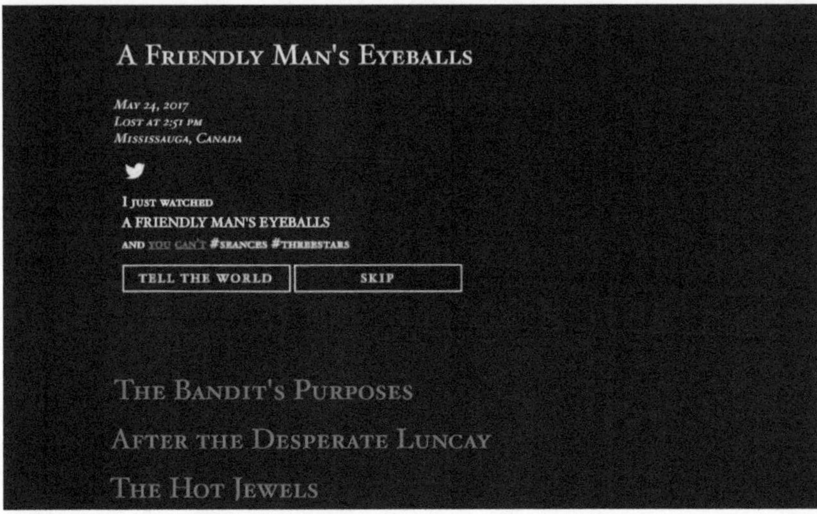

FIGURE 6.3 | SCREENGRAB OF MY OWN VIEWING EXPERIENCE OF THE NEVER-BEFORE-SEEN *A FRIENDLY MAN'S EYEBALLS*, WHICH, THE TEXT TELLS US, IS NOW LOST.

media that have emerged throughout this book. Most importantly, *Séances* performs intermedial and transmedial instances of haunting that are particularly generative for thinking through the relationship between media, technology, and the supernatural today.

Through utilizing simulated celluloid decay alongside explicitly digital glitch effects, in manufacturing uniqueness, loss, and erasure, and in recreating the liveness and collectivity of theatrical performance, *Séances* encompasses the ghostly qualities of media as well as the transmediality of the ghost. The use of glitch aesthetics evokes the problematics of access and erasure addressed in chapter 5, while the combinatory structure of the *Séances* website enacts a logic of contagion. Similarly, Maddin's peculiar method of adaptation, in which the spirit of lost films is conjured, resonates with found-footage horror film as discussed in chapter 4; the project constitutes a spectral iteration of found-footage filmmaking practice, in that archival and historical footage is "found" within the enchanted space of the séance. The inaccessible works of Murnau, Griffith, Ophuls, and others become phantom documents; their original titles and plot descriptions inspired Maddin's adaptations, while the short films he produces constitute a mere shadow of the lost work, a fleeting impression of the original. Through the conceit of the film shoot as séance, the lost footage from early cinema circulates through the ether and materializes on the film set to be documented by our team of cinematographic spirit photographers. Of course, this found lost footage quickly becomes lost found footage as the works deteriorate and are ultimately erased upon viewing on the website.

Moreover, *Séances* exploits online streaming as a new format of home video and, in so doing, spectralizes modes of video distribution. Likewise, the computer screen as the chief interface for film, video, and digital images in contemporary media culture is commensurate with chapter 4's problematization of medium specificity and chapter 3's examination of televisual liveness and broadcast transmission. The computer screen operates as a pre-eminent site of convergence that collapses distinctions between television, film, video, and print text. Moreover, television's capacity for instantaneous transmission and its attendant collapse of temporal and spatial distance is exacerbated by the affordances of digital networked circulation through the internet. In relation to paranormal reality television specifically, *Séances* contributes to the geo-logics of ghost-hunting TV, not only by mobilizing the nowness of televisual discourse but also through algorithmic mapping and transmission. As chapter 3 asserts, the variety of ghost-hunting technologies on display in paranormal reality television function to detect spectral presences and translate them into transmittable data that, in turn, quantify ghosts as measurable geological phenomena. Similarly, Maddin and the Johnsons function as spirit photographers, for the spectres of cinema manifest themselves through "celluloid decasia, pixel datamoshing, and, finally, autodestruction."[6] Perhaps most profoundly, though, *Séances* stages a spectral return of the cinema itself by renewing the loss of the photographic image.

Derived from the Old French *seoir* (a sitting) and the Latin *sedēre* (to sit), a séance is defined by the *Oxford English Dictionary* as a meeting or discussion, a sitting or gathering of a group of people for the purposes of instruction or discussion. In this context, a séance may also be applied to a public cinema screening in which a group of people gather to watch a film. In addition to conjuring lost or inaccessible film images, then, *Séances* aims to recover this fading experience of liveness, presence, and collectivity of cinema spectatorship. The films were shot in public with the welcomed presence and energy of a live audience (perhaps a prerequisite for cinematic conjuring); indeed, the live performance component of the project was designed to *require* audience presence and attention in order to function properly. Debuting at the Tribeca Film Festival in 2016, the live performance consisted of a small theatre where the automatically generated films were projected. Maddin oversaw the proceedings as a showman and self-proclaimed charlatan facilitating the cinematic séance. In the *Séances Project Manual*, Maddin writes, "If anyone in the audience breaks concentration, coughs or fidgets too much, or leaves the screening room altogether, the video cameras installed in the theatre detect this sag in attention and the picture quality of the projection grows weaker, snowier, sometimes in little hiccups of degeneration, sometimes into a steady slide into decasia."[7] The deteriorating image and sound quality as a result of audience inattention, Maddin writes, "reinforces the consequences of not joining in the séance spirit of collective concentration."[8] The presence and attention of audience members, then, are required in order to ensure a successful cinematic séance. The project thus emphasizes the meeting, sitting, and gathering of the séance as an essential attribute of the cinematic experience.

This emphasis on presence and attention is also evident in the planned operation of the interactive website as articulated in the project manual. When a film has been conjured, the viewer is unable to pause, stop, or rewind during playback; this encourages the viewer to watch the entirety of the film or close their browser. Closing the browser also results in the erasure of the film, meaning that it will never be viewable again. In a portion of the website that itself remains unrealized, the manual describes viewers being placed in a virtual waiting room on the website. Here, the viewer waits for two to four other website visitors from anywhere in the world to join the séance. This group of people will all share the experience of watching the same automatically generated film together in the virtual space of the NFB website. As with the live performance, Maddin outlines the "consequences of inattention" in the online component, writing that "should any of the visitors drop out of the viewing experience once it has begun – either by minimizing or closing their browser window or by otherwise making it non-active – the signal will 'weaken' for the remaining visitors, and this weakening will intensify the more visitors drop out."[9] In both the public screening and the interactive website, audience attention is given primacy, so much so that the quality of the image deteriorates amidst signs of distraction, akin to a weakening spirit battery in a nineteenth-century séance. The public meeting of audiences – whether physical or virtual – is therefore a celebrated component of cinematic experience. Far from the fears associated with cinemagoing articulated by Justice Joseph McKenna in 1915, the *Séance*s project revels in the pleasures of publicity, in being immersed within the hypnotic and oneiric experience of film along with other patrons in a gathering, sitting, or meeting place. It is the séance of cinema itself that is conjured in Maddin's project, one that remains an increasingly fleeting experience subject to loss and erasure.

Paul Flaig and Katherine Groo point to *Séances* as indicative of a contemporary interest in silent film and early cinema in the twenty-first century. Amidst the rapid shifts in film technologies and modes of distribution and exhibition, renewed fascination with early cinema reveals a curiosity and nostalgia for a bygone era of moving-image culture.[10] Its perceived foreignness has paradoxically rendered early silent cinema a form of new media, an unfamiliar novelty invoked in works as varied as *Hugo* (Martin Scorsese, 2012), *The Artist* (Michel Hazanavicius, 2011), *Holy Motors* (Leos Carax, 2012), and, of course, Guy Maddin's entire filmography. Flaig and Groo cite Maddin as "one of the most consistently creative of new silent cinema practitioners," and his *Séances* project represents the culmination of his artistic practice.[11] The project evinces a "complex layering of temporality" that simultaneously exhibits cinema's past, present, and virtual future, an untimely contamination endemic to the spectral.[12]

The cinema has here emerged as a spectre in itself, a fading half-presence that lingers on in the new media landscape of the twenty-first century. The old and lost films of early cinema attain this ghostliness, Murray Leeder suggests, because "they are both too departed and too present, something that ought to be lost but remains nonetheless."[13] In ruminating upon the return of early cinema, Leeder considers why the spectral turn in film studies has occurred now, in the twilight of the new millennium. Leeder points to digitization, which he suggests has occasioned reflections on the newness of old media.[14] He also identifies shifts in our conception of history and in the role of the archive, the latter of which is "structured as much by its gaps [as by] what it preserves."[15] While Leeder describes Maddin's reimagined films as artificial copies, as "fakes, ersatzes," he argues that *Séances* produces its own mode of superimposition, haunting the virtual space of the internet with vanished eras of cinema history.[16]

Displaying the temporal recursivity proper to the ghost, I conclude by returning to a question posed at the outset of this book: "What does the ghost look like?" As this book has demonstrated, the ghost is a transmedial figure and is the confluence of its textual, photographic, cinematic, televisual, videographic, and networked representations. The ghost, then, is itself haunted by media images and sounds, each contributing to contemporary conceptions of spectrality and haunting. Spectral images continue to materialize and vanish among a variety of platforms, demonstrating the myriad ways in which media technologies function as evidentiary documents of the supernatural while also demonstrating that media have always already been haunted by spirits.

NOTES

CHAPTER ONE

1 Roland Barthes reflects upon the melancholic and piercing experience of photographic temporality as he views a photograph of his dead mother when she was a child: "In front of the photograph of my mother as a child, I tell myself: she is going to die: I shudder … *over a catastrophe which has already occurred*." Barthes, *Camera Lucida*, 96.
2 Davis, *Haunted Subjects*, 2. Emphasis in original.
3 Waskul and Waskul, *Ghostly Encounters*, 67–9.
4 Ibid., 68.
5 Radford, "The Curious Question."
6 Derrida, *Specters of Marx*, 5.
7 Radford, "The Curious Question."
8 Leeder, *Modern Supernatural*, 5.
9 *Oxford English Dictionary*, s.v. "paranormal, Etymology."
10 Bordwell, *Poetics of Cinema*, 12.
11 Ibid.
12 For an in-depth analysis of the formal construction of the jump scare in horror film, see: Hart, "I'M SCREEEEEEEEEAMING!!!!," 59–88.
13 Harvey, *Photography and Spirit*, 10.
14 Ibid., 13.
15 Ibid., 16.
16 Ibid. 19.
17 Ibid.
18 Ibid.
19 Ibid.
20 Owens, *The Ghost*, 164.
21 Ibid.
22 Ibid., 93.
23 Ibid., 94.

24 Ibid.
25 Ibid., 127–9.
26 Abbott, "Spectral Vampires," 6.
27 Leeder, *Modern Supernatural*, 51.
28 Abbott, "Spectral Vampires," 9.
29 Carlson, "Charles Dickens," 35.
30 Ibid., 34–5.
31 Pepper was inspired by Henry Dircks's design, which similarly used a pane of glass and light as a projection method. However, Pepper's innovation was to tilt the glass 45° so that the illusion would be visible to the entire audience. See Carlson, "Charles Dickens," 39.
32 Ibid.
33 Owens, *The Ghost*, 169.
34 Ibid.
35 Ibid.
36 Luckhurst, "The Contemporary London Gothic," 527.
37 Derrida, *Specters of Marx*, 202.
38 Blanco and Peeren, "Introduction," 7.
39 Laclau, "The Time Is Out of Joint," 201.
40 Fisher, *Ghosts of My Life*, 22.
41 Quoted in Chakrabarty, "Introduction," 3.
42 Ibid., 7.
43 Lim, *Translating Time*, 14.
44 Chakrabarty, "Introduction," 8.
45 Ibid.
46 Lim, *Translating Time*, 11.
47 Chakrabarty, "Introduction," 237.
48 Ibid., 238.
49 Derrida, *Specters of Marx*, xvii–xix.
50 Ibid., xviii. Original emphasis.
51 Ibid., 11. Original emphasis.
52 Blanco and Peeren, "Introduction," 9.
53 Lim, *Translating Time*, 32.
54 Ibid., 26.
55 Sconce, *Haunted Media*, 4.
56 Ibid., 6.
57 Ibid., 10.
58 Gunning, "Invisible Worlds," 52.
59 Gunning, "In Your Face," 1.

60 Ibid., 2.
61 Gunning, "To Scan a Ghost," 96.
62 Ibid., 95.
63 Ibid., 96.
64 Ibid., 97.
65 Gunning, "In Your Face," 2.
66 Gunning, "Phantom Images," 18.
67 Ibid., 24.
68 Turvey, *Doubting Vision*.
69 Bazin, "In Quest of *Télégénie*," 46.
70 Doane, "Information, Crisis, Catastrophe," 222.
71 Williams, "The Liveness of Ghosts," 149.
72 Lauro and Paul, "Make Me Believe!," 231.
73 Ibid., 224.
74 See: Galloway, "Protocol vs. Institutionalization," 187–98.
75 I borrow the phrase "postmodern fantastic" from Lauro and Paul, "Make Me Believe!"

CHAPTER TWO

1 Gunning, "Flickers," 21.
2 Wertheimer, "Mutual Film Reviewed," 159.
3 Ibid.
4 Quoted in Wertheimer, "Mutual Film Reviewed," 160.
5 Quoted in Gunning, "Flickers," 22.
6 Ibid., 23.
7 Ibid., 25.
8 Ibid., 26.
9 Ibid., 23.
10 *Death Bed: The Bed That Eats* (George Berry, 1977); *Christine* (John Carpenter, 1983); *The Refrigerator* (Nicholas Jacobs, 1991); and *The Mangler* (Tobe Hooper, 1995) are notable, if disreputable, examples.
11 Benjamin, "The Work of Art," 221.
12 Kracauer, "Basic Concepts," 145.
13 Ibid., 144
14 Ibid., 145.
15 Kracauer writes, "Imagine a film which, in keeping with the basic properties, records interesting aspects of physical reality but does so in a technically imperfect manner; perhaps the lighting is awkward or the editing uninspired.

Nevertheless, such a film is more specifically a film than one which utilizes brilliantly all the cinematic devices and tricks to produce a statement disregarding camera-reality." Ibid.

16 Ibid., 150–1.

17 Ibid., 153.

18 Miriam Hansen clarifies that for Kracauer, the term "nature" "becomes the allegorical name for any reality that posits itself as given and immutable." See Hansen, *Cinema and Experience*, 35.

19 Kracauer, "Basic Concepts," 152.

20 Turvey, *Doubting Vision*.

21 Ibid., 11.

22 Jean Epstein, "On Certain Characteristics," 295.

23 Ibid., 296.

24 Ibid., 293–4.

25 Dulac, "Visual and Anti-Visual Films," 32.

26 In "The Essence of Cinema," Dulac writes, "The cinema is an eye wide open on life, an eye more powerful than our own and which sees things we cannot see" (ibid., 39).

27 Ibid., 40.

28 Benjamin, "The Work of Art," 236–7.

29 Balázs, "Der Sichtbare Mensch," 39–40.

30 Ibid., 40.

31 Balázs, "The Play of Facial Expressions," 34–5.

32 Canudo, "The Birth of Sixth Art," 58.

33 Ibid., 59. Original emphasis.

34 Ibid.

35 Ibid., 64–5.

36 Faure, "The Art of Cineplastics," 256.

37 Gromaire, "A Painter's Ideas," 178.

38 Moussinac, "On Cinegraphic Rhythm," 281–2.

39 Kracauer, "Photography," 48. Original emphasis.

40 Ibid., 56.

41 Ibid.

42 Hansen, *Cinema and Experience*, 33.

43 Ibid.

44 Kracauer, "Photography," 61.

45 As Miriam Hansen articulates, "Kracauer pinpoints the significance of photographic media for the direction of the present, the fate of modernity." *Cinema and Experience*, 35. Later on in her text, Hansen reiterates: "Whether or not such collective self-representation will have a chance to prevail is a matter of

the 'go-for-broke game' of history by which the technological media could either advance or defeat the liberatory impulses of modernity." *Cinema and Experience*, 53.

46 Sconce, *Haunted Media*, 22.

47 Cloutier, "Mumler's Ghosts," 20.

48 Sconce, *Haunted Media*, 24.

49 Emerling, *Photography*, 1.

50 Talbot titled his 1844 book, the first on the subject of photography, *The Pencil of Nature*.

51 Chéroux, "Ghost Dialectics," 48.

52 Montebello and Monterosso, "Forward," 9.

53 Tucker, "The Social Photographic Eye," 40–2.

54 Vogel, *Chemistry of Light and Photography*, 205.

55 For more on the development of scientific illustrated journals and magazines, see Tucker, "Testing the Unity of Science and Fraternity," in *Nature Exposed*, esp. 110–19.

56 Puglionesi, *Common Phantoms*, 18.

57 Ibid.

58 Ibid., 11.

59 Ibid., 27.

60 Ibid., 69.

61 Tucker, *Nature Exposed*, 111.

62 This is a reference to the graphophone, an improved phonograph designed by Alexander Graham Bell and Charles Tainter. Echoing Talbot's description of photography as the "pencil of nature," its etymology, according to the *Oxford English Dictionary*, derives from the Greek *γράφειν* (to write) and *φωνή* (voice, sound).

63 Doane, *Emergence of Cinematic Time*, 69.

64 Gunning, "What's the Point," 40.

65 Ibid., 70.

66 Taylor, *The Veil Lifted*, vi–vii.

67 For example, Georgiana Houghton, a medium and spirit photographer discussed later in this chapter, criticized the spirit photos of William Mumler. See: Tucker, *Nature Exposed*, 90.

68 Natale, *Supernatural Entertainments*, 141.

69 As discussed in the introduction, John Harvey has traced the shifting visual representation of ghosts in art and literature that is particularly relevant here. See Harvey, *Photography and Spirit*, 10–20.

70 Apraxine and Schmit, "Photography and the Occult," 12.

71 Taylor, *The Veil Lifted*, 10.

72 Ibid., 10–11.
73 Cloutier, "Mumler's Ghosts," 21.
74 Ibid.
75 Mnookin, "The Image of Truth," 30.
76 Ibid., 34.
77 Ibid., 30.
78 Ibid., 34–41.
79 Ibid,. 41.
80 Coates, *Photographing the Invisible*, 19.
81 Coates recounts the testimonies of several prestigious individuals in *Photographing the Invisible*, 19–27.
82 Taylor, *The Veil Lifted*, 12–13.
83 Cloutier, "Mumler's Ghosts," 22. He is not alone, of course, as most magicians and illusionists denounced the practice, going so far as to parody séances in their stage acts. As Tom Gunning has written, "Rarely claiming supernatural powers … nineteenth-century magicians most frequently operated within the realm of demystification. Frequently parodying and mocking their spiritualist counterparts, such magicians claimed no extrahuman aid, yet fervently concealed the secrets behind their illusions." Gunning, "Flickers," 29.
84 Cloutier, "Mumler's Ghosts," 22–3.
85 Ibid., 22.
86 Brewster, *The Stereoscope*, 205.
87 Natale, *Supernatural Entertainments*, 58.
88 Ibid., 2.
89 Coates, *Photographing the Invisible*, 2.
90 Ibid., 2–3.
91 Quoted in Houghton, *Chronicles*, 18.
92 Gunning, "In Your Face," 1–2. The trip wire apparatus used by Cathcart in the film is reminiscent of the similar setup Muybridge employed when he famously photographed a running horse.
93 Quoted in Beckman, *Vanishing Women*, 87.
94 Fischer, "The Reciprocal Adaptation," 178–9.
95 Beckman, *Vanishing Women*, 87.
96 It should be noted that Schrenk-Notzing did not regard the ectoplasmic materializations as ghosts, but rather as an unconscious substance generated by the psyche.
97 Beckman, *Vanishing Women*, 91.
98 Ibid., 78.
99 Gunning, "In Your Face," 4–5.
100 Zimmerman, *Reel Families*, ix.

101 Wasson, “Electric Homes!,” 2.

102 Ibid., 3.

103 Johnson, “Are We in the Movies Now?,” 136.

104 Ibid., 140.

105 Kattelle, “The Evolution,” 56–7.

106 This anxiety is still evident today, of course, as “media effects” arguments pertaining to the undue influence of media images on youth, particularly violent images, remain a topic of debate in popular discourse. This will re-emerge in chapter 4’s discussion of the Slender Man mythology.

107 It should be noted, however, that this shot does not contain the graininess or scratches of the 8mm reels, thus signalling that we are in the present moment and are identifying with the omniscient camera of classical Hollywood rather than the first-person perspective of a killer.

108 Here, it becomes clear that Bughuul does not have a mouth and he never speaks during the film. This would seem to cement his status as an iconic entity enmeshed in the cinematic imaginary and outside the realm of language.

109 Baudrillard, *Evil Demon*, 13.

110 Baudry, “The Apparatus,” 209.

111 ‘Subterranean screening room’ is Tom Gunning’s phrase describing Plato’s allegory. Gunning, “Flickers,” 28.

112 Baudry, “Ideological Effects,” 359.

113 Dayan, “The Tutor-Code,” 112.

114 Ibid.

115 Jay, “Scopic Regimes,” 5–6.

116 Dayan, “The Tutor-Code,” 111.

117 Ibid., 114.

118 Ibid., 115.

119 In addition to illuminated images of individuals, it is often argued in paranormal circles that the presence of ghosts is marked by balls of light called “orbs.”

120 Burch, “Charles Baudelaire,” 12.

121 Ibid., 6.

122 Paolo Cherchi Usai has defined the cinema as “the art of moving image destruction” precisely because of the damage and decay done to the filmstrip upon each projection. See: Usai, *Death of Cinema*, 6.

123 Bazin, “The Myth of Total Cinema,” 17.

124 Ibid., 21.

125 Ibid.

126 Ibid., 17–18.

127 Ibid., 17.

128 Ibid., 18. Bazin describes this as a reversal of causation – he wants to suggest that the true inventors of the art of film stem not from those technological inventions that led to moving pictures, but from the idea of cinema that led to the creation of the technologies.
129 Burch, "Charles Baudelaire," 7.
130 It is worth noting that the French term for a camera lens is *objectif.*
131 See: Althusser, "Ideology," 170–7.
132 Colin McCabe has noted that it is surprising Roland Barthes does not mention Bazin's essay since *Camera Lucida* shares striking similarities with "Ontology of the Photographic Image." Noted in Mulvey, *Death 24× a Second*, 54.
133 Bazin, "The Ontology," 9.
134 Ibid., 13.
135 Ibid., 12.
136 Ibid., 14.
137 Ibid., 15.
138 See Rosen, *Change Mummified*, 4–43.
139 Mulvey, *Death 24× a Second*, 56.
140 Bazin, "The Ontology," 16.
141 Bazin, *What Is Cinema?*, 10.
142 Barthes, *Camera Lucida*, 88.
143 Baudrillard, *Evil Demon*, 13.
144 In an interview with Alan Cholodenko, Baudrillard acknowledged the influence of a "Manichean element" in his theories. See: "Evil Demon of Images," 83.
145 For a fuller explanation of the Manichean religion see Gunning, "Flickers," 34.
146 Gunning, "Flickers," 34.
147 Rodowick, *Virtual Life of Film*, 10.
148 Ibid., 9.
149 Doane, "The Indexical," 129.

CHAPTER THREE

1 Historic Hotels Worldwide, "1886 Crescent Hotel and Spa."
2 Prices for the ghost tour are set at $22.50 per person. America's Most Haunted Hotel, "Tickets."
3 This phrasing appears on the hotel's website encouraging guests to bring along their cameras to document their experiences. Significantly, uniqueness is highlighted as a key feature of the ghost tour, a paradoxical notion given the centrality of repetition and return in cases of haunting.
4 Knable, "Reality TV Gives Boost."

5 Lawrence, *Ghost Channels*, 9.

6 Baron Karl von Reichenbach was a German chemist and scientist who conducted a series of experiments beginning in 1839 concerning psychic phenomena and sensitivities. He was particularly associated with his attempts to demonstrate "od," a vital force akin to mesmerism and animal magnetism. See his encyclopedia entry in: Melton, *Encyclopedia*, 1:1298.

7 "Committees," *Journal of the Society for Psychical Research* [hereafter *JSPR*], 13.

8 "General Meeting," *JSPR*, 35.

9 Ibid.

10 The organization maintains that sensational characteristics or occurrences are "extremely rare" and are more prevalent in popular entertainment magazines than actual encounters with the paranormal. "General Meeting," *JSPR*, 35.

11 Ibid., 36.

12 Ibid.

13 Ibid.

14 Ibid.

15 "Lectures," *JSPR*, 8.

16 Ibid.

17 Castle, *Female Thermometer*, 17.

18 Radford, "The Curious Question."

19 Bernico, "Apocryphal Media," 67. On the EMF reader specifically, Bernico notes, "The EMF reader actually detects EMF fields, but it doesn't tell the user about the origins of those fields – the combination of a device that has real, practical and scientific utility (not to mention the fact that it's relatively cheap and easily obtainable), and that is infused with the mythology of paranormal detection, is apocryphal in the sense that in paranormal research, the effect it produces surpasses the importance of what the device actually does" (69).

20 Andriopoulos, "Psychic Television," 632.

21 Quoted in ibid., 627.

22 Hernan and Dade-Robinson, "Atmospheres of Digital Technology," 219.

23 Ibid.

24 Ibid. The authors go on to state, "The adoption of ethereal theories to account for scientific as well as mystical matter should be understood within the context of the reaction against materialism, especially in Physics during the late nineteenth century."

25 Andriopoulos, "Psychic Television," 625–6.

26 Ibid., 625.

27 Ibid., 630.

28 Ibid., 623.

29 Ibid., 622.
30 Ibid., 625.
31 Ibid., 623.
32 Bazin, "Television Is Unbeatable," 48.
33 Bazin, "Long Live Radio!," 75.
34 Ibid., 49.
35 Bazin, "In Quest of *Télégénie*," 46.
36 Ibid.
37 Bazin writes, "As for me, each time I meet one of the presenters of the TV news or even a TV actor in the street, I have to supress a spontaneous urge to shake their hand, as though they knew me from having seen me daily in front of my screen." Bazin, "Aesthetic Future," 40.
38 Bazin suggests that the revelation of human authenticity is an inevitability in television: "[télégénie] always reveals, if not one or several moral qualities, then at the very least a certain human authenticity." Bazin, "The Aesthetic Future," 42.
39 Ibid., 41
40 Ibid,. 42.
41 Andrew, *André Bazin's New Media*, 8.
42 See Rosen, *Change Mummified*, esp. 11–21.
43 Bazin writes, "For the first time, the image of things is also the image of their duration, like a mummification of change." Bazin, *What Is Cinema?*, 9. See also Rosen, *Change Mummified*, 21–2.
44 Bazin, "Death Every Afternoon," 30.
45 Bazin, "The Aesthetic Future," 41.
46 See Andrew, *André Bazin's New Media*, 13.
47 Doane, "Information, Crisis, Catastrophe," 222.
48 Ibid., 223.
49 Doane notes that the Greek etymology of crisis, *krisis*, means "decision." Ibid.
50 Rather than the condensed temporality of the crisis which unfolds in time, the catastrophe has no extended duration and "happens all at once," according to Doane. Ibid.
51 For a philosophical discussion of how media of recording and transmission, what Jacques Derrida calls "teletechnologies," preserve, archive, and transmit an experience of liveness even when the content is pre-recorded, see Derrida and Steigler, *Echographies of Television*, esp. 36–40.
52 Derrida and Steigler, *Echographies of Television*, 38.
53 Ibid.
54 Ibid.
55 Fisher, *Ghosts of My Life*, 21.

56 Jane Feuer, "The Concept of Live Television," 13.

57 Ibid., 15.

58 Ibid., 16–17.

59 Ibid., 18.

60 Ibid., 16.

61 Friedman, "Introduction," 2.

62 In 1952, Edward Berry Roberts wrote, "More than prose, more than the stage, more than motion pictures – oh, so much more than radio – television, with its immediacy, gets to the heart of the matter, to the essence of character, to the depicting of the human being who is *there*, as if under a microscope, for our private contemplation, for our approval, our rejection, our love, our hate, our bond of brotherhood recognized." Quoted in Boddy, "Live Television," 81. See also Gould, "A Plea."

63 Sconce, *Haunted Media*, 17. Emphasis in original.

64 Ibid., 128–34.

65 Significantly, Erik Born notes that the German word for television, *Fernseher*, referred to "telescope" until the end of the nineteenth century. The verb *fernsehen*, to watch television, referred to both psychic visions and remote viewing, aligning television's seeing-at-a-distance with paranormal connotations. See Born, "The Promise of Television."

66 Sconce, *Haunted Media*, 174.

67 Zolides, "The Truth," 188.

68 Leeder, "*Ghostwatch*," 174.

69 Ibid.

70 Sconce, *Haunted Media*, 17.

71 Lawrence, *Ghost Channels*, 3.

72 Williams, "The Liveness of Ghosts," 149.

73 Ibid.

74 See Zolides, "The Truth."

75 Although it is certainly true that evidence such as thermal images constitute "spectacle" of a sort. Additionally, *Ghost Hunters* also employs POV shots and reaction shots in order to record the affective experience of the investigators.

76 King, "Official Website."

77 Ibid.

78 While early seasons depict Wilson and Hawes during their day job, the show eventually abandons this pretense.

79 Lauro and Paul, "Make Me Believe!," 229.

80 Ibid.

81 Renner, "Negotiations of Masculinity," 203.

82 Ibid.

83 For a more detailed analysis of *Queer Ghost Hunters*, see Chabot, "Queer Spectralities."

84 In what I call an action headshot, footage of the team member in the act of investigating is freeze-framed, with their name and role within the group displayed. Typically, the action headshot will depict the team member peering pensively into the distance, emphasizing their role as investigators.

85 With the strength of twelve men, an employee recounts, this woman pushed the employees away from her.

86 Edensor, "The Ghosts," 830.

87 Ibid.

88 Ibid., 829.

89 At the end of Kubrick's *The Shining*, a long zooming shot reveals Jack Torrance present in a photograph on the wall of the hotel, a photograph taken in 1924. The existence of the photograph suggests that either Jack is the reincarnation of the man in the photo, a suggestion borne out by Jack's spectral encounter with the waiter Grady, or Jack has been absorbed and incorporated into the history of the hotel.

90 Edensor, "The Ghosts," 829.

91 Ibid.

92 Quoted in Edensor, "The Ghosts," 834.

93 Ibid., 836.

94 Ibid., 830–1.

95 Ibid, 831.

96 Holloway and Kneale, "Locating Haunting," 303.

97 Waskul and Waskul, *Ghostly Encounters*, 61.

98 Ibid., 63.

99 Ibid., 67.

100 Quoted in Stollznow, "Stanley Hotel."

101 Stollznow, "The Stanley Hotel."

102 Ibid.

103 Radford, "Ghost-Hunting Mistakes."

104 Cohen, *Stone*, 9.

105 Ibid., 8.

106 Ibid., 12.

107 Ibid., 78.

108 Ibid.

109 Ibid., 106.

110 Ibid., 85.

111 Ibid., 83–4 at 80.

112 Hawes and Wilson capture the voice of a girl apparently saying "hello" and laughing while they are investigating a basement walkway in the hotel. Because the ghost seemingly responds and reacts to Hawes and Wilson, this would constitute an instance of intelligent haunting.

113 Todorov defines the fantastic as a literary genre in which the veracity of the supernatural is left ambiguous for the entirety of the narrative. In Henry James's *The Turn of the Screw* (1898), it remains unresolved: Is the manor in Bly truly haunted, or are the events of the novella the result of the governess's deteriorating mental condition? A literary work remains in the realm of the fantastic as long as it sustains this hesitation, this ambiguity, this undecidability. Once a narrative reveals the supernatural to be real, the work becomes an example of the "fantastic-marvellous"; conversely, if the supernatural is disproven with a rational explanation, the work is categorized as the "fantastic-uncanny." The fantastic, then, is a unique genre, for it is rare for a work to sustain this ambiguity for its entirety. Todorov cites James's novella as one such work. See Todorov, *The Fantastic*, esp. 41–57.

114 Lauro and Paul, "Make Me Believe!," 224.

115 Ibid., 231.

116 Williams, "The Liveness of Ghosts," 155. Original emphasis.

117 Ibid., 160.

118 Ibid., 155.

119 Villarejo, *Ethereal Queer*, 1.

CHAPTER FOUR

1 Herbert, "Nostalgia Merchants," 4.

2 Ibid., 5–6.

3 Ibid.

4 Ibid.

5 See Menta, "Stranger Things."

6 Herbert, "Nostalgia Merchants," 9–10.

7 Diane Garrett wrote an obituary for the format published in *Variety* that identifies the cause of death as "loneliness." See Garrett, "VHS Tapes Die of Loneliness."

8 Heller-Nicholas, *Found-Footage Horror*, 11.

9 Wax, "The Dizzy Spell."

10 Jackson, *Technology*, 58–60; Benson-Allott, *Killer Tapes*, 178–9.

11 Marc Olivier remarks that the configuration of the television monitors resembles that of a Nam June Paik art installation. Olivier, "Glitch Gothic," 265.

12 Hilderbrand, *Inherent Vice*, xiii.

13 Hilderbrand describes the kinds of damage unique to video in the following passage: "videotape's wear tends toward the softening interference of muffled rainbow flares (called video moiré), skewed images at the top and bottom of the frame (called flagwaving or skew error, caused by stretched or distorted tapes), white specks (called dropout), lines of distortion (called noise bars), exaggerated pixels, jittery framing, and muted sounds." Hilderbrand, *Inherent Vice*, 15.

14 Ibid., 6.

15 For a fascinating discussion of vinyl record collecting and the objecthood of music, see "Lost in the Shuffle: Record Collecting and the Twilight of Music as Object," in Reynolds, *Retromania*, 86–128.

16 Benjamin, "The Work of Art," 221.

17 Tashiro, "Contradictions of Video Collecting," 17. For a comprehensive examination of the pleasures of rewatching and repeat viewing, see "Once Is Not Enough: The Functions and Pleasures of Repeat Viewings," in Klinger, *Beyond the Multiplex*, 135–90.

18 Edensor, "The Ghosts," 829.

19 Olivier, "Glitch Gothic," 253.

20 Ibid., 269.

21 Edensor, "The Ghosts," 236.

22 Olivier, "Glitch Gothic," 265.

23 Sean Cubitt has written that "video" is an umbrella term denoting a wide variety of formats including "VHS, S-VHS and VHS-C, V 2000, Betamax, U-matic, Hi-brand, Beta SP, Video-8 and Hi-S8, MII, MAC, and D-MAC, and so on." To this list, we may add the myriad digital formats and codecs that have been developed since this book's publication. See: Cubitt, *Videography*, xii.

24 Berko, "Video," 289.

25 Greenberg, *From BetaMax to Blockbuster*, 42.

26 Wasser, *Veni, Vidi, Video*, 48.

27 Greenberg, *From BetaMax to Blockbuster*, 42.

28 Newman, *Video Revolutions*, 9.

29 Berko, "Video," 292.

30 Ibid.

31 Greenberg, *From BetaMax to Blockbuster*, 43.

32 Ibid., 43–44.

33 For an examination of various failed home video formats, see: Wasser, *Veni, Vidi, Video*, 60–76.

34 Herbert, *Videoland*, 22–3; Hilderbrand, *Inherent Vice*, 8; Newman, *Video Revolutions*, 37.

35 Paul Virilio describes the effects of the VCR in the following terms: "The machine, the VCR, allows man to organize a time which is not his own, *a deferred time*, a time which is somewhere else – and to capture it … the VCR … creates two days: a reserve day which can replace the ordinary day, the lived day." Quoted in Friedberg, "The End of Cinema," 445.

36 Greenberg, *From BetaMax to Blockbuster*, 26.

37 Wasser, *Veni, Vidi, Video*, 72–3.

38 Ibid., 94.

39 For a more detailed examination of the transition from videotapes as time-shifting devices to pre-recorded feature films, see: Wasser, *Veni, Vidi, Video*, 76–103.

40 Berko, "Video," 290.

41 Spielmann, *Video*, 3.

42 Hilderbrand, *Inherent Vice*, 6.

43 Ibid.

44 Baron, *The Archive Effect*, 17–18.

45 Ibid., 22.

46 Ibid., 49.

47 Scheible, "Video after Video Stores," 57.

48 Ibid., 59. Original emphasis.

49 Greenberg, *From BetaMax to Blockbuster*, 21–5.

50 Ibid., 23.

51 Hilderbrand, *Inherent Vice*, 63.

52 Greenberg, *From BetaMax to Blockbuster*, 30.

53 For a detailed account of the emergence of the video store as an economic and cultural institution, see Herbert, *Videoland*.

54 Tashiro, "Contradictions of Video Collecting," 15.

55 Bjarkman, "To Have and to Hold," 537–8.

56 For a comprehensive study of the use of limited editions to confer uniqueness and value to works of video on the contemporary art market, see "The Limited Edition," in Balsom, *After Uniqueness*, 127–65.

57 Lucas Hilderbrand uses the phrase "objects of passion" to describe the bootleg circulation and collection of video as well as the role of pornography in the development of home video industries. Hilderbrand, *Inherent Vice*, 34. Similarly, Barbara Klinger opens her chapter on video collecting with an epigraph by Jean Baudrillard stating that everyday objects are "objects of passion," aligning emotional investment in private property with the acquisition of videotapes. See: Klinger, *Beyond the Multiplex*, 54.

58 Benson-Allott, *Killer Tapes*, 117.
59 Benjamin, "Unpacking my Library," 60.
60 Ibid.
61 Egan, "The Celebration," 201.
62 Gray, "Saving the Scream Queens."
63 Ibid.
64 Ibid.
65 Bjarkman, "To Have and to Hold," 537–8.
66 Benjamin, "Unpacking my Library," 64.
67 Sturken, "The Politics of Video Memory," 4.

CHAPTER FIVE

1 Baron, *Archive Effect*, 17–23.
2 The term "creepypasta" is derived from the portmanteau "copypasta" meaning "copy and paste." Whereas copypasta refers to the circulation of short texts through online forums and email, creepypastas consist of the dissemination of short texts, videos, images, and audio with specifically supernatural or paranormal themes. See Boyer, "The Anatomy of a Monster," 243n10.
3 Chess and Newsom, *Folklore*, 5.
4 Ibid.
5 Quoted in Chess and Newsom, *Folklore*, 8.
6 Chess and Newsom write, "Though the storytelling has moved from traditional storytelling places to online spaces, the folkloric qualities remain when stories are told around digital campfires." *Folklore*, 77.
7 Peck, "Tall, Dark, and Loathsome," 334.
8 Ibid., 337.
9 Ibid., 342.
10 Ibid., 343–4.
11 Ibid., 334, 344.
12 Boyer, "The Anatomy of a Monster," 245.
13 For more on Trender Man and related posts, see: https://knowyourmeme.com/memes/slender-man#trender.
14 For more detailed information of Slender Man's spread through the internet, see *Know Your Meme* at https://knowyourmeme.com/memes/slender-man#spread.
15 In *Specters of Marx*, Derrida writes that "the specter is a paradoxical incorporation, the becoming-body, a certain phenomenal and carnal form of the spirit" (5). Ernesto Laclau describes the essence of spectrality as a foundational "undecidability between flesh and spirit" wherein the spectre embodies

a "paradoxical incorporation" through its return to, and passage through, the body. Laclau, "The Time Is Out of Joint," 201.

16 Blackman, *Haunted Data*, 56.
17 Figures accessed 31 May 2023.
18 Jenkins, *Convergence Culture*, 10.
19 Ibid., 10–12.
20 Ibid., 2.
21 Ibid., 3.
22 Peck, "Tall, Dark, and Loathsome," 338; Chess and Newsom, *Folklore*, 25.
23 Chess and Newsom, *Folklore*, 28.
24 Ibid., 29.
25 Jenkins, Ford, and Green, *Spreadable Media*, 1.
26 Ibid., 12.
27 Ibid., 11.
28 Ibid., 18.
29 Ibid., 19.
30 Ibid., 20.
31 Ibid., 21.
32 Ibid.
33 Ibid., 132.
34 Ibid., 135.
35 Jenkins, Ford, and Green identify soap operas as the epitome of the transmedial text because of their sometimes decades-long investment in a particular story world.
36 Jenkins, Ford, and Green, *Spreadable Media*, 2.
37 Chess and Newsom, *Folklore*, 77.
38 Wendy Hui Kyong Chun, "Introduction," 3.
39 Galloway, *Interface Effect*, 2.
40 Mirzoeff, "Ghostwriting," 251.
41 Ibid., 251–2.
42 Peck, "Tall, Dark, and Loathsome," 346.
43 Alexander Galloway, "Protocol vs. Institutionalization," 195. Emphasis in original.
44 Ibid., 187–9.
45 Ibid., 187.
46 Ibid., 195.
47 Manon and Temkin, "Notes on Glitch," 1.
48 Moradi et al., "Introduction," 8.
49 Nunes, "Error, Noise, and Potential," 3.
50 Manon and Temkin, "Notes on Glitch," 7.

51 Quoted in Nunes, "Error, Noise, and Potential," 1.
52 Hill, "Revealing Errors," 27.
53 Ibid., 29.
54 Manon and Temkin, "Notes on Glitch," 1.
55 Ibid., 7.
56 Nunes, "Error, Noise, Potential," 13.
57 Ibid., 5–7.
58 Manon and Temkin, "Notes on Glitch," 8.
59 Ibid., 2.
60 Ibid., 3, my emphasis.
61 Ibid., 8–9.
62 Bazin, "The Ontology," 13.
63 Ibid., 12.
64 Of course, the photographer, even in the earliest incarnations of the medium, decided where to place the camera, the angle of the photograph, and how to stage the scene, thus undermining the sense of pure objectivity evident in Bazin's writing.
65 Bazin, "The Myth of Total Cinema," esp. 18–21.
66 Benjamin, "The Work of Art," 221.
67 Ibid., 222–3.
68 Ibid., 221.
69 Ibid., 224.
70 For example, Rudolf Arnheim, Roland Barthes, and, more recently, D.N. Rodowick have also theorized the relationship between mechanical, analogue artwork and reality. See: Arnheim, *Film as Art*, esp. 8–34; Barthes, *Camera Lucida*, esp. 3–60; and Rodowick, "Lost in Translation: Analogy and Index Revisited," in *Virtual Life of Film*, 110–18.
71 Doane, "The Indexical," 129.
72 Rodowick, *Virtual Life of Film*, 10.
73 Ibid., 9.
74 Grant, "Digital Anxiety," 171.
75 Ibid., 170.
76 Quoted in Soderman, "The Index and the Algorithm," 157.
77 Ibid., 159.
78 Gunning, "What's the Point," 40.
79 Ibid.
80 Ibid.
81 Nunes, "Error, Noise, and Potential," 11.
82 Soderman, "The Index and the Algorithm," 162.
83 Ibid.

84 Quoted in Doane, "The Indexical," 135. Original emphasis.
85 Olivier, "Glitch Gothic," 267.
86 Ibid., 253.
87 Mirzoeff, "Ghostwriting," 242.
88 Ibid., 243.
89 Chun, "Introduction," 3.
90 Ibid.
91 Ibid.
92 Ibid.

CHAPTER SIX

1 Semley, "Guy Maddin."
2 Maddin states, "I've been literally haunted by the idea that there are these really intriguing titles by some of my favourite filmmakers that I'd never get to see, whether it's because they're lost for the time being, or permanently. I told myself years ago that the only way I'd get to see any version of these is if I made the adaptation myself and watched it." Ibid.
3 Toronto International Film Festival, "Essential Cinema."
4 This site can be accessed here: http://seances.nfb.ca.
5 Quoted in Everett-Green, "Seances."
6 Flaig and Maddin, "The Biggest Kuleshov Experiment," 316.
7 Maddin, Johnson, and Kotyk, *Séances Project Manual*, 25. I am indebted to James Cahill for providing me with a copy of the project manual.
8 Ibid.
9 Ibid., 17.
10 Flaig and Groo, "Introduction," 2–3.
11 Ibid., 13.
12 I borrow this phrase from Constance Balides's analysis of Scorsese's *Hugo* in which she writes, "[*Hugo*] enacts a complex layering of temporality in which it references two past times of cinema – the silent era and the 1950s – while it engages the spectator in the ongoing present of the film experience." Balides, "Intertext as Archive," 146.
13 Leeder, *Modern Supernatural*, 192.
14 Ibid.
15 Ibid.
16 Ibid., 196–7.

BIBLIOGRAPHY

Abbott, Stacey. "Spectral Vampires: *Nosferatu* in the Light of New Technology." In *Horror Film: Creating and Marketing Fear*, edited by Steffen Hantke, 3–22. Jackson: University Press of Mississippi, 2004.

Althusser, Louis. "Ideology and Ideological State Apparatuses (Notes Toward an Investigation)." In *Lenin and Philosophy and Other Essays*, translated by Ben Brewster, 127–86. New York: Monthly Review Press, 1971.

America's Most Haunted Hotel. "Tickets." http://www.americasmosthauntedhotel.com/tickets-tours-in-eureka-springs.

Andrew, Dudley, ed. *André Bazin's New Media*. Berkeley: University of California Press, 2014.

Andriopoulos, Stefan. "Psychic Television." *Critical Inquiry* 31, no. 3 (2005): 618–37.

Apraxine, Pierre, and Sophie Schmit. "Photography and the Occult." In *The Perfect Medium: Photography and the Occult*, edited by Clément Chéroux et al., 12–19. New Haven: Yale University Press, 2005.

Arnheim, Rudolph. *Film as Art*. Berkeley: University of California Press, 1957.

Balázs, Béla. "The Play of Facial Expressions." In *Béla Balázs: Early Film Theory*, translated by Rodney Livingstone, edited by Erica Carter, 33–7. New York: Berghahn Books, 2010.

– "Der Sichtbare Mensch." In *Theory of Film: Character and Growth of a New Art*, translated by Edith Bone, 39–45. New York: Dover, 1970.

Balides, Constance. "Intertext as Archive: Méliès, Hugo, and New Silent Cinema." In *New Silent Cinema*, edited by Paul Flaig and Katherine Groo, 135–58. New York: Routledge, 2016.

Balsom, Erika. *After Uniqueness: A History of Film and Video Art in Circulation*. New York: Columbia University Press, 2017.

Baron, Jaimie. *The Archive Effect: Found Footage and the Audiovisual Experience of History*. London: Routledge, 2014.

Barthes, Roland. *Camera Lucida: Reflections on Photography*, translated by Richard Howard. New York: Hill and Wang, 1981.

Baudrillard, Jean. *Evil Demon of Images*. Sydney: Power Institute of Fine Arts, 1987.

– "Evil Demon of Images." In *The Baudrillard Reader*, edited by Steve Redhead, 83–98. New York: Columbia University Press, 2008.

Baudry, Jean-Louis. "The Apparatus: Metapsychological Approaches to the Impression of Reality in the Cinema." In *Film Theory and Criticism*, 6th ed., edited by Leo Braudy and Marshall Cohen, 206–23. New York: Oxford University Press, 2004.

– "Ideological Effects of the Basic Cinematographic Apparatus." In *Film Theory and Criticism*, 6th ed., edited by Leo Braudy and Marshall Cohen, 355–65. New York: Oxford University Press, 2004.

Bazin, André. "The Aesthetic Future of Television." In *André Bazin's New Media*, edited and translated by Dudley Andrew, 37–43. Berkeley: University of California Press, 2014.

– "Death Every Afternoon." In *Rites of Realism: Essays on Corporeal Cinema*, edited by Ivone Margulies, translated by Mark A. Cohen, 27–31. Durham: Duke University Press, 2003.

– "Long Live Radio! Down with the 8th Art!" In *André Bazin's New Media*, edited and translated by Dudley Andrew, 75–8. Berkeley: University of California Press, 2014.

– "The Myth of Total Cinema." In *What Is Cinema?, vol. 1*, translated by Hugh Gray, 17–22. Berkeley: University of California Press, 2005.

– "The Ontology of the Photographic Image." In *What Is Cinema?, vol. 1*, translated by Hugh Gray, 9–16. Berkeley: University of California Press, 2005.

– "In Quest of Télégénie." In *André Bazin's New Media*, edited and translated by Dudley Andrew, 44–7. Berkeley: University of California Press, 2014.

– "Television Is Unbeatable for Live Coverage." In *André Bazin's New Media*, edited and translated by Dudley Andrew, 48–50. Berkeley: University of California Press, 2014.

– *What Is Cinema?* Translated by Timothy Barnard. Montreal: Caboose Press, 2009.

Beard, David. "Introduction: Paranormal TV." *Horror Studies* 4, no. 2 (2013): 151–8.

Beckman, Karen. *Vanishing Women: Magic, Film, and Feminism*. Durham: Duke University Press, 2003.

Benjamin, Walter. "Unpacking My Library: A Talk about Book Collecting." In *Illuminations: Essays and Reflections*, translated by Harry Zohn, edited by Hannah Arendt, 59–68. New York: Schocken Books, 2007.

– "The Work of Art in the Age of Mechanical Reproduction." In *Illuminations: Essays and Reflections*, translated by Harry Zohn, edited by Hannah Arendt, 217–52. New York: Schocken Books, 2007.

Benson-Allott, Caetlin. *Killer Tapes and Shattered Screens: Video Spectatorship from VHS to File Sharing*. Berkeley: University of California Press, 2013.

Berko, Lili. "Video: In Search of a Discourse." *Quarterly Review of Film Studies* 10, no. 4 (1985): 289–307.

Bernico, Matthew. "Apocryphal Media: An Archaeology of Mediated Paranormal Presence." *Artnodes* 21 (2018): 65–72.

Bjarkman, Kim. "To Have and to Hold: The Video Collector's Relationship with an Ethereal Medium." In *Television: The Critical View*, 7th ed., edited by Horace Newcomb, 530–56. Oxford: Oxford University Press, 2007.

Blackman, Lisa. *Haunted Data: Affect, Transmedia, and Weird Science*. London: Bloomsbury Academic, 2019.

Blanco, María del Pilar, and Esther Peeren. "Introduction: Conceptualizing Specters." In *The Spectralities Reader: Ghosts and Haunting in Contemporary Cultural Theory*, edited by María del Pilar Blanco and Esther Peeren, 1–27. New York: Bloomsbury, 2013.

Boddy, William. "Live Television: Program Formats and Critical Hierarchies." In *Fifties Television: The Industry and Its Critics*, 80–92. Urbana: University of Illinois Press, 1990.

Bordwell, David. *Poetics of Cinema*. New York: Routledge, 2008.

Born, Erik. "The Promise of Television." *The Promise of Cinema*, 14 October 2017. https://www.thepromiseofcinema.com/index.php/the-promise-of-television/index.html.

Boyer, Tina Marie. "The Anatomy of a Monster: The Case of Slender Man." *Preternature: Critical and Historical Studies on the Preternatural* 2, no. 2 (2013): 240–61.

Brewster, David. *The Stereoscope, Its History, Theory, and Construction*. London: John Murray, 1856.

Burch, Noël. "Charles Baudelaire Versus Doctor Frankenstein." In *Life to Those Shadows*, edited and translated by Ben Brewster, 6–23. Berkeley: University of California Press, 1990.

Burger, Alissa. "*Ghost Hunters*: Simulated Participation in Televisual Hauntings." In *Popular Ghosts: The Haunted Spaces of Everyday Culture*, edited by

María del Pilar Blanco and Esther Peeren, 162–74. New York: Continuum, 2010.

Cahill, James Leo, and Timothy Holland. "Double Exposures: Derrida and Cinema, an Introductory Séance." *Discourse* 32, nos. 1–2 (2015): 3–21.

Canudo, Ricciotto. "The Birth of the Sixth Art." In *French Film Theory*, vol. 1: *1907–1929*, edited by Richard Abel, 58–65. Princeton: Princeton University Press, 1988.

Carlson, Marvin. "Charles Dickens and the Invention of the Modern Stage Ghost." In *Theatre and Ghosts: Materiality, Performance, and Modernity*, edited by Mary Luckhurst and Emilie Morin, 27–45. Houndmills: Palgrave Macmillan, 2014.

Castle, Terry. *The Female Thermometer: Eighteenth-Century Culture and the Invention of the Uncanny*. Oxford: Oxford University Press, 1995.

Chabot, Kevin. "Queer Spectralities and Untimely Subjects: *Queer Ghost Hunters* and Paranormal Reality Television." *Canadian Journal of Film Studies* 28, no. 2 (2019): 1–22.

Chakrabarty, Dipesh. "Introduction: The Idea of Provincializing Europe." In *Provincializing Europe: Postcolonial Thought and Historical Difference*, 3–46. Princeton: Princeton University Press, 2000.

Chéroux, Clément. "Ghost Dialectics: Spirit Photography in Entertainment and Belief." In *The Perfect Medium: Photography and the Occult*, edited by Clément Chéroux et al., 45–71. New Haven: Yale University Press, 2005.

Chess, Shira, and Eric Newsom. *Folklore, Horror Stories, and the Slender Man: The Development of an Internet Mythology*. New York: Palgrave, 2015.

Chun, Wendy Hui Kyong. "Introduction: Did Somebody Say New Media?" In *New Media, Old Media: A History and Theory Reader*, edited by Wendy Hui Kyong Chun and Thomas Keenan, 1–10. New York: Routledge, 2006.

Cloutier, Crista. "Mumler's Ghosts." In *The Perfect Medium: Photography and the Occult*, edited by Clément Chéroux et al., 20–8. New Haven: Yale University Press, 2005.

Coates, James. *Photographing the Invisible: Practical Studies in Spirit Photography, Spirit Portraiture, and Other Rare but Allied Phenomena*. London: L.N. Fowler and Co., 1911.

Cohen, Jeffrey Jerome. *Stone: An Ecology of the Inhuman*. Minneapolis: University of Minnesota Press, 2015.

"Committees." *Journal of the Society for Psychical Research* 1, no. 1 (February 1884): 13.

Davies, Owen. *The Haunted: A Social History of Ghosts*. New York: Palgrave Macmillan, 2007.

– *Haunted Subjects: Deconstruction, Psychoanalysis, and the Return of the Dead*. Houndmills: Palgrave Macmillan, 2007.

Dayan, Daniel. *Specters of Marx: The State of the Debt, the Work of Mourning, and the New International*, translated by Peggy Kamuf. New York: Routledge, 2006.

– "The Tutor-Code of Classical Cinema." In *Film Theory and Criticism*, 6th ed., edited by Leo Braudy and Marshall Cohen, 106–17. New York: Oxford University Press, 2004.

Derrida, Jacques, and Bernard Stiegler. *Echographies of Television: Filmed Essays*, translated by Jennifer Bajorek. Cambridge: Polity, 2022.

Dickey, Colin. "The Broken Technology of Ghost Hunting." *The Atlantic*, 14 November 2016. https://www.theatlantic.com/science/archive/2016/11/the-broken-technology-of-ghost-hunting/506627.

Doane, Mary Ann. *The Emergence of Cinematic Time: Modernity, Contingency, the Archive*. Cambridge, MA: Harvard University Press, 2002.

– "The Indexical and the Concept of Medium Specificity." *Differences* 18, no. 1 (2007): 128–52.

– "Information, Crisis, Catastrophe." In *Logics of Television: Essays in Cultural Criticism*, edited by Patricia Mellencamp, 222–39. Bloomington: Indiana University Press, 1990.

Dulac, Germaine. "The Essence of Cinema: The Visual Idea." In *The Avant-Garde Film: A Reader of Theory and Criticism*, edited by P. Adam Sitney, 36–42. New York: NYU Press, 1978.

– "Visual and Anti-Visual Films." In *The Avant-Garde Film: A Reader of Theory and Criticism*, edited by P. Adam Sitney, 31–5. New York: NYU Press, 1978.

Edensor, Tim. "The Ghosts of Industrial Ruin: Ordering and Disordering Memory in Excessive Space." *Environment and Planning D: Society and Space* 23 (2005): 829–49.

Egan, Kate. "The Celebration of a 'Proper Product': Exploring the Residual Collectible through the 'Video Nasty.'" In *Residual Media*, edited by Charles Acland, 200–21. Minneapolis: University of Minnesota Press, 2007.

Emerling, Jae. *Photography: History and Theory*. New York: Routledge, 2012.

Epstein, Jean. "On Certain Characteristics of Photogénie." In *Jean Epstein: Critical Essays and Translations*, edited by Sarah Keller and Jason N. Paul, 292–6. Amsterdam: Amsterdam University Press, 2012.

Everett-Green, Robert. "Seances: Guy Maddin's Film Generator Is an Endless Cinematic Experience." *Globe and Mail*, 2 May 2016.

Faure, Elie. "The Art of Cineplastics." In *French Film Theory*, vol. 1: *1907–1929*, edited by Richard Abel, 258–67. Princeton: Princeton University Press, 1988.

Feuer, Jane. "The Concept of Live Television: Ontology as Ideology." In *Regarding Television: Critical Approaches*, edited by E. Ann Kaplan, 12–22. Frederick: University Publications of America, 1983.

Fischer, Andreas. "'The Reciprocal Adaptation of Optics and Phenomena': The Photographic Recording of Materializations." In *The Perfect Medium: Photography and the Occult*, edited by Clément Chéroux et al., 171–216. New Haven: Yale University Press, 2005.

Fisher, Mark. *Ghosts of My Life: Writings on Depression, Hauntology, and Lost Futures*. Winchester: Zero Books, 2014.

– "What Is Hauntology?" *Film Quarterly* 66, no. 1 (2012): 16–24.

Flaig, Paul, and Katherine Groo. "Introduction: Celluloid Specters, Digital Anachronisms." In *New Silent Cinema*, edited by Paul Flaig and Katherine Groo, 1–16. New York: Routledge, 2016.

Flaig, Paul, and Guy Maddin. "The Biggest Kuleshov Experiment Ever: A Conversation with Guy Maddin about *Séances*." In *New Silent Cinema*, edited by Paul Flaig and Katherine Groo, 315–29. New York: Routledge, 2016.

Friedberg, Anne. "The End of Cinema: Multimedia and Technological Change." In *Reinventing Film Studies*, edited by Christine Gledhill and Linda Williams, 439–52. London: Oxford University Press, 2001.

– "Introduction." In *Reality Squared: Televisual Discourse on the Real*, edited by James Friedman, 1–22. New Brunswick: Rutgers University Press, 2002.

Galloway, Alexander. *The Interface Effect*. Cambridge: Polity Press, 2012.

– "Protocol vs. Institutionalization." In *New Media, Old Media: A History and Theory Reader*, edited by Wendy Hui Kyong Chun and Thomas Keenan, 187–98. New York: Routledge, 2006.

Garrett, Diane. "An Obituary: VHS Tapes Die of Loneliness at Age 30." *Variety*, 14 November 2006.

"General Meeting." *Journal of the Society for Psychical Research* 1, no. 3 (April 1884): 35–8.

Gordon, Avery. *Ghostly Matters: Haunting and the Sociological Imagination*. 2nd ed. Minneapolis: University of Minnesota Press, 2008.

Gould, Jack. "A Plea for Live Video. Switch to Film for TV was a Major Mistake." *New York Times*, 7 December 1952.

Grant, Barry Keith. "Digital Anxiety and the New Verité Horror and SF Film." *Science Fiction Film and Television* 6, no. 2 (2013): 153–75.

Gray, David. "Saving the Scream Queens: Why Yale University Library Decided to Preserve Nearly 3,000 Horror and Exploitation Movies on VHS." *The Atlantic*, 21 August 2015.

Greenberg, Joshua M. *From BetaMax to Blockbuster: Video Stores and the Invention of Movies on Video*. Cambridge, MA: MIT Press, 2008.

Gromaire, Marcel. "A Painter's Ideas about the Cinema." In *French Film Theory*, vol. 1: *1907–1929*, edited by Richard Abel, 174–81. Princeton: Princeton University Press, 1988.

Gunning, Tom. "Flickers: On Cinema's Power for Evil." In *Bad: Infamy, Darkness, Evil, and Slime on Screen*, edited by Murray Pomerance, 21–38. Albany: SUNY Press, 2004.

– "In Your Face: Physiognomy, Photography, and the Gnostic Mission of Early Film." *Modernism/Modernity* 4, no. 1 (1997): 1–29.

– "Invisible Worlds, Visible Media." In *Brought to Light: Photography and the Invisible, 1840–1900*, edited by Corey Keller, 51–66. San Francisco: San Francisco Museum of Modern Art, 2008.

– "Phantom Images and Modern Manifestations: Spirit Photography, Magic Theater, Trick Films, and Photography's Uncanny." In *Cinematic Ghosts: Haunting and Spectrality from Silent Cinema to the Digital Era*, edited by Murray Leeder, 17–38. New York: Bloomsbury Academic, 2015.

– "To Scan a Ghost: The Ontology of Mediated Vision." *Grey Room* 26 (2007): 94–127.

– "What's the Point of an Index? Or, Faking Photographs." *Nordicom Review* 25, nos. 1–2 (2004): 39–49.

Hansen, Miriam. *Cinema and Experience: Siegfried Kracauer, Walter Benjamin, and Theodor W. Adorno*. Berkeley: University of California Press, 2012.

Hart, Adam Charles. "I'M SCREEEEEEEEEAMING!!!! The Lowly Art of the Jump Scare." In *Monstrous Forms: Moving Image Horror across Media*, 59–88. New York: Oxford University Press, 2020.

Harvey, John. *Photography and Spirit*. London; Reaktion Books, 2007.

Heller-Nicholas, Alexandra. *Found Footage Horror Films: Fear and the Appearance of Reality*. Jefferson: McFarland, 2014.

Herbert, Daniel. "Nostalgia Merchants: VHS Distribution in the Era of Digital." *Journal of Film and Video* 69, no. 2 (2017): 3–19.

– *Videoland: Movie Culture at the American Video Store*. Berkeley: University of California Press, 2014.

Hernan, Luis, and Martyn Dade-Robertson. "Atmospheres of Digital Technology: Wireless Specters and Ghosts outside the Machine." *Digital Creativity* 27, no. 3 (2016): 214–33.

Hilderbrand, Lucas. *Inherent Vice: Bootleg Histories of Videotape and Copyright*. Durham: Duke University Press, 2009.

Hill, Annette. "Armchair Ghost Hunters." In *Paranormal Media: Audiences, Spirits, and Magic in Popular Culture*, 66–88. London: Routledge, 2011.

Hill, Benjamin Mako. "Revealing Errors." In *Error: Glitch, Noise, and Jam in New Media Cultures*, edited by Mark Nunes, 27–43. New York: Continuum, 2011.

Historic Hotels Worldwide. "1886 Crescent Hotel & Spa." https://www.historichotels.org/hotels-resorts/1886-crescent-hotel-and-spa.

Holloway, Julian, and James Kneale. "Locating Haunting: A Ghost–Hunter's Guide." *Cultural Geographies* 15, no. 3 (2008): 297–312.

Houghton, Georgiana. *Chronicles of Spirit Photography*. London: E.W. Allen, 1882.

Hudson, Martyn. *Ghosts, Landscapes, and Social Memory*. New York: Routledge, 2017.

Jackson, Kimberly. "Scopic Regimes of Modernity." In *Vision and Visuality*, edited by Hal Foster, 3–28. New York: New Press, 1999.

– *Technology, Monstrosity, and Reproduction in Twenty-First Century Horror*. New York: Palgrave Macmillan, 2013.

Jenkins, Henry. *Convergence Culture: Where Old and New Media Collide*. New York: NYU Press, 2008.

Jenkins, Henry, Sam Ford, and Joshua Green. *Spreadable Media: Creating Value and Meaning in a Networked Culture*. New York: NYU Press, 2013.

Johnson, Stacey. "Are We in the Movies Now?" *Cinèmas: Revue d'Études Cinematographie / Journal of Film Studies* 8, no. 3 (1998): 135–58.

Kaplan, Louis. *The Strange Case of William Mumler, Spirit Photographer*. Minneapolis: University of Minnesota Press, 2008.

Kattelle, Alan. "The Evolution of Amateur Motion Picture Equipment, 1895–1965." *Journal of Film and Video* 38, nos. 3–4 (1986): 47–57.

King, Stephen. "Stephen King: The Official Website." http://stephenking.com/library/novel/shining_the_inspiration.html.

Klinger, Barbara. *Beyond the Multiplex: Cinema, New Technologies, and the Home*. Berkeley: University of California Press, 2006.

Knable, Kate. "Reality TV Gives Boost to Business." *Arkansas Business*, 9 January 2012.

Kracauer, Siegfried. "Basic Concepts." In *Film Theory and Criticism*, 6th ed., edited by Leo Braudy and Marshall Cohen, 143–53. New York: Oxford University Press, 2004.

– "Photography." In *The Mass Ornament: Weimar Essays*, edited by Thomas Y. Levin, 47–63. Cambridge, MA: Harvard University Press, 1995.

Laclau, Ernesto. "The Time Is Out of Joint." In *Ernesto Laclau: Post-Marxism, Populism, and Critique*, edited by David Howarth, 199–212. London: Routledge, 2014.

Lauro, Sarah Juliet, and Catherine Paul. "'Make Me Believe!': Ghost-Hunting Technology and the Postmodern Fantastic." *Horror Studies* 4, no. 2 (2013): 221–39.

Lawrence, Amy. *Ghost Channels: Paranormal Reality Television and the Haunting of Twenty-First Century America*. Jackson: University Press of Mississippi, 2022.

"Lectures." *Journal of the Society for Psychical Research* 1, no. 1 (February 1884): 8–9.

Leeder, Murray. "*Ghostwatch* and the Haunting of Media." *Horror Studies* 4, no. 2 (2013): 173–86.

– *The Modern Supernatural and the Beginnings of Cinema*. London: Palgrave Macmillan, 2017.

Lim, Bliss Cua. *Translating Time: Cinema, the Fantastic, and Temporal Critique*. Durham: Duke University Press, 2009.

Luckhurst, Roger. "The Contemporary London Gothic and the Limits of the 'Spectral Turn.'" *Textual Practice* 16, no. 3 (2002): 527–46.

Maddin, Guy, Evan Johnson, and Robert Kotyk. *Séances Project Manual*. Cinema Ateliar Tovar, 2012.

Manon, Hugh, and Daniel Temkin. "Notes on Glitch." *World Picture* 6 (Winter 2011): 1–15.

Melton, Gordon J., ed. "Reichenbach, Baron Karl von (1788–1869)." In *Encyclopedia of Occultism and Parapsychology*, 5th ed., 2 vols. Farmington Hills: Gale Group, 2001.

Menta, Anna. "Stranger Things' VHS Packaging Is Confusing '80s Kids Everywhere." *Newsweek*, 16 October 2017.

Mirzoeff, Nicholas. "Ghostwriting: Working Out Visual Culture." *Journal of Visual Culture* 1, no. 2 (2002): 239–54.

Mnookin, Jennifer. "The Image of Truth: Photographic Evidence and the Power of Analogy." *Yale Journal of Law and the Humanities* 10, no. 1 (1998): 1–74.

Montebello, Philippe, and Jean-Luc Monterosso. "Forward." In *The Perfect Medium: Photography and the Occult*, edited by Clément Chéroux, 1–11. New Haven: Yale University Press, 2005.

Moradi, Iman, Ant Scott, Joe Gilmore, and Christopher Murphy, eds. *Glitch: Designing Imperfections*. New York: Mark Batty, 2009.

Moussinac, Léon. "On Cinegraphic Rhythm." In *French Film Theory*, vol. 1: *1907–1929*, edited by Richard Abel, 280–2. Princeton: Princeton University Press, 1988.

Mulvey, Laura. *Death 24× a Second: Stillness and the Moving Image*. London: Reaktion Books, 2006.

Natale, Simone. *Supernatural Entertainments: Victorian Spiritualism and the Rise of Modern Media Culture*. University Park: University of Pennsylvania Press, 2016.

Newman, Michael Z. *Video Revolutions: On the History of a Medium*. New York: Columbia University Press, 2014.

Nunes, Mark. "Error, Noise, and Potential: The Outside of Purpose." In *Error: Glitch, Noise, and Jam in New Media Cultures*, edited by Mark Nunes, 3–25. New York: Continuum, 2011.

Olivier, Marc. "Glitch Gothic." In *Cinematic Ghosts: Haunting and Spectrality from Silent Cinema to the Digital Era*, edited by Murray Leeder, 253–70. New York: Bloomsbury Academic, 2015.

Owens, Susan. *The Ghost: A Cultural History*. London: Tate, 2017.

Oxford English Dictionary. s.v. "paranormal (*adj. & n.*), Etymology," July 2023. https://doi.org/10.1093/OED/7155939929.

Peck, Andrew. "Tall, Dark, and Loathsome: The Emergence of a Legend Cycle in the Digital Age." *Journal of American Folklore* 128, no. 509 (2015): 333–48.

Pratt, Aaron T. "Horror and Exploitation on VHS: The History of Home Video Comes to Yale." *Journal of Visual Culture* 14, no. 2 (2015): 332–5.

Puglionesi, Alicia. *Common Phantoms: An American History of Psychic Science*. Stanford: Stanford University Press, 2020.

Radford, Benjamin. "The Curious Question of Ghost Taxonomy." *Skeptical Inquirer* 42, no. 3 (May–June 2018). https://skepticalinquirer.org/2018/05/the-curious-question-of-ghost-taxonomy.

– "Ghost-Hunting Mistakes: Science and Pseudoscience in Ghost Investigations." *Skeptical Inquirer* 34, no. 6 (November–December 2010). https://skepticalinquirer.org/2010/11/ghost-hunting-mistakes.

Renner, Karen J. "Negotiations of Masculinity in American Ghost-Hunting Reality TV." *Horror Studies* 4, no. 2 (2013): 201–19.

Reynolds, Simon. *Retromania: Pop Culture's Addiction to Its Own Past*. New York: Faber and Faber, 2011.

Rodowick, D.N. *The Virtual Life of Film*. Cambridge, MA: Harvard University Press, 2007.

Rosen, Philip. *Change Mummified: Cinema, History, Theory*. Minnesota: University of Minnesota Press, 2001.

Sayad, Cecilia. "Found-Footage Horror and the Frame's Undoing." *Cinema Journal* 55, no. 2 (2016): 43–66.

Scheible, Jeff. "Video after Video Stores." *Canadian Journal of Film Studies* 23, no. 1 (2014): 51–73.

Sconce, Jeffrey. *Haunted Media: Electronic Presence from Telegraphy to Television*. Durham: Duke University Press, 2000.

Semley, John. "Guy Maddin Haunts the Lightbox with His Cinematic Spooks." *Torontoist*, 13 September 2010. https://torontoist.com/2010/09/guy_maddins_haunts_the_lightbox_with_his_cinematic_spooks.

Soderman, Braxton. "The Index and the Algorithm." *Differences* 18, no. 1 (2007): 153–86.

Spielmann, Yvonne. *Video: The Reflexive Medium*. Translated by Anja Welle and Stan Jones. Cambridge, MA: MIT Press, 2008.

Stollznow, Karen. "The Stanley Hotel: An Investigation." 21 December 2009. https://skepticalinquirer.org/exclusive/stanley_hotel_an_investigation.

Sturken, Marita. "The Politics of Video Memory: Electronic Erasures and Inscriptions." In *Resolutions: Contemporary Video Practices*, edited by Michael Renov and Erika Suderberg, 1–12. Minneapolis: University of Minnesota Press, 1996.

Talbot, William Henry Fox. *The Pencil of Nature*. London: Longmann's, 1844.

Tashiro, Charles. "The Contradictions of Video Collecting." *Film Quarterly* 50, no. 2 (1996): 11–18.

Taylor, John Traill. *The Veil Lifted: Modern Developments of Spirit Photography*. London: Whittaker and Co., 1894.

Telotte, J.P. "The Blair Witch Project: Film and the Internet." *Film Quarterly* 54, no. 3 (2001): 32–9.

Todorov, Tzvetan. *The Fantastic: A Structural Approach to a Literary Genre*. Translated by Richard Howard. Ithaca: Cornell University Press, 1975.

Toronto International Film Festival. "Essential Cinema." http://collection.tiff.net/mwebcgi/mweb/mweb/mweb?request=record;id=24;type=901.

Tucker, Jennifer. *Nature Exposed: Photography as Eyewitness in Victorian Science*. Baltimore: Johns Hopkins University Press, 2005.

– "The Social Photographic Eye." In *Brought to Light: Photography and the Invisible, 1840–1900*, edited by Corey Keller, 37–50. San Francisco: San Francisco Museum of Modern Art, 2008.

Turvey, Malcolm. *Doubting Vision: Film and the Revelationist Tradition*. Oxford: Oxford University Press, 2008.

Usai, Paolo Cherchi. *The Death of Cinema: Theory, Cultural Memory, and the Digital Dark Age*. London: British Film Institute, 2001.

Villarejo, Amy. *Ethereal Queer: Television, History, Desire*. Durham: Duke University Press, 2014.

Vogel, Hermann Wilhelm. *The Chemistry of Light and Photography*. New York: D. Appleton and Company, 1875.

Waskul, Dennis, and Michelle Waskul. *Ghostly Encounters: The Hauntings of Everyday Life*. Philadelphia: Temple University Press, 2016.

Wasser, Frederick. *Veni, Vidi, Video: The Hollywood Empire and the VCR*. Austin: University of Texas Press, 2001.

Wasson, Haidee. "Electric Homes! Automatic Movies! Efficient Entertainment! 16mm and Cinema's Domestication in the 1920s." *Cinema Journal* 48, no. 4 (2009): 1–21.

Wax, Emily. "The Dizzy Spell of 'Blair Witch Project.'" *Washington Post*, 30 July 1999.

Wertheimer, John. "Mutual Film Reviewed: The Movies, Censorship, and Free Speech in Progressive America." *American Journal of Legal History* 37, no. 2 (1993): 158–89.

Williams, Karen. "The Liveness of Ghosts: Haunting and Reality TV." In *Popular Ghosts: The Haunted Spaces of Everyday Culture*, edited by María del Pilar Blanco and Esther Peeren, 149–61. New York: Continuum, 2010.

Zimmermann, Patricia. *Reel Families: A Social History of Amateur Film*. Bloomington: Indiana University Press, 1995.

Zolides, Andrew. "The Truth Is in Their Faces: MTV's *Fear* and the Rise of 'Personal Affect' in Paranormal Horror." *Horror Studies* 4, no. 2 (2013): 187–200.

INDEX